The Hills of Faraway

A Guide to Fantasy

DIANA WAGGONER

The Hills of Faraway

A Guide to Fantasy

ATHENEUM
NEW YORK
1978

TO LANNY

"please be with me"

Library of Congress Cataloging in Publication Data

Waggoner, Diana.
    The hills of faraway.

    Bibliography: p.
    Includes indexes.
    1. Fantastic literature—Bibliography.
2. Fantastic literature—History and criticism.
I. Title.
Z6514.F35W33   [PN56.F34]   809.3′876   76–900
ISBN 0–689–10846–X

Copyright © 1978 by Diana Waggoner
All rights reserved
Published simultaneously in Canada by
McClelland and Stewart Ltd
Composition by Kingsport Press, Kingsport, Tennessee
Printed and bound by Halliday Lithograph Corporation,
West Hanover and Plympton, Massachusetts
Designed by Harry Ford
First Edition

PREFACE
AND
ACKNOWLEDGEMENTS

THIS BOOK was not intended, nor is it presented, as a complete, encyclopedic history of fantasy. It is instead an introduction to fantasy as a literary form; the historical and bibliographical materials included are illustrative. Most previous work on the theory of fantasy has appeared within studies of other forms—science fiction, "weird" or horror fiction, epic and mythic literature—or in studies of individual authors. No single work has dealt with fantasy alone—with all of fantasy, and with nothing but fantasy. The lack of critical consensus about what fantasy is and what it consists of has caused the current critical situation: an amazing outburst of creativity in the writing of fantasy matched by a near-total vacuum in criticism. Many critics—notably Eleanor Cameron, L. Sprague De Camp, and Lloyd Alexander, all fantasists themselves—have written excellent studies of some aspects of fantasy; none has tried to consider fantasy as a whole. This book is an attempt to remedy this situation. It is offered to the many readers, students, and librarians interested in fantasy today, in hopes that it will enunciate and clarify the principles that define fantasy as a form.

I would like to express my particular gratitude to two writers whose work has influenced, inspired, and delighted me. Northrop Frye's *Anatomy of Criticism* and J. R. R. Tolkien's "On Fairy-Stories" have provided the theoretical framework and the vocabulary with which I have tried to elucidate the meaning of fantasy. Tolkien's magnificent fantasy *The Lord of the Rings* has been a never-failing source of joy and refreshment: it is the one work which has most stimulated my interest in and love for fantasy, and thus is the principal inspiration of my work. My debt to both these men is immeasurable.

Many friends have given me their time, efforts, and interest in my work, and I would like to thank them all for their kindness and generosity. The UCLA Graduate School of Library and Information Science, under whose auspices I wrote the Specialization Paper on which this

book is based, provided me with timely financial aid. My advisers, Miss
Betty Rosenberg and Mr. Jerome Cushman, were helpful, encouraging,
and enthusiastic about the project from its start. Mr. Cushman's faith
in the book, and his practical aid, have heartened and reassured me
many times. I am indebted to Priscilla Moxom of the Los Angeles Public Library, Sherri Gottlieb and Gil Lamont of the Change of Hobbit
Bookstore, and Jane White of the Beverly Hills Public Library for their
help while I was researching the book. I must also thank Bill Glass for
his unfailing interest and support. David Ossman very kindly read the
manuscript and offered many valuable suggestions. Dorothea Racionzer
and Donna Henry were generous and indefatigable helpers. Finally, I
would like to thank my husband, Lanny Waggoner, whose loving en-
couragement made the book possible, and to whom it is dedicated. Any
merit the work may have is owed to these friends and colleagues; errors
and omissions, of course, are entirely my own.

Diana Waggoner
February, 1977

CONTENTS

ILLUSTRATIONS

(Following page 72)

The jacket of the first American edition of *The Lord of the Rings*.

Copyright © 1965 by J. R. R. Tolkien. Reprinted by permission of Houghton Mifflin Company and George Allen & Unwin, Ltd.

Cover painting for the first Ballantine edition of *The Lord of the Rings*.

Reprinted by permission of Ballantine Books, Inc.

The Hobbit, frontispiece by J. R. R. Tolkien.

Copyright © 1966 by J. R. R. Tolkien. Reprinted by permission of Houghton Mifflin Company and George Allen & Unwin, Ltd.

"The Man in the Moon Came Down Too Soon" by Pauline Baynes from *The Adventures of Tom Bombadil* by J. R. R. Tolkien.

Copyright © 1962 by George Allen & Unwin, Ltd.

"The Last Shore" by Tim Kirk from The Tolkien Calendar 1973.

Reprinted by permission of Ballantine Books, Inc.

A Calormene nobleman by Pauline Baynes from *The Horse and His Boy* by C. S. Lewis.

Copyright 1954 by Macmillan Publishing Co. Inc. Reprinted by permission of Macmillan Publishing Co. Inc., Collins Publishers and Geoffrey Bles.

Jacket painting by Peter Schaumann for *The Forgotten Beasts of Eld* by Patricia McKillip.

Copyright © 1974 by Patricia McKillip. Reprinted by permission of Atheneum Publishers.

"Magelight" by Gail Garraty from *The Farthest Shore* by Ursula LeGuin.

Copyright © 1972 by Ursula LeGuin. Reprinted by permission of Atheneum Publishers.

Illustration by Helen Stratton for *The Princess and Curdie* by George MacDonald.

"Toad's Last Song" by Ernest H. Shepard from *The Wind in the Willows* by Kenneth Graham.

Copyright 1933 by Charles Scribner's Sons. Reprinted by permission of Charles Scribner's Sons.

ix

From *The Bee-Man of Orn* by Frank R. Stockton, illustrated by Maurice Sendak.

> Copyright © 1964 by Maurice Sendak. Reproduced by permission of Holt, Rinehart and Winston, Publishers.

The Psammead by H. R. Millar from *Five Children and It* by E. Nesbit.

From *Knight's Castle* by Edward Eager, illustrated by N. M. Bodecker.

> Copyright © 1956 by Harcourt Brace Jovanovich, Inc. and reproduced with their permission.

From *Mistress Masham's Repose* by T. H. White, illustrated by Fritz Eichenberg.

> Reprinted by permission of G. P. Putnam's Sons. Copyright 1946 by T. H. White; renewed.

Cover painting by Gervasio Gallardo for *Lud-in-the-Mist* by Hope Mirrlees.

> Reprinted by permission of Ballantine Books.

Chapter One illustration from *The Wood Beyond the World* by William Morris.

Cover art from *A Fish Dinner in Memison* by E. R. Eddison.

> Reprinted by permission of Ballantine Books, Inc.

A cover illustration by Frank Frazetta, from *The Frank Frazetta Calendar 1978.*

> Copyright © 1977 by Frank Frazetta. Reprinted by permission of the artist and Peacock Press/Bantam Books.

Cover art by J. Jones for *The Incomplete Enchanter* by DeCamp and Pratt.

> Reprinted by permission of Pyramid Publications.

Cover drawing by Bert Tanner for *Magazine of Fantasy and Science Fiction.*

> Copyright © 1966 by Mercury Press Inc. Reprinted by permission.

Cover painting by Ian Miller for *Kai Lung's Golden Hours* by Ernest Bramah.

> Reprinted by permission of Ballantine Books, Inc.

The Hills of Faraway

A Guide to Fantasy

Take me to the apple-laden land . . .

C. S. Lewis *after Sappho*

CHAPTER ONE

Theory of Fantasy

FANTASY LITERATURE, in recent years, has reached a position of mass popularity; but this popularity has been accompanied by considerable confusion about what it is and what it means. Some of the world's most diverse works of fiction are in fantasy's realm: everything from Tolkien to Tarzan, in fact. Yet this realm is not as great as some think it is. Not even all that is of Faerie is fantasy. This confusion comes about partly from the common uses of the term "fantasy" to mean one of two things: the exercise of the mind's powers of imagination; or daydreams of sexual, financial, or political power, and their literary expressions. But fantasy literature is not such an escape from reason. It begins, as every work of fiction does, with a vision or an idea, but it expresses the vision in a literary form that demands the strictest adherence to reason, logic, and order from its creator. Chesterton remarks that fantasy reminds us that "the soul is sane, but the universe is wild and full of marvels"; and Lloyd Alexander has aptly said that the Muse of fantasy "wears good, sensible shoes. No foam-born Aphrodite, she vaguely resembles my old piano teacher, who was keen on metronomes. . . ."[1]

If this is so, then why are so many readers and critics confused? The answer is that fantasy, as a literary genre, is not primarily about the material it uses—the symbols and dream-stuff, myths and images, which are the flesh and blood on its skeleton of rationality. Fantasy deals with mythopoeic archetypes of great antiquity and power—enchanters, princesses, quests, dark towers, hidden cities, haunted forests, walled gardens—as well as with myths of less age but no less force like the Old West, the atomic bomb, or the power of telepathy. But use of

1. Lloyd Alexander, "The Flat-Heeled Muse," in *Horn Book Reflections: On Children's Books and Reading*, ed. by Elinor W. Field, Boston, Horn Book, 1969, p. 242.

these symbols and images is not confined to fantasy, nor does it make a work a fantasy. What is important is the treatment of this mythopoeic material. Fantasy places the material in a fictional framework within which it is treated as empirical data, the common stuff of ordinary reality. A fantasy world is a secondary reality whose metaphysical premises are different from those of the real world, but whose inhabitants are men and women like ourselves, who live in their reality just as we do in ours.

Fantasy treats mythopoeic materials thus, "realistically," not to debunk them nor to analyze them, but to give them new life. Every successful fantasy, explicitly or implicitly, tries to establish another universe as a mirror or metaphor for our own. In J. R. R. Tolkien's terminology, it substitutes a Secondary World for our Primary one.[2] The means to this end are inextricably tied to the secular mode of modern thought: the conviction that everything, even the mythopoeic or "supernatural," must be perceptible, touchable, proven, *accountable*, to be "real." Tolkien called this means the "creation of literary belief," a redefinition of Coleridge's "suspension of disbelief."

Subcreation and literary belief

The Primary World is the world of living reality, the material, phenomenal world in which the laws of nature are never suspended, in which history has taken a certain course and no other, in which time flows forward, not backward, and in which the only certainty is death. In Tolkien's view, all this, including ourselves, was created by a Creator: therefore we cannot truly create. Tolkien's friend C. S. Lewis said that "we can only re-combine elements borrowed from the real universe; no one can imagine a new primary colour or a sixth sense."[3] He did not mean that no one can imagine the possible existence of such colors and senses, even give them names—but what colors are they? What sensations do they receive? A combination of (say) red and purple and yellow is not wholly new, not something outside previous experience. If new colors should be found on the distant planets of Arcturus or Rigel, they will not have been created by us.

But the act of recombination that we perform is not merely analogous to the divine Creation: it is part of our created nature and essential to our souls, a gift from the Creator. So Tolkien calls it "subcreation," exercised by man as sub-Creator. In literature, subcreation is the

2. J. R. R. Tolkien, "On Fairy-Stories," in his *Tree and Leaf*, Boston, Houghton Mifflin, 1965, p. 37.
3. C. S. Lewis, *Miracles: a Preliminary Study*, New York, Macmillan, 1947, p. 33.

act of putting a world into a story in order to make fiction with the "inner consistency of reality."[4] The world of the story is not the Primary World, but a new, Secondary World. When one reads *Pride and Prejudice*, for example, one must "suspend disbelief" in the existence of Elizabeth Bennet, for she never existed in the Primary World; her story is possible, but not actual. Even in biography some suspension of disbelief is necessary. Elizabeth and Essex are not the same people in the work of Hilaire Belloc as they are in the work of Lytton Strachey.

But Tolkien considers "suspension of disbelief" an inaccurate description of what is really happening:

> What really happens is that the story-maker proves a successful sub-creator. He makes a Secondary World which your mind can enter. Inside it, he relates what is "true"; it accords with the laws of that world. You therefore believe it, while you are, as it were, inside. The moment disbelief arises, the spell is broken; the magic, or rather art, has failed. You are then out in the Primary World again, looking at the little abortive Secondary World from outside. If you are obliged, by kindliness or circumstance, to stay, then disbelief must be suspended (or stifled), otherwise listening and looking would become intolerable. But this suspension of disbelief is a substitute for the genuine thing, a subterfuge we use when condescending to games or make-believe, or when trying (more or less willingly) to find what virtue we can in the work of an art that has for us failed.[5]

Tolkien further argues that what he calls Enchantment is the equivalent of art in creating literary belief in fantasy. Art is the "operative link between imagination and . . . Sub-creation"[6]; when it is applied to the mythopoeic material of fairy-story it becomes Enchantment (if successful) and creates fantasy. This point can be confusing, for Tolkien ties it to his own mystical beliefs about elves and "elvish craft." It is not necessary to give the art of writing fantasy a special name, and, indeed, Tolkien seems to imply that Enchantment is the highest form of art, while mere realism, however artful, must take a lower place. But then he says himself that art and Enchantment are the same process: only the materials used differ. Perhaps Tolkien's prejudices about modern literature, with its anomie, its disillusionment, its elitist nature, and its alienation from the past and from the ordinary mass of men, led him to slight it in favor of the fairy-story and fantasy literature he preferred both personally and morally. I do not believe that he meant to argue

4. Tolkien, p. 46.   5. Tolkien, p. 37.   6. Tolkien, p. 47.

that any form of literature was intrinsically superior, as a form, to any other.

Given, then, that the processes of creating ordinary realistic fiction and fantasy are the same: how does the need for literary belief particularly apply to fantasy? The answer is that fantasy requires more effort from the reader in establishing literary belief than does any other kind of fiction. To read realistic fiction, such as *Pride and Prejudice*, one must assume the characters could actually exist in the Primary World in order to "believe" in the story. This is the basic metaphysical assumption the reader must make for any work of realistic fiction, and is, in a way, its reason for being.

Literary realism and its effects

The literature of realism arose as a revolt against the excesses of pre-realistic literature, particularly the excesses of medieval romance. As early as the end of the sixteenth century, Cervantes had killed the romance with *Don Quixote*, a novel which was both the culmination and the greatest parody of the romance form, and which introduced a new style of prose narrative in what Northrop Frye calls the "low mimetic" mode.[7] Low mimetic writing deals with the life of ordinary people, with the everyday life we live, seen from the inside, where the mythic and high mimetic modes treat the life of heroes and kings, seen from the outside. During the century after the appearance of *Don Quixote*, the rise of scientific, empirical rationalism and materialism created a mental climate in which literary realism, based on observation, logic, and reason, could flourish. Verisimilitude to the phenomena of everyday life, as lived by real people whatever their social station, became all-important. If readers no longer gave credence to the supernatural in the Primary World—if the supernatural's influence could not be measured—then the supernatural could not be credible in a Secondary World, either. People might still believe in supernatural powers, though they were far less credulous than before, but it was their belief that prompted their behavior, not the supernatural itself.

Realism could not dominate literature, alone, for long; if it gave the mind's intellectual faculties an importance they had never previously enjoyed, it also slighted the mind's other faculties and denigrated their roles in human existence. But its division of phenomena into two classes—the natural or "real" and the supernatural—had an irrevocable effect on literary thought, leading to the rise of the "sentimental" forms of fiction which compose the class of modern speculative fiction. The

7. Northrop Frye, *Anatomy of Criticism: Four Essays*, Princeton, N.J., Princeton University Press, 1957.

term "sentimental" is used by Northrop Frye to denote sophisticated re-creations of naive or archaic literary forms.[8] It is just this division into classes by which we may understand the fundamental difference between the genres of modern speculative fiction, including fantasy, and the pre-realistic genres of myth, epic, romance, legend, folktale, allegory, utopia, and imaginary voyage.

Such pre-realistic genres made no distinctions between natural and supernatural phenomena, except in theological or religious senses; the supernatural might require a special, "religious" attitude, but it was an acknowledged part of the whole universe, inextricably entangled with every natural object and event. Its existence was taken for granted; it was not in any way divorced from the rest of reality. Dante's *Divine Comedy*, for example, treats Hell, Purgatory, and Paradise with the respect and awe proper to religious matters, but never suggests that they and ordinary reality are not organically related. If the life of our world were less than the invisible life of the afterworld, it was less hierarchically, not less validly real. Everything existed in a vast unity within the mind of God.

But this image of the universe as a single unified whole was destroyed by modern secular rationalism. The supernatural, if it existed at all, was not part of the "real" world; therefore it could not be accepted in fiction. Supernatural-seeming events were credited to psychological sources or coincidence or (worse) the scheming of evil men trying to hold mankind in the bondage of superstition. The writers of the Enlightenment tended to emphasize superstition when they discussed the supernatural; Victorian writers tended to rely on coincidence or "Divine Providence," which mostly meant the writers' own skill in making up plots. Twentieth-century writers tend to credit psychological sources. This has led to the current supremacy of what Robert Scholes calls "post-realistic fabulation" in his *The Fabulators*.[9] The fabulators are the natural heirs of realism, just as, in painting, Cézanne was the heir of Delacroix. They have broadened the scope of realism to describe the natural world as seen by the subconscious mind. Just as *Don Quixote* was the culmination of the romance, Joyce's *Ulysses* (influenced by E. T. A. Hoffman and Lewis Carroll) was the culmination of the realistic novel. It fully expressed the possibilities of the older narrative form, while remaking it into a new form. *Ulysses* demonstrated that the realistic approach could handle description of both everyday life and the irrational phenomena of the unconscious mind. Previous novelists had dealt with the irrational by observing its results in outward

8. Ibid.
9. Robert Scholes, *The Fabulators*, New York, Oxford University Press, 1967.

action—madness—or by casting their narratives in the form of dreams. Carroll's *Alice* is the most successful attempt to bridge the gap between the conscious and unconscious minds with dream-narrative. When Joyce realized that the unconscious itself could be described by the techniques of realistic observation, the way lay open for the "comic allegorists . . . innovators in form and verbal technique" [10] of contemporary fiction: Vladimir Nabokov, John Barth, Jorge Luis Borges, Tom Pynchon, Donald Barthelme, Kurt Vonnegut, Richard Brautigan, and many others.

The fabulators' observation of the irrational includes the supernatural, thanks especially to the work of the psychologist Carl Jung, whose research into myth, symbol, and archetype has offered them means to go beyond mere description of the irrational. They can distort the patterns of existence in ways analogous to the distortion that insanity, especially schizophrenia, imposes on reality. By exploring deeply within the psyche, they can tap the sources of linguistic symbolism, thus revealing a new perspective on language and on mythmaking. The fabulators have transformed literary realism from the low mimetic to the ironic mode, and have re-created pre-realistic literature by substituting the unity of the human mind for the unity of God's universe. Literary belief can therefore be given to the supernatural as an expression of the unconscious.

Speculative fiction

But this leaves one question unanswered: what if the supernatural were, after all, *real*—not a chimera of the unconscious mind, not a plot of "illuminati" to keep the masses quiet, not the meshings of coincidence and fate? This seminal question created modern speculative fiction. In the same way that realism had rebelled against the excesses and conventions of pre-realistic literature, speculative fiction rebelled against the excesses and conventions of realism. If romance had been illogical, realism was over-logical; it could not encompass the whole of life, even by referring to the psychology of the unconscious. To argue that the symbols of the numinous were mere representations of human psychology was to overlook the possibility that they might refer to objectively real things. Ghosts, magic, alternate universes, unreasonable horrors, the unimaginable future, even God, might not be superstitions or convenient philosophical assumptions or evidence of madness, but living, if unprovable, reality. The idea that everything real was per-

10. Mark R. Hillegas, *Shadows of Imagination: the Fantasies of C. S. Lewis, J. R. R. Tolkien, and Charles Williams*, Carbondale, Illinois, Southern Illinois University Press, 1969, p. xiii.

ceptible was itself only an assumption. Speculative fiction appeared to provide a means by which realism could speculate on unprovable realities and readers could give them literary belief.

But the term "speculative" indicates how much this class of narrative depends on the realism it rebels against. Realism forced writers to treat the supernatural as a class apart from the rest of reality. They had to be "realistic" about it; they had to adhere strictly to realistic conventions. The supernatural could not be routinely accepted, on its own terms, in a story. It had to conform to the accepted rules of ordinary existence, to be accounted for. Pre-realistic literary forms were thus imitated or updated by writers who had learned to accept realism as the standard of prose narrative. They therefore applied realistic criteria to the material they used. It is these criteria which must be satisfied in order to give the "inner consistency of reality" to works of speculative fiction, so that the reader may give them literary belief.

Of all the genres of speculative fiction—allegory, satire, utopia, imaginary voyage, traveler's tale, ghost story, the Perrault fairy tale, the "art fairy tale," or *Kunstmärchen,* the Oriental tale (imitating the *Thousand and One Nights*), the dream-story, the Gothic novel, the horror story, science fiction, and fantasy—fantasy has the greatest impact, because in it the gap between the natural and the supernatural is at its widest. The metaphysical assumptions the reader must make are the means of bridging this gap; so they are the most extreme and far-reaching.

We have, so far, discussed four broad classes of fiction: speculative fiction, realism, post-realistic fabulation, and pre-realistic literature. Speculative fiction can be briefly defined as a class of modern, "sentimental" literature that treats supernatural and/or nonexistent phenomena (such as the future) as a special class of objectively real things or events, using the low mimetic mode. Realism explains the supernatural away as lies, coincidence, or illusion, while post-realistic fabulation is a fuller development of realism. Pre-realistic literature does not consider the supernatural to be divorced, as a class of things, from the rest of reality; it does not need special treatment, except in the religious sense.

Fantasy's basic assumption and its consequences

Fantasy is distinct among the genres of speculative fiction in that it goes to the farthest extreme to establish realistic credentials—a history and background—for the supernatural. It might be argued that the purity of a vision of the numinous is spoiled by "explaining" it. Yet even Dante prepares the reader for the Beatific Vision by first taking him through all the circles of Heaven and Hell. A world of fantasy is not the Primary World; its internal laws are different from ours, and so preparation and explanation are necessary. In such worlds the supernatural is not merely a possibility, but actual fact. A numinous power—an *ultimate* power, for good or evil—orders the world and impels the story, acting directly upon its characters and events. In the Primary World, the existence and activity of such powers are a matter of religious faith; in the fantasy's Secondary World, their existence and activity are subject to material proof.

It is not enough for the reader of fantasy to make the assumption that the characters in a story could exist. He must assume that their whole universe, and the power that created it, could exist. The major consequence of this is that fantasy, though bound like all art to emotional reality, is more free from physical reality than any other form of literature. It is far less limited in this respect than its sister genre, science fiction, which (as will be discussed later) must always pay lip service to an ideal of scientific plausibility.

Another consequence of this necessary assumption is: a fantasy that fails to establish a credibly numinous universe fails not only in a formal sense, but fails entirely, regardless of the quality of the writing or the artistic goals of the author. The establishment of the numinous power's existence is the basic premise from which the fantasy must develop; if the premise is false—or overlooked—the fantasy is maimed. This is not to say that the author must state, in so many words, that some supernatural power is behind the story. Its existence is implicit in those fantasies based on "magical" impossibilities: talking animals, alternate universes, new worlds, Perrault fairy tales, and so forth. More explicit or active acknowledgement of the numinous is found in the many fantasies using "magic" itself as a basis, or which are religiously oriented (usually Christian). For if there were no supernatural power, bad or good, behind the magic of enchanters, witches, or Faerie, then magic would merely be a kind of science originating in the natural world. But whether the author's view of the numinous is active or passive, it must be there, or the work is not fantasy. A well-written book like Roald Dahl's *Charlie and the Chocolate Factory* can be a complete failure as fantasy; a piece of hack work like A. Merritt's *The Moon Pool* can succeed, at least on a formal level. *Charlie* takes place in a no-world, a bedtime-story place without rules, order, history, or future; *The Moon Pool*, claptrap that it is, is set in a world that is consistent in its silliness.

A third consequence is that even the most comic fantasy must contain a basic sense of seriousness: it must be presented as "true."

Any attempt by the author to peek from behind the scenes will instantly shatter the fragile illusion. To present a fantasy as *merely* a story or a dream is a contradiction in terms. It is possible, as Tolkien points out, to write a story reproducing dream-experience and to be extremely successful at it, as Carroll was with *Alice*. Both *Alice's Adventures in Wonderland* and *Through the Looking Glass* are set within dreams, and their internal logic and abrupt transitions are those of dreams. The common identification of *Alice* with fantasy probably derives from the equally common, equally mistaken identification of it with children, who usually lack the sophistication to appreciate it. Carroll expresses the dream-experience with unmatched skill, but dream is not vision, and dream-story is not fantasy. The mechanism of the dream-story ensures that everything happens not only within the Primary World, but within the psyche. There are fantasies which purport to take place in dreams, notably Mark Twain's *Connecticut Yankee*, Fletcher Pratt's *The Blue Star*, and E. R. Eddison's *The Worm Ouroboros*. But in all three cases, the dream-frame is merely a clumsy device to set the plot in motion; the plot itself is not presented as a dream. Indeed, in the two latter stories, the author promptly forgets all about the "dream" with which the story began.

A fourth consequence of our basic assumption is that all supernatural elements in the story, especially supernatural persons, must be motivated and believable. They must have a history; it may not be actually written down in the book, but it must have existed. This point marks the distinction between fantasy and horror and ghost stories. The ghost fantasy, like Thorne Smith's *Topper*, takes place in another universe; the ghost story, like Mrs. Oliphant's "The Library Window," takes place in the Primary World, with the ghost cast as an intruder into ordinary reality. The ghost is more a part of the setting—a piece of the furniture—than it is a character. In "The Library Window," a girl is fascinated by a man whom she watches through the window every evening, until she finds that the window is a fake, a blind, to give the library building symmetry. She can see the man because he is the ghost of her ancestress's murdered lover, but she never meets him; he is an object, not a person. This lovely, atmospheric story is unsatisfactory as fantasy, precisely because it never deals with the ghost as a personality. Presumably, all ghosts want revenge, or rest, or to give warning to the living; but in a ghost story this is merely stated, never developed. In a ghost fantasy, on the other hand, ghosts are characters, people, not props. They are observed from the inside, just like the living characters; their hopes are as important as any other characters' are, and they interact with, as well as influence, the others. In *Topper*, George and

Marion Kirby are characters who happen to be dead—"ghosts"—but who act very much alive; they have powers the living do not, but are otherwise just like them. The ghost in a ghost story is an object, at best the remains of a personality; an intruder from the "unknown," whom even the living characters are not always sure is real. But the whole point of fantasy is to establish a credible universe, not an "unknown" one. The ghost in a ghost fantasy is a sort of living creature in a world that allows supernatural creatures to coexist with humanity—a world, therefore, with different metaphysical premises from ours.

The horror story is farther from fantasy than the ghost story, for similar reasons. Creatures of fantasy, of Faerie, may be frightening. The mantichore, the griffin, the chimera, the vampire, the werewolf, the witch, and the ogre terrify; but they are not, generally, found in the horror story, and their function is entirely different. When the hero of a fantasy meets an evil or terrifying being, he meets it on equal ground. He changes because of it, whether it tempts him, defeats him, persuades him, or surrenders to him; he may even be able to sympathize with it, understanding though rejecting it. The horror story relies on monsters and evil spirits—giant insects and gorillas, defrosted dinosaurs, extra-terrestrial beings, "things" from the slime, the Red Death, "presences of evil"—whose distinguishing characteristics are that they are evil for the sake of evil, irrational, and purposelessly destructive. Like the ghost of the ghost story, they are not persons, but props. The hero of a horror tale has no relationship or interaction with the monstrous being he meets; he is unchanged by the experience, for his only feelings are of revulsion and disgust, whether he wins or loses. Hence the term "horror," which indicates instinctive, unthinking aversion and repugnance. The horrifying creatures of fantasy exist as a means to an end, which is the proving or breaking of the protagonists. The horror of the horror story is an end in itself, and the final victory or defeat of the protagonists has nothing to do with their merit or their personalities. For instance, in Arthur Machen's short story "The Novel of the White Powder," an innocent young man is erroneously given a horrible drug instead of his prescription; when he takes it, he turns into a mass of slime. His fate is literally an accident; he has no choice, no will, no temptation, and no hope. Fantasy requires that evil pose a moral dilemma; horror story supplies only the titillation of evil.

But it is not only supernatural persons who must be realistically motivated; it is every supernatural element. Protagonists are not given magical aid as an end in itself, but, again, as means to their proving or breaking. Here, fantasy shows its greatest dependence on and resemblance to the mythopoeic material of fairy-story from which it is made. The numinous power that orders the world and impels the adventure of the story ordains that magical aid should be given to the protagonist so that he may achieve a good end to the adventure—not so that he will always have magical ice cream cones whenever he wants them. This does not mean that the protagonist *will* achieve a good end. It means that he will be helped to try. The existence of a supernatural moral order does not guarantee success to the hero and defeat to the villain; it shows why moral standards are necessary. This is taken for granted in fairy-story, where the protagonist must use his good sense and his virtue in order to apply any magical aid he gets. Fantasy must be no less true to this emotional reality than any other literary type.

Didactic genres of speculative fiction

Similarly, this moral order does not exist as a didactic model for the Primary World; it is metaphorical, not allegorical or ideological. There are many didactic genres of speculative fiction, with their own histories. It may further clarify the position of fantasy to consider these other forms and their differences from it and each other. They include satire, allegory and parable, utopia and dystopia, the *Kunstmärchen*, the imaginary or cosmic voyage, the traveler's tale, and science fiction.

Satire is an attitude more than a form; anyone can hold follies and vices up to scorn. The classical satire, however, is what Northrop Frye calls "Menippean satire" in his *Anatomy of Criticism*: a work in which all characters and events are subordinated to an ideological scheme that the author imposes on his material. Satire, therefore, belongs with allegory and parable, utopia and dystopia, which share a common prophetical intent. Unlike fantasy, they are not genuinely interested in creating a new world, but in finding similes for the aspects of human behavior and society they wish to criticize. The realms of enchantment they may describe do not exist for their own sake, and the reader finds his way into them almost by accident. *The Pilgrim's Progress* is the most conspicuous example of allegory. Its strength is the accuracy of Bunyan's assessment of human activities and the fervor and beauty with which his vision is set down. But Bunyan did not intend to create a new world within which to consider human activities; he wanted to influence the behavior of his readers by dressing spiritual realities in physical form. Allegory can approach fantasy only if the author is willing to sacrifice his scheme to the spirit of his story. Bernard Shaw points out that "allegory is never quite consistent except when it is written by someone without dramatic faculty, in which case it is unreadable . . . the more consistent, the more unreadable." [11]

11. George Bernard Shaw, *The Perfect Wagnerite*, New York, Dover, 1967, p. 28.

Allegory is directed toward the individual: consider the typical parable—the Good Samaritan, the Prodigal Son—with its point, or moral. As I. F. Clarke has pointed out in his two bibliographies of utopian fiction,[12] utopias and dystopias are directed at society as a whole. The utopian society is our own with its defects remedied according to the notions of the author; the dystopia is our society with its defects taken to a logical extreme. Many people confuse utopian or dystopian works, like Orwell's *1984* or Huxley's *Brave New World*, with science fiction, which often contains utopian elements. Yet, though technological progress plays a major role in both books, neither is primarily concerned with the effect of that progress on society, as science fiction would be. They are, rather, concerned with the development of concepts that the authors represent as existing in the present, though technological progress may be the means to their ultimate realization. Depersonalization and doublethink exist today; test-tube babies and televisions that watch people have not yet appeared. Or, imagine a means of efficient teleportation by machine, described in a novel. Science fiction would concern itself with the new mode of transportation's effect on people; a utopia or dystopia would show how teleportation fitted in with sociological tendencies already established. A single work may do both. The distinction is one of primary emphasis.

Utopian fiction tends to date quickly. It is a rare writer whose plans and dreams for the future are not outstripped and made to look tame, or horrible, by history. For example, Edward Bellamy's *Looking Backward*, published in the 1890s, gave a great impetus to liberal socialism and the labor movement when it first appeared. Today, its conception of universal conscription into an Army of workers seems both naive and oppressive, its materialism drab, and its treatment of women patronizing. Utopias are inevitably bound to a single time and place. Their philosophy may endure through the ages; but their new worlds are soon perceived as mere distorted mirrors of the world of their creation.

The *Kunstmärchen* ("art-folktale") has had an intriguing history. It was the product of the German Romantics in their effort to "turn away from . . . the realms of rational experience." [13] Fantasy and fabulation both owe a debt to it, through its two most famous writers, E. T. A. Hoffmann, author of the *Tales*, and Novalis, the mystic. Hoffmann in-

12. I. F. Clarke's two studies are *The Tale of the Future* (London, Library Association, 1962, 216 pp.) and *Voices Prophesying War, 1763–1984* (London, Oxford University Press, 1970).

13. Marianne Thalmann, *The Romantic Fairy Tale: Seeds of Surrealism*, translated by Mary B. Corcoran, Ann Arbor, University of Michigan Press, 1964, p. 122.

fluenced Edgar Allan Poe in particular; through him, the modern fabulators drew the idea of mixing the imaginary with the irrational in their representations of psychological reality. Novalis's religious ideas exercised a formative effect on the mind of the first true fantasist, George MacDonald, who took from him the inspiration of using a naive form to express a mystical or supernatural reality.

Yet the *Kunstmärchen* was moribund from its beginning, and it perished by the mid-nineteenth century, because its originators did not use the strengths of the archaic folktale form (German, *Hausmärchen*) from which it sprang. The *Kunstmärchen* was not a tale, but a vehicle for philosophical speculation on a "higher reality." [13] As such, it was sister to Shaw's unreadably consistent allegory. An air of detachment characterizes it, because its originators were not concerned with the form for its own sake, but as an opportunity to display their philosophical ideas. A well-known example is Friedrich de la Motte Fouqué's stiff, disjointed *Undine* (1811), in which a selfish, willful water nymph receives a soul on marrying a human, then is rejected by her husband and returns to her fairy relatives. Undine's possession of a soul, however, has no effect on her nature. She is forced to carry out the harsh fairy law and kill her husband, whom she still loves, when he is unfaithful to her; then she transforms herself into a brook winding round his grave. She suffers, commits a sin, and experiences remorse, but there is no mention of redemption, which might seem to be the main justification of her gaining a soul. If Undine could not abandon her fairy nature, then there is no point in her having a soul. The story represents a total lack of understanding of the folktale, which it resembles only on the surface; the author's pretentious artiness kills its vitality. Compare *Undine* with Hans Christian Andersen's fairy tale "The Little Mermaid," which uses the same motifs. The Mermaid suffers and loves in order to receive a soul and the chance of salvation; Undine receives a soul, suffers and loves, but no salvation is offered to her. The Andersen story presents an experience of harmony; *Undine* presents one of alienation and despair, which ill accords with the folktale form in which it is cast. Andersen's story is a classic, while *Undine* is merely a curiosity.

The imaginary voyage, cosmic voyage, and Robinsonade are closely related, and elements of all three are found in other speculative genres. Philip Gove has written an excellent scholarly study entitled *The Imaginary Voyage in Prose Fiction*,[14] and Roger Lancelyn Green

14. Philip Babcock Gove, *The Imaginary Voyage in Prose Fiction: a history of its criticism and a guide for its study, with an annotated check list of 215 imaginary voyages from 1700 to 1800*, New York, Columbia University Press, 1941, xii, 445 pp. (Columbia University Studies in English and Comparative Literature No. 152).

has written an equally excellent popular book called *Into Other Worlds: Space Flight in Fiction from Lucian to Lewis*.[15] Strong leanings to allegory are characteristic of these genres. The hero voyages, on earth or in the Ptolemaic heavens, to exotic locations with utopian or dystopian qualities, undergoing a spiritual metamorphosis parallel to his physical journey. Apuleius's *Golden Ass*, the *Odyssey*, Lucian of Samosata's *Voyage to the Moon*, the *Divine Comedy*, *The Pilgrim's Progress*, *Gulliver's Travels*, and David Lindsay's fantasy *A Voyage to Arcturus* all include imaginary voyages. Such a voyage represents the intersection of the allegory and the utopia. It is a spiritual journey through a physical setting in which every element has a signification, to societies which are distorted mirror images of real society.

The Robinsonade is, of course, named for *Robinson Crusoe*, and is the story of a castaway—a voyage cut short—in an isolated setting, which the author can use to describe his idea of the basic elements separating man from beast. Neither imaginary voyage nor Robinsonade is much written today, since modern geographical knowledge makes literary belief impossible, except in science fiction, where lonely planets stand in for desert islands. But most science-fiction writers prefer to compare humans to aliens in order to discuss human-ness, rather than putting a single human by himself on a planet. Loneliness is the chief essential of a Robinsonade.

The traveler's tale is included here because of its resemblance to the imaginary voyage, though it rarely has a didactic purpose, and inclines more to simple storytelling. This form, too, is not much used today, since literary belief in it depends largely on geographical ignorance and the concealment of great distance. The classical traveler's tale, like those of Sir John Mandeville, is not really fiction at all; it is an early form of geographical writing. Modern geographical information comes from photographs and television, which have done away with the men "whose heads do grow beneath their shoulders," the mantichores, dragons, unicorns, and other monsters and marvels of a more credulous past. Within fantasy, however, a variation on the traveler's tale still maintains its vitality: the "lost city" or "lost civilization" story, a theme which Edgar Rice Burroughs exploited so thoroughly in his Tarzan books that a host of imitators is still faithfully grinding them out. The lost city is somewhere in the wilds of Africa, or the Amazon jungles, or Central Asia (before the Communists brought in commissars and vaccinations). It is invariably ruled by a beautiful white woman, who either orders the hero's arrest and sacrifice to the gods, or

15. Roger Lancelyn Green, *Into Other Worlds: Space Flight in Fiction from Lucian to Lewis*, London, Abelard-Schumann, 1957, 184 p.

who depends on the hero to save her from her rebellious native subjects, or both. Burroughs was an American imitator of that master of romantic adventure, H. Rider Haggard, the Ian Fleming of his day, whose *She* (1886) is one of the few tales of this type with any claim to artistic respectability. Just as early traveler's tales were mostly inventions, lost-city tales are mostly hack work. Contemporary writers in the genre have eliminated the overt racism that makes much of the early work unreadable, from Haggard right up to the 1950s, but artistic quality has probably declined. As fantasy, this form of the traveler's tale has retained its popularity, even adding elements of "magic" of the witch-doctor or jungle-priestess variety; but its charm is usually wasted on all but adolescents.

Science fiction

Of all the didactic genres, science fiction is the most vital, and the most often confused with fantasy. A common misconception is that the two genres are one and the same, or, alternatively, that one is a subcategory of the other. The well-known science-fiction writer, Brian Aldiss, says that it is "impossible to separate science fiction from science fantasy, or either from fantasy, since both genres are part of fantasy. . . . But fantasy in a narrower sense, as opposed to science fiction, generally implies a fiction leaning more towards myth or the mythopoeic than towards an assumed realism." [16] Aldiss' terminology is both confusing and misleading, since he uses the same term—"fantasy"—to mean two different things, and since we have seen already that fantasy relies upon a genuine, not an "assumed," realism. *The Wizard of Oz* is not less "realistic" in its treatment of its themes than a science fiction novel like Arthur C. Clarke's *Childhood's End*, whose subject is the absorption of humanity into a godlike Overmind. Yet *The Wizard of Oz* is a myth, while *Childhood's End* propounds an objective future possibility. The relationship between fantasy and science fiction is not that of two strands twisted together into a rope, but of two colors next to each other on a spectrum. They neighbor each other because the new worlds they create are similar; the "rhetorical strategy" [17] each uses to create literary belief is likewise similar.

To clarify this point, let us consider three attempted definitions of fantasy and science fiction. John R. Pfeiffer observes, in his *Fantasy and Science Fiction: A Critical Guide*, that " 'Speculative fiction' is a

16. Brian Aldiss, *Billion Year Spree: the True History of Science Fiction*, Garden City, N.Y., Doubleday, 1973, pp. 8, 9.
17. Robert M. Philmus, *Into the Unknown: the Evolution of Science Fiction from Francis Godwin to H. G. Wells*, Berkeley, University of California Press, 1970, p. vii.

term offered as a substitute for 'fantasy' . . . a perfectly valid label for works such as Walter Pater's *Marius the Epicurean* which is both fiction and speculative philosophy—but not fantasy." [18] This is a misinterpretation. The term "speculative fiction" was coined by Robert A. Heinlein more than twenty years ago as a convenient expression that would cover many genres, including fantasy, not as a substitute for "fantasy." Heinlein did not intend the adjective "speculative" to mean only meditative philosophy, but specifically included what he called "undisguised fantasy," "science fiction," "sociological speculation," "space opera," and other forms, giving examples in each category.[19] It is true that the several genres of speculative fiction contain "fantastic" or magical elements and employ "fantasy," in the sense of "the exercise of the imagination," rather than being confined to strict representation of the material world. But there is no reason why a work of speculative philosophy, like *Marius*, and a work of speculative imagination, like *The Wizard of Oz*, should not be included in a larger class.

Russel Nye, author of *The Unembarrassed Muse*, is more helpful, stating that "Fiction of fantasy, that is, of the unexplained impossibility, is of course as old as fairy tale and myth. Fiction of science—of the explicable possibility—depended on the post-Newtonian world's faith in science's ability to explain and shape experience. . . . Poe established the essential difference between fantasy and science fiction . . . by ruling that every departure from the norm of behavior of men and matter must be explained rationally and must be scientifically plausible." [20] Nye is not quite correct in saying that fantasy is "unexplained," since it uses magic, or the assumption of a new universe, or both, to explain its effects. But he is right to point to "science's ability to explain and shape experience," and scientific plausibility, as the basis of the difference between the two genres.

When Kingsley Amis defined science fiction in his *New Maps of Hell*, he mentioned a point that helps to explain why so many readers

18. John R. Pfeiffer, *Fantasy and Science Fiction, a Critical Guide*, Palmer Lake, Colorado, Filter Press, 1971, p. 2. It is doubtful whether Pfeiffer has any real grasp of the distinction between science fiction and fantasy, for two reasons. The first is his comment that realism is an "aesthetic aberration" in literature, because the majority of readers prefer "fantasy" in the form of Westerns, mysteries, pornography, television, and nursery rhymes. He confuses the literature of wishfulfillment with true fantasy. The second is the fact that his guide fails to note whether any specific book listed in it is science fiction or fantasy. This is a disservice to the inexperienced reader for whom his book is intended; the audiences for the two genres are not identical.

19. Robert A. Heinlein, "Ray Guns and Rocket Ships," *Library Journal*, Vol. 78 (July 1953), pp. 1188–89.

20. Russel Nye, *The Unembarrassed Muse: the Popular Arts in America*, New York, Dial, 1970, pp. 270–271.

confuse science fiction with fantasy. He wrote that science fiction was "that class of prose literature treating of a situation which could not arise *in the world we know,* but which is hypothesized on the basis of some innovation in science or technology. . . ." (Italics added).[21] In other words, the story must take place in a world different from the one we know, a newly created world in which some fundamental assumption about the way things work is different. But where fantasy's change of assumptions is metaphysical, science fiction's is only physical, since it must conform to an ideal of scientific plausibility (or, at least, pseudo-scientific plausibility). The "technologically miraculous"[22] is not the same as the supernaturally miraculous, though its effect on the ignorant may be the same.

Science fantasy

In science fantasy, the shadowy area between the genres where technological and supernatural miracles blend, the use of the term "science" is an attempt to legitimize situations that depend on fantastic assertions. For example, in Ursula K. Le Guin's *The Lathe of Heaven* (1971), a man whose dreams can change reality is manipulated by a scientist with a machine that augments brain waves. Such "bio-feedback" machines already exist and are used in research into the nature of sleep and dreaming; they are "scientific." But the idea that a man's dreams can change the actual past and present is clearly fantastic. The science of the story may indicate the author's desire to gain serious sociological consideration for her ideas beyond any purely literary criticism. Other science fantasies lean more towards pure fantasy, emphasizing storytelling. Andre Norton's *Star Gate* (1958) is a good example: the "science" provides a plausible background for a story relying on supernatural powers and a quasi-medieval setting.

To distinguish true science fiction from science fantasy, space opera, and adventure fantasy, all of which may use scientific or pseudo-scientific elements, the reader must note the writer's attitude towards his material. As Amis points out, and as we saw in our discussion of utopias, science fiction is primarily interested in the effects of science and technology on the Primary World—future history from the point of view of our highly technological society. "Future history" is a common science fiction term and has been applied to the work of several science fiction writers, notably Robert Heinlein himself. But in science fantasy, the development of the scientific or techno-

21. Kingsley Amis, *New Maps of Hell: a Survey of Science Fiction*, New York, Harcourt, 1960, p. 18.
22. Frye, p. 49.

logical innovation is not so important, and in outright fantasy, it is usually not mentioned at all. Take the old notion of the "ray gun." Suppose that it is cheap, silent, popular, and easily recharged at any electrical outlet. What would be the effect of such a weapon on people's daily lives? What if an energy crisis far greater than today's cut off the source of the gun's charges? How would police work be affected by a gun whose effects were not distinguishable ballistically from any other gun's effects? This is the sort of question science fiction asks. A fantasy might use a "ray gun" instead of a sword, but it would not be interested in questions like these.

When a science-fiction writer invents a new planet, he is imagining an extension of the Primary World, separated from us only by distance or time. The universe operates in the same way there as here; neither we nor the story's character's can have any certainty of a supernatural order, for the certainty of faith is not the same as the certainty of material proof. It is possible for a science-fiction writer to imagine a world with physical laws *different* from ours; but inside the story neither the reader nor the characters would be able to credit the change to a supernatural power. It is also possible for science fiction to deal with religion. Walter Miller's *A Canticle for Leibowitz*, in which the major characters are Catholic monks in a post-atomic future, is such a book. But although the characters believe in their God, He is not a character in the story. On the other hand, James Blish's A *Case of Conscience* (1958), published as "science fiction," is about a priest who discovers that an alien race has been used by Satan to "prove" that there is no God. Although Satan himself is not seen, he is a real character in the universe of the book, which is therefore science fantasy. Science fiction may be about knowledge, but its knowledge is confined to the physical universe, however distorted. In every fantasy, a numinous power, active or passive, exists in the universe of the story.

In order to distinguish between science fiction and fantasy, consequently, the reader cannot depend on the subject matter of the narrative in question. Anne McCaffrey's *Dragonflight* is often called fantasy because its characters live in a quasi-medieval society and fly on the backs of "dragons," with whom they communicate by telepathy. But the story takes place in the far future on a distant planet; the dragons are indigenous semi-intelligent animals, not supernatural beasts; and the gift of telepathy is specifically described as a mental power susceptible to scientific interpretation. On the other hand, Leonard Wibberley's *The Mouse That Roared* might seem to be science fiction because it centers round an atomic air-raid drill and a "Q-bomb"; but Grand Fenwick bears an anything but superficial resemblance to Oz

and Pantouflia, because it exists in the same kind of fantasy world: a
world in which some power watches over the heroes. The real crux of
the difference lies in the writer's attempt to present his ideas within the
context of new assumptions about the way the world works. The science
fiction story is set in a world which, however much it may differ from
the Primary World in detail, follows the laws of physical reality as we
know them. The story may modify those laws according to whatever
hypothesis the writer wants to consider, but the modification must be
scientifically plausible and bound to Nature. But fantasy, though it
may use "science," is not bound to Nature, but to something beyond
Nature. Fantasy's rhetorical strategy resembles science fiction's, but it is
radical where science fiction's is limited by science.

Fairy-story and fantasy

We come now to the distinction between fantasy itself and the
mythopoeic material of fairy-story which it uses. Fairy-story, as defined
by Tolkien, includes folktales, legends and ballads, medieval romances,
Perrault and Andersen, beast-fables, even Eloi and Morlocks. But fairy-
stories are not necessarily about fairies—Tinker Bell or the Queen of
Elfland; they are about Faerie, the

> realm or state in which fairies have their being. Faerie contains
> many things besides elves and fays, and besides dwarfs, witches,
> trolls, giants, or dragons; it holds the seas, the sun, the moon, the
> sky; and the earth, and all the things that are in it: tree and bird,
> water and stone, wine and bread, and ourselves, mortal men, when
> we are enchanted.[23]

Faerie is not another universe or a Secondary World; it is a source
of symbols out of which tales may be told and fantasy subcreated.
Fairy-story is not the same thing as "fairy tale," a better term for which
is probably "folktale," because fairy-story is not a form, but a mass of
material on which form may be imposed.

But this may be misinterpreted. Eleanor Cameron has said:

> Because Tolkien considers fantasy an attribute of the fairy tale,
> and because, in general usage, the words are closely related, I want
> to be specific about fantasy as it is thought of currently in chil-
> dren's literature. When we speak of the literature of magic, we
> recognize that fairy tales are fantasy, but that they are only one
> kind, and that all fantasies written today are not fairy tales. When
> we speak of fantasy, we mean tales in which humans, usually
> children, are enabled to experience events which are impossible

23. Tolkien, p. 9.

according to the laws of reality. The word *magic* need never be mentioned, and yet we take for granted that events are happening because of magic. Fairy tales take place in the world of magic, where magic is natural and beasts and trees speak. . . .[24]

But Tolkien does not consider fantasy to be an "attribute" of fairy-story (not "fairy tales"); he considers it the *result* of the subcreative imagination applied to fairy-story. Cameron's judgments are usually both sensitive and reliable; but many fantasies are *not* about "humans, usually children" who experience impossible events in the "world of reality," and many books set in the world of magic are *not* "fairy tales." Think of *The Wind in the Willows*, in which there is no magic as such; even if it is set in the world of magic, it is not a "fairy tale," nor are Tolkien's *The Hobbit*, Le Guin's *A Wizard of Earthsea*, or many others.

Nor does fairy-story necessarily employ magic. When Tolkien discusses magic, he mentions it only to dispose of it. To him, magic is a base mechanical craft, which at worst is power-hungry and at best is but a poor metaphor for the enchantment of true subcreation. Magic may be used by the supernatural power behind the Secondary World, or it may be a sort of shorthand reference to that power; but it is that power's presence, not magic, which fairy-story and fantasy have in common. As Cameron rightly says, in fairy-story this presence is taken for granted. In fantasy, this presence must be realistically established.

Fairy-story is Tolkien's term for the mass of tales about Faerie; he does not use the term "fairy tale" interchangeably with it, preferring "folktale." This leaves "fairy tale" free to describe a special subgenre of fantasy: the sophisticated modern re-creation of the naive folktale or *Hausmärchen*, also sometimes called the "Perrault fairy tale," after its first author. The Perrault fairy tale is not a form, or a revival, of the *Kunstmärchen*, since it is not used as a vehicle for philosophy, but written for its own sake. Many modern fantasists have written fairy tales; the greatest are those of Hans Christian Andersen. Consider the most famous of Andersen stories, "The Ugly Duckling," which, again, contains no "magic." The Perrault fairy tale holds a special position among the subgenres of fantasy, not because of the use or disuse of magic, but because it creates a new universe in an abbreviated form. It is not as complete as the fantasy universe; it uses naive character and story motifs, like the youngest prince, the helpful servant, the wicked stepmother, the lovely princess. One of the ways in which fantasy can

24. Eleanor Cameron, *The Green and Burning Tree: on the Writing and Enjoyment of Children's Books*, Boston, Little, Brown, 1969, p. 10.

be distinguished from fairy tale is fantasy's transformation of the fairy-story material to give the characters personalities instead of occupational labels.

The beast-fable is related to fantasy in much the same way as is the allegory. Tolkien points out that:

> Beasts and birds and other creatures often talk like men in real fairy-stories. In some part (often small) this marvel derives from one of the primal "desires" that lie near the heart of Faerie: the desire of men to hold communication with other living beings. But the speech of beasts in a beast-fable . . . has little reference to that desire, and often wholly forgets it. The magical understanding by men of the proper languages of birds and beasts and trees, that is much nearer to the true purposes of Faerie.[25]

In a beast-fable, "the animal form is only a mask upon a human face, a device of the satirist or the preacher. . . ."[26] Beast-fable is a form of parable, a didactic genre. A satirical attitude does not make a story into a "Menippean satire"; if that were so, Tolkien's own *Farmer Giles of Ham* would not qualify as fantasy. But the satire of beast-fable is aimed at some particular foible of human nature, like greed, selfishness, or pride. The satire of fantasy is more subtle. It laughs at human nature itself, at being human as contrasted to being something else. Just as the utopia is not really concerned with the new world it depicts, so the beast-fable is not really concerned with communicating to other living beings, but with the faults of humans. Where the folktale and fairy tale label individuals by social position, the beast-fable exaggerates some characteristic of human personality: *sly* fox, *loyal* dog, *vain* lion, *humble* mouse. It shows animals not as they are—individuals of a species—but in anthropomorphic terms. Communion with other living beings cannot occur when the others are merely ourselves in costume.

Only when an animal tale begins to consider the animals as individuals, not as representatives of some human tendency, does it become fantasy. There are books in which the animal characters, though they may seem at first glance to be disguised humans, at second glance seem more like real animals than ever. They are animals disguised as humans, rather than the reverse. Human characters are not always necessary. Tolkien considered *The Wind in the Willows* beast-fable, but it little resembles the other examples he gives: "Brer Rabbit," "Reynard the Fox," or "The Three Little Pigs."[27] Real animals do not always resemble their counterparts in fable; Mr. Toad is not just a comment on vainglory.

25. Tolkien, p. 15.   26. Ibid.   27. Tolkien, p. 15, pp. 75–76.

It is the difference in attitude toward the raw material that distinguishes fantasy from the rest of fairy-story. Fantasy has contributed to fairy-story as much as fairy-story has given it: Munchkins, hobbits, marsh-wiggles, Shangri-La, Islandia, Alderley Edge, Dr. Dolittle, Tarzan, Winnie-the-Pooh, and many more have all been put in Tolkien's great Cauldron of Story by fantasy. But all these elements come from books whose rationalistic attitude towards them has made them what they are. Pre-realistic and fairy-story forms of narrative often seem illogically and unaccountably told to us today. For example, in Rabelais' *Gargantua*, the monstrous infant, newly born, eats whole oxen in his cradle. In *Gulliver's Travels* the island of Balnibarbi hangs suspended between two gigantic magnets, apparently undisturbed by the winds. In Cyrano's *Voyage to the Moon*, the hero ascends to the Moon assisted only by vials of evaporating dew. Exaggeration and lack of internal consistency do not necessarily harm the artistic impact of these stories. But exaggeration and inconsistency cannot be used in the same way by a modern author, who must set up a logical superstructure, implicit or explicit, on which to hang his tale. The events, characters, style, and setting of a fantasy may resemble or imitate those of fairy-story or pre-realistic fiction. But the internal logic of each type is predicated on different assumptions.

The author of an honest fantasy must convince the reader of two things: first, that his world is plausible; second, that the story he sets in that world is plausible. The reader must be willing to enter not only into the events, but into the world of the events. A fantasy that relies upon the conventions of fairy-story to establish literary belief cannot succeed, because these conventions will not stand up to realistic criteria. A fairy godmother cannot merely appear: she must be established, accounted for, and given a motivation, for she is not a prop, but a character. She cannot just pop out of the woodwork when the protagonist is in difficulties. The same is true for all other supernatural elements within the fantasy, especially the basic one, the numinous power that oversees the world. Where a realistic writer must be true to life, the fantasist must invent a new life and make it believable both on its own terms and by realistic standards. Thus, fantasy is securely bound to realism, while the pre-realistic author and the post-realistic fabulator—the mythmaker and the ironist—approach each other in the realms of unreason.

Fantasy's characteristic elements

Among the various genres of speculative fiction, only two, science fiction and fantasy, can carry the possibilities of speculative writing to their logical conclusion by creating wholly new worlds. Their association in the minds of readers and writers is no accident; but science fiction is bound to its sociological and technological bases in the real world. Only fantasy allows the writer the godlike power of creating characters, settings, worlds, and powers wholly different from our own. A science-fiction book can contain a new planet and populate it with a race of alien beings, but they must exist within Nature as we know it. A fantasy can describe beings totally divorced from Nature, yet free to act within it; it can change the past and present, as well as imagine the future; and it can change the very nature of the universe. The fantasist's imagined world must make emotional sense, but need make physical sense only on its own terms. The mythmaker, the realist, and the fabulator must report on actuality, psychological or physical; the science-fiction writer may extend actuality, but he cannot cross its boundaries. The fantasist alone creates new actualities to describe.

Fantasy is the most visionary of fictional genres: tied as all art is to emotional truth, it is freer than any other literary form to escape mere actuality. It is often misused. In the hands of a hack, it becomes sensational and wish-fulfilling; in the hands of a prig, it becomes sanctimonious, didactic, and condescending. But this is true of any form. On the other hand, merely sensational or sanctimonious fantasy is instantly recognizable, because it fails formally as well as artistically. It is unable to sustain literary belief and to allow the reader to enter fully into the newly created world. Some readers are unable to give literary belief to fantasy, either because the notion of a numinous creation is distasteful to them, or because they associate fantasy with childishness. To them fantasy, good or bad, has no appeal, and no distinctions. They lack what Tolkien calls the "primal desire at the heart of Faerie . . . the realization, independent of the conceiving mind, of imagined wonder." [28] The lover of fantasy does not, in the end, read it for its beautiful symbols, its princesses and quests. He reads it to experience the world in which princesses and quests must exist—to experience it as a consistent reality as well as a vision. The realism that gives fantasy its distinctive structure is the background of the work, just as the sky is the background of the stars. The artist's vision is expressed with intellectual consistency and plausibility, but it is, nonetheless, a vision.

Fantasy is not dialectical or allegorical, a battle between Niceness and Nastiness with imaginative trappings. Taking a realistic approach to the materials of myth, romance, legend, and folklore means giving them a history, actualizing what was only imagined before—in short,

28. Tolkien, p. 14.

reporting on a reality, not forcing elements into a pre-ordered mold. Fantasy masters the author and takes control of his imagination. Like both history and myth, it develops according to its own internal logic. C. S. Lewis wrote: "Into an allegory a man can put only what he already knows; into a myth he puts what he does not yet know and would not come to know in any other way." [29] Even a bad fantasist tries to be a creator; a good one creates more than he tried to, and his work takes on its own life.

Sheer inventiveness and "style," meaning a unique sensibility, may enhance fantasy, but they are not always necessary to it. The greatest pitfall for inexperienced fantasists is too much reliance on invention and not enough on realism. Fantasy's power does not derive from its separation from reality, but from its simplicity and self-limitation, its rules of procedure, and its internal logic. The supernatural is important not because it offers excitement and fun and escape, but because it provides laws and moral values. Once the reader accepts the basic premises of the new world, everything in it follows organically and realistically from them. To create a genuine Secondary World, the fantasist must convince us that his creation is not only plausible, but necessary; that it follows not only logically, but desirably, from its premises. The inventions and beauty of the story may produce, as fairy-story does, enchantment based on symbolism—the symbols of great emotional archetypes rising up out of our imaginations and our feelings. But the true enchantment of fantasy is produced by the formal framework that forces us to open our minds to new concepts of creation, and to judge them intellectually as well as emotionally. Our reason must be as much engaged as our hearts.

These two bases of mood and form are fantasy's contribution to the metaphysical expansion of the range of human possibilities. The degree to which a fantasy is removed from the Primary World is, too often, misleading. It is not by inventiveness and queerness that a fantasy succeeds, but by how convincingly "realistic" it is. The act of casting a spell is a practical activity, though its elements must be geared to an emotional reality that may be tenuous and inscrutable. The fact that fantasy has at hand all the paraphernalia of Faerie—ready-made, so to speak—leads many to confuse the activity of fantasy with the material it uses. It also provides a simple shorthand for lazy writers, who abuse the form with trite references to magic, wishes, exotic personages, and over-decorated locations. But such symbols are only the

29. Peter Milward, "C. S. Lewis on Allegory," in *Eigo Seinen* (*The Rising Generation*), Vol. 114, No. 4 (April 1, 1968), p. 229. The quotation is from a letter written by Lewis to Milward on Sept. 22, 1956.

flesh of fantasy. The real strength—the bones—comes from the author's attitude towards the symbols. What counts is not the new world itself, but how well human beings can deal with it; not whether it is enchanted, but whether it is enchanting. And yet the author must make it possible for the reader, and the characters, to love it and appreciate it for itself and to live in it to their fullest extent. It must provide another life: another standard by which to evaluate human life in the Primary, the real, world. Fantasy is not allegorical, but metaphorical. The purpose of allegory is to direct. The purpose, or perhaps the *use*, of fantasy is to enlighten and clarify.

Fantasy combines the best elements of fairy-story, realism, and fabulation. Like fairy-story, it works with psychological, emotional symbols that possess great evocative power in themselves and in their referents. The divine, the magical, the heroic, the lovely, the wicked, and the good are embodied in rational form so that they can be dealt with in ordinary, personal terms. Like realism, fantasy allows the reader to identify with the protagonist and experience his adventures just as he would if he were in the protagonist's place. Like fabulation, fantasy encompasses all of life: the conscious and the unconscious, the temporal and the eternal, the real and the ideal. The separation of the worlds of reality and imagination that fantasy forces on the writer enables him to see more clearly just what the relationship between the ordinary and the numinous is. Once that is understood, he and the reader are free to enter the newly created world and surrender to the newly created myth. The fantasist does not merely employ materials of myth and romance; he is employed by them. No artist, it might be said, creates art. He only gives it being. But because fantasy is concerned with the numinous, the true fantasist's art takes on a specially numinous power. The great paradox and reward of fantasy is that the artist's ability to perceive the sundering of the natural and supernatural worlds is his ability to express an emotional experience of harmony and reunification.

Fantasy awakens within us a new vision, not of strange or exotic dreams, but of ordinary reality. We do not need new colors or a sixth sense, but to be able to really see the old colors and really use the old senses. Like beauty, fantasy enables us to get the most out of what we already have. Those who read fantasy in order to escape into a world of gorgeousness and adventure are missing the point; fantasy restores our own world to us. Sometimes it seems that our life is full of tragedy, grief, and evil, the realized visions of greed, error, pride, hatred, and selfishness. To read fantasy is to escape evil, not to ignore it, but to recognize good; to escape reality in order to see it as it really is—to see, as Rupert Brooke said, "no longer blinded by our eyes."

CHAPTER TWO

Some Trends in Fantasy

FROM ITS BEGINNINGS, fantasy has been written as much for adults as for children. We forget that Charles Perrault was a courtier of Louis XIV who composed his tales for the delectation of sophisticated lords and ladies, not for the children to whom we have relegated "Cinderella" and "Puss-in-Boots." Those adults who love fantasy do not enjoy it only for sentimental reasons; for example, *The Wind in the Willows* is a classic of English literature—not just of children's literature. It is not true that an appetite for fantasy is especially strong in children, compared with adults, although it is true that fantasy has long been out of fashion among adult literary critics. But nothing in fantasy makes it inherently suitable for children.

James Higgins says in his *Beyond Words: Mystical Fancy in Children's Literature* that "The fairy tale, like the child, is a wild flower. It thrives on a hillside of uncultivated innocence, nourished by the elemental passions beneath the sod . . . which contribute to the sacredness of man. . . ." [1] This is a highly sentimental view both of the fairy tale and of childhood. Children spend a great deal of their time being "cultivated," or taught; they absorb (among other things) a comprehensive knowledge of the "elemental passions," which, far from being hidden "beneath the sod," are apparent to any person of normal intelligence: love, envy, conscience, the power of the social group, dislike, sympathy. Higgins draws a picture of carefree merriment sporting on the green, a picture only occasionally true to life. The problems of childhood seem as great to the child as those of maturity to the adult. Fairy tales and fantasy are not "innocent"; they incorporate elements of myth and dream, which have intense psychological meanings. They often have a burden of satire, moralizing, heroic behavior-models, or

1. James E. Higgins, *Beyond Words: Mystical Fancy in Children's Literature*, New York, Teachers' College Press, 1970, pp. 4–5.

wonderment, none of which are hidden somewhere beneath the surface. As Tolkien points out, even Peter Rabbit did not gambol about on the green, but met a prohibition and suffered the consequences of defying it. If children do like fantasy, it is not because both it and they are naive.

Nor do they like it, if they do, because they cannot distinguish between fantasy and reality. Helen Lourie says: "Children pass easily from the incomprehensible adult world to the equally mysterious world of fantasy . . . they have acquired less disbelief to be suspended before they can enter into the Kingdom of Never-Never." [2] Andrew Lang says: "They represent the young age of man true to his early loves, and have his unblunted edge of belief, a fresh appetite for marvels." [3] But this implies that the "adult world" is somehow identical with the "real world," that children are therefore not part of the real world, and that their lack of experience with the real world makes them ready to swallow anything; that an appetite for marvels is stronger in children than in adults, which appetite makes them more credulous. It is true, as Tolkien observes, that a child's inexperience may cause him to mistake the fantastic for the real in a particular case; it is not true that, once the difference is pointed out, he cannot understand why there is a difference. We have seen that an appetite for marvels is not the key to a liking for fantasy. History, travel, and science provide marvelous experiences for anyone willing to receive them; a dinosaur is not less marvelous than a dragon.

It is extremely doubtful that the percentage of children who do like fantasy is greater than the percentage of adults who do, always allowing for those persons over the age of eighteen who refuse to allow themselves to like it because they mistakenly think it "childish." C. S. Lewis says, "When I became a man I put away childish things, including the fear of childish things and the desire to be very grownup." [4] The ability to give literary belief to fantasy is not inherent in all children, any more than it is inherent in all people; literary tastes form at a very early age if they form at all. Most people probably find it difficult to enter fantasy worlds, which means that fantasy's audience will always be relatively small, but it will not be further fragmented by arbitrary age groupings. When considering the history of fantasy, it is

2. Helen Lourie, "Where is Fancy Bred?" in Sheila Egoff, G. T. Stubbs, & L. F. Ashley, eds., *Only Connect: Readings on Children's Literature*, New York, Oxford University Press, 1969, p. 109.

3. Quoted by J. R. R. Tolkien, "On Fairy-Stories," in his *Tree and Leaf*, Boston, Houghton Mifflin, 1965, p. 36.

4. C. S. Lewis, "On Three Ways of Writing for Children," in Sheila Egoff et al., op. cit., p. 147.

important to realize that adult and children's fantasies are equally significant and influential.

It is also important to realize that fantasy did not arise in a vacuum. Besides the literary forms that we have already discussed, fantasy drew inspiration from many areas which experienced an "information explosion" during the nineteenth century. Among them were, first, the rediscovery of the great national epic literatures of the world—not just Homer and Virgil, but the *Nibelungenlied*, the *Kalevala*, the *Arabian Nights*, the *Shah-Namah*, the *Mahabharata*, the *Mabinogion*, the *Song of Roland, Beowulf*, the *Morte d'Arthur*, and the Icelandic *Eddas* and sagas. Second, the great folk-tale collections, especially those of the Brothers Grimm, Andrew Lang, and Joseph Jacobs, and the scholarly compilations of other types of folklore, like the *Popular Ballads* of Francis James Child. Third, the progress made in the study of philology and mythology by the Grimms, Lang, Max Muller, Sir James Frazer, and others. Fourth, the new scientific and geographic knowledge of the world: the discoveries of explorers and archaeologists; a new rigorousness in historical research. Fifth, research in anthropology, which stimulated interest in non-Western religions, including Oriental, African, Polynesian, and Amerindian beliefs. Sixth, developments in other arts: the Pre-Raphaelite movement; Aestheticism; the folk nationalism of composers such as Wagner, Grieg, Dvorak, and others.

The result of the interaction of all these influences was that fantasy diversified early; there is no single, central fantasy tradition, though some trends have been more important than others. The only criterion of a fantasy is, as we have seen, that it create a new universe by causing the reader to change some basic physical, historical, or geographical assumption about the Primary World, not as a scientific or pseudo-scientific speculation, but as a vehicle for a new reality that gives the reader a new perspective on the Primary World. This new reality must be internally consistent and logically developed. Neither magic, a heroic tone, nor a total divorcement from the Primary World is necessary to a fantasy, while inventing an "imaginary country" like Ruritania for a story does not make it a fantasy. Eight major trends, or strains, in the history of fantasy may be identified according to their dominant mood: (1) mythopoeic, (2) heroic, (3) adventurous, (4) ironic, (5) comic, (6) nostalgic, (7) sentimental, and (8) horrific. The subject arrangement appended to this Introduction (Appendix D) identifies several subgenres, according to whether the numinous power implied in a work takes an active or passive hand in the story's events.

1. *Mythopoeic fantasy*

Mythopoeic fantasy holds the place of honor, because its first practitioner, George MacDonald, was also the first fantasist to wholly escape both the limitations of the fairy tale (on the model of Hans Christian Andersen) and the pompous moralizing of previous attempts at fantasy. His first fantastic novel, *Phantastes* (1858), was the story of a young man's journey through a spiritual landscape similar to that of a medieval romance. MacDonald was a minister, but he was no cheap moralizer, either in his adult books or in his stories for children. His books are more mystical than sermonizing. In this they differ profoundly from previous works of a fantastic nature. Adult stories emphasized either exotica (as in the Oriental tale) or heavy-handed allegory; children's books were preachy and didactic.

MacDonald avoided falling into either of these literary traps, because his message could not be *told*; it had to be felt. Consequently, his writing conveyed a feeling of the supernatural, the mystical, and the spiritual. He neither talked down to the reader, nor looked over his head to someone else at whom his books were really aimed, as did Charles Kingsley, also a clergyman. Compare the death of Diamond, in MacDonald's *At the Back of the North Wind* (1871), with that of Ellie in Kingsley's *The Water-Babies* (1863). Diamond has known from the start that death is the only way into the North Wind's country, to which he longs to go. Ellie's death is gratuitous. She falls and hits her head on a rock, in the middle of a discourse on evolution by a Professor who is supposed to be minding her. Kingsley makes it quite clear to the reader that the Professor's ungodly beliefs are directly responsible for the child's accident, adding some coyly sarcastic comments on the stupidity of overeducated people. The difference between Kingsley and MacDonald is the difference between an order and a hint.

To escape the confines of the fairy tale, MacDonald made both characters and settings specific. He did not invent a whole new country, with a definite geography and history, until his last book, *Lilith* (1895), and it was more like Elfland than Middle-Earth. But neither did he say that his tales took place "once upon a time," nor did he rely for characterization on the folk-tale motifs of Youngest Son and Beautiful Princess and Helpful Fairy. *At the Back of the North Wind* is set in the London Dickens knew; Curdie and Irene of *The Princess and the Goblin* (1872) are not at all like Jack the Giant Killer and Briar Rose. He had a sense of humor, but never exercised it at the expense of the story; he never sneered at the fantasy form. Nor did he overrate it.

Although MacDonald was strongly influenced by the *Kunstmärchen* tradition, especially Novalis, he never succumbed to the temptation of sacrificing his story to his message, because the story was the message.

G. K. Chesterton wrote about *The Princess and the Goblin:*

> The commonplace allegory takes what it regards as the com-
> monplaces or conventions necessary to ordinary men and women,
> and tries to make them pleasant or picturesque by dressing them
> up as princesses or goblins or good fairies. But George MacDonald
> did really believe that people were princesses and goblins and good
> fairies, and he dressed them up as ordinary men and women. The
> fairy-tale was the inside of the ordinary story and not the outside.[5]

Yet MacDonald did not force human life to submit to his con-
victions about an overriding moral order in the universe. For example,
in *The Pilgrim's Progress* we see Christian making his way along a
road. Sometimes it dips into a dark valley, sometimes reaches a city,
sometimes runs smoothly along the heights; sometimes Christian is
sidetracked away from it; but the road always remains, its starting-
point and destination clearly marked. In *Lilith,* MacDonald's best
work, the starting-point is a mirror through which Vane, the hero, sees
the new world—but he does not always see the same scene through it.
Far from desiring to travel in the new world, he is at first terrified of,
then resigned to it; yet although he knows he need not go there, he
cannot keep away from the mirror. Once there, he meets people who
talk in riddles, as he wanders across an unmarked countryside. He rejects the aid of all who, at first, offer to help him. He meets no one like
Faithful or Mr. Valiant-for-Truth or Mr. Standfast; instead, he meets
Mr. Raven, who is sometimes a bird and sometimes Adam, and has
been his father's librarian, and Lona, who is both Lilith's daughter and
Lilith herself, as she ought to have been. The journey to spiritual truth
in MacDonald is not a pilgrimage along a highway, but a solitary expedition through an unknown, unmapped country of indescribable
beauty and terror.

What MacDonald did to fantasy was to take moralizing out and
put in morality, which was derived from the basic assumptions of the
new universe he described. He did not personify spiritual qualities in
human form; he showed them operating in real people. At the same
time, he proved that the fantasy form could support serious consideration of religious and psychological questions. This is the object of

5. G. K. Chesterton, *GKC as MC, Being a Collection of Thirty-seven Intro-
ductions,* selected and edited by J. P. de Fonseka; Freeport, N.Y., Books for Libraries
Press, 1967 (1929), pp. 166–167.

mythopoeic fantasy: to introduce living spiritual beings into the ordinary human world. Every story, whether set in a wholly new universe or in our own world, deals with the attempts of ordinary humans—ordinary sinners—to come to terms with new demands placed on them by beings of numinous power. In real life, MacDonald could say, "God requires you to do such-and-such"; in fantasy, he could say, "North Wind" or "the old princess" or "Mr. Raven requires you to do such-and-such," showing the human characters meeting their spiritual mentors face to face. Having brought these supernatural powers into the story in the form of characters enabled him to show why moral imperatives in the ordinary world demand certain kinds of behavior. Mythopoeic fantasy is essentially evangelistic, but MacDonald managed to keep it from being merely didactic.

Other mythopoeic fantasists have not always been so successful, especially since G. K. Chesterton imparted a Tory, conservative cast to mythopoeic fantasy, which many people find repulsive. If MacDonald was primarily interested in the search for the immutable Truth, Chesterton was far more interested in Justice, believing that the truth was already known and had only to be accepted. He made mythopoeic fantasy aggressive, attacking other beliefs in a surreal Holy War; he was the first mythopoeic fantasist to equate disbelief in Christianity with stupidity rather than with evil. Chesterton himself was too intelligent and too kind to make his work into a literary type of muscular Christianity, but his influence on other fantasists has not always been good.

Charles Williams has suffered most from Chesterton's influence, since it has been chiefly responsible for the limiting of Williams's audience. Williams, besides being a poet and playwright of considerable lyric ability, was interested in the occult and in various out-of-the-way elements of supernatural lore, and his seven "theological thrillers" each center around some numinous object or notion—the Celestial Virtues realized as gigantic animals, the Tarot deck, the Seal of Solomon, the Grail, a succubus, Simon the Magus, and the Doppelganger—which he dealt with imaginatively and originally. His plots were fast-moving and exciting, his characters believable and likable, if a bit priggish, and his prose was quietly powerful. But, except for a tiny minority of readers, Williams's effects do not quite come off. As Roger Sale points out,[6] the problem is that his work is aimed at those who already agree with him. Readers who are not yet convinced find that he is not interested in their reasons for disagreeing—that he has no respect for the right

6. Roger Sale, "England's Parnassus: C. S. Lewis, Charles Williams, and J. R. R. Tolkien," *Hudson Review*, Vol. 17 No. 2 (Summer 1964), p. 212 ff.

to hold what is from his point of view an incorrect opinion. He has an absolutist's temperament and a fanatical conscience, which is both shaming and repellent. For the few readers he does attract, he is perfect, always concerned with principles and motivations, always sure of his ground, always making intuitive leaps from logic to inspiration, always earnest, always resolute.

Through Williams, Chesterton's influence reached C. S. Lewis, whose native admiration for MacDonald was too often subject to his fear that he ought to be more like Chesterton, and his combativeness, which made him more Chestertonian than Chesterton himself. Lewis was a true child of Mercury and Philology, an intellect drunk on language, with a facility for metaphor less skillful writers can only envy. At his worst Lewis has the defects of his virtues. His wit becomes glibness, his argument becomes casuistry, his deepest beliefs become debating-points. At his best Lewis is capable of explosions of brilliance and of tender sensitivity. He was that rare thing, a writer with an idiosyncratic style that never palled. The most characteristic things in Lewis are his descriptions of other-worldly landscapes: the trembling silence of the grove of Meldilorn; the fragrant seas and glowing sky of Perelandra; the flowering glades of Narnia. His imagination worked in colors like bright enamel and with the precision of a diamond tool. He was perhaps more capable than MacDonald of capturing the spirit, the mood, of a mystical experience.

But the influence of Williams and Chesterton encouraged Lewis to slight his visionary qualities and concentrate on theological argument, with poor results. In *That Hideous Strength* (1945), the most Williams-like of all Lewis's novels, the characters are mere caricatures of both the good qualities he approved and the bad ones he abhorred. All his prejudices—against science, against journalism, against vivisection, against sociology—are laid on to the villains, who are eventually dispatched in one of the most savage scenes in modern literature, in which a horde of maddened wild animals invades a dinner party. In *The Voyage of the "Dawn Treader"* (1952), one of the Narnia books for children, the three protagonists meet Christ (Aslan) in the form of a Lamb who cooks them a dinner of fish. In *The Last Battle* (1956), the final Narnia story, a girl character loses her entire family at one blow—parents, brothers, sister, cousin, godparents—for the sin of being overly interested in lipstick and stockings. Lewis's emphasis on evangelism led him to condemn modern life wherever he considered it, which naturally spoiled his depiction of modern life in fiction. He simply could not cope with the effects of his arguments in ordinary human society.

His real strength—depicting the supernatural itself—is unsurpassed by any other mythopoeic fantasist, even MacDonald. He created a whole new mythology in his adult fantasies, the Perelandra trilogy, blending the Olympian gods with medieval angelology. In the Narnia books, he successfully combined the lesser Olympians—Bacchus and the Maenads, fauns, dryads, and centaurs—with more homely, English creatures like dwarfs, giants, talking animals, witches, and the inimitable Marsh-wiggles. What Lewis contributed to mythopoeic fantasy was specificity, which it had never had before. The vagueness and moodiness, the misty uncertainty, which most people associate with religious experience, have no place in Lewis's work. He pointed out that a mystical vision, far from being vague and unreal, should be more vivid, more real, more memorable than ordinary life. Williams had seen this, but had been unable to escape the habit of wrapping mystical experience in an obscuring veil; Chesterton never concerned himself with internal consistency; MacDonald lacked Lewis's lucidity. Lewis alone among mythopoeic fantasists convinces the reader of the vibrant reality of religious experiences, while conveying the mystical, supra-rational, ecstatic, entranced qualities that we think characteristic of them.

The only mythopoeic fantasy that approaches Lewis's power is David Lindsay's *A Voyage to Arcturus* (1920), a difficult, unforgettable, almost irrational book. Though it uses some of the trappings of science fiction, no book less like science fiction has ever been published. The world of Tormance, through which Maskull, the hero, travels, is full of irreconcilable landscapes and alien personas, unnamable temptations and fascinations, and new colors and sensations under the furious light of a double sun. The book's power does not come from Maskull's actual journey, although some incidents are compelling, but from the passion with which Lindsay delineated his unearthly vision. *A Voyage to Arcturus* is perhaps the only mythopoeic fantasy that does not evangelize the reader. Its hallucinogenic intensity overpowers him. The book has had no successors, and only one predecessor in literature, Coleridge's "Kubla Khan." Compared with it, Vane's troubled quest in *Lilith* seems like a pleasant afternoon stroll; the massacre of the villains in *That Hideous Strength* seems humanly reasonable, if not agreeable. But it offers experiences unobtainable, even inconceivable, elsewhere in literature.

Mythopoeic fantasy since Lewis tends to be derivative and didactic. A children's writer, Madeleine L'Engle, won the Newbery Medal with *A Wrinkle in Time* (1962), a book often mistaken for science fiction because of its "tesseract" and missing scientist. But Mrs. Who, Mrs. Which, and Mrs. Whatsit are angels, and the tesseract that got Meg's father into trouble can only be broken by love. A sequel, *A Wind in the Door* (1973), increases the moralizing of the first book, which at least had an organically developed plot and credible motivations; the sequel depends entirely on external moral lessons that L'Engle tries to impose on her readers. The scene in which Meg saves the unkind school principal, who has always disliked her, is downright embarrassing. Unless mythopoeic fantasists are content to let their stories tell themselves, mythopoeic fantasy will probably not develop farther than it has already.

2. *Heroic fantasy and adventure fantasy*

Heroic fantasy has received the greater part of critical attention in recent years, largely because of the influence and importance of J. R. R. Tolkien. Lin Carter's *Imaginary Worlds* (1973) argues that heroic fantasy is the mainstream of fantasy, but as he concentrates on horror and adventure fantasy, and states that children's books do not qualify, his case is not very coherent.[7] As a re-creation of the medieval epic and romance forms, heroic fantasy lends itself to the creation of wholly different geographies, but it is not confined to them. Heroic behavior is possible in any setting and is the real criterion of this type. It means that physical courage and exciting events are not enough; every action must have a serious purpose. Adventure fantasy is an unambitious form of heroic fantasy, with the heroism left out. The reader identifies with the hero not because he is good, but because he is strong, clever, and resourceful. His conflicts with his opponents are interesting only as action; he does not necessarily deserve to win. Adventure fantasy is still being written according to the conventions of pulp fiction and comic books, though in the last few years some authors have tried to impart more of the tone of heroic fantasy. But most adventure fantasy remains what it has always been—escapist trash.

Heroic fantasy, like mythopoeic fantasy, emphasizes a conflict between good and evil, but it is not explicitly religious; in fact, religion is rarely even mentioned. The characters of heroic fantasy have other things to do; they are already on the side of good, and do not need to be converted by supernatural beings who demand that they overcome themselves. They help others fight evil. The first heroic fantasies are those of William Morris, the poet, printer, designer, Pre-Raphaelite, and early Socialist, whose seven prose romances were inspired and influenced by Icelandic sagas. His first two, *The House of the Wolfings* and *The Roots of the Mountains*, were vaguely historical, set in Mid-

7. Lin Carter, *Imaginary Worlds: the Art of Fantasy*, New York, Ballantine, 1971, pp. 6–7.

dle Europe during the Dark Ages. They depicted the wars of the Goths against the Romans and the Huns, respectively. These historical novels were "utopian" in the sense of having an impossibly ideal social organization: Morris believed that human happiness had reached a high point in the homely, rustic chivalry of early Gothic culture. His first fantasy, *The Story of the Glittering Plain* (1891), is also set in a primitive Teutonic society, but introduces magic into the story. In this book Morris left historic Europe for a world of his own making, which better expressed his vision of the ideal medieval culture. In the four books that followed, Morris left the Dark Ages for the high Middle Ages: warriors became knights, maidens became ladies, magic became sophisticated. As C. S. Lewis once said, Morris was not really interested in the Middle Ages, but in the image of them that the Romantics had established in the public imagination, the mythology of chivalry.

This Middle Ages of Morris's imagination was not an earthly paradise; it was full of robbers, raiders, witches, slavers, murderers, and wild ravening beasts. But the medieval setting provided a simple and believable social system within which to consider the conflict between good and evil, setting up resonances and connotations in the minds of readers that could be used to advantage. It gave an atmosphere that was congenial to Morris's temperament and ideas and did not need much development. It had virtues that went to the heart of Morris' beliefs: rural quietude, simple faith, pride in craftsmanship, physical courage, and a good deal of freedom, as opposed to sophistication, complexity, self-doubt, vulgarity, caution, and conformity.

It was perhaps too simple, too believable: too many fantasists found it too easy to imitate. The hallmark of heroic fantasy, and of adventure fantasy, thanks to Morris, is a quasi-medieval setting. Few writers bother to develop such a background beyond a few scattered references to castles, knights, feudal dues, and courtly behavior, which, by calling up all the well-known images of medieval life current in popular culture, are supposed to serve as Secondary Worlds. There are no surprises in such work. Good and evil become mere labels pasted on the characters, who function within the framework of a Secondary Reality that is, at best, tenuous.

Some of this oversimplification taints Morris's work, particularly the automatic identification of the protagonist with "good," whatever his actual behavior is like. His inner nobility (usually a reflection of his social status) protects him from the consequences of evil behavior—even his own. Morris never explores questions of morality; mistakes must be expiated, but no special blame attaches to them. What is important is that the protagonist's quest should come to a successful conclusion, not that the quest itself should express a valid moral system. And yet the atmosphere of Morris's fantasies is genuinely heroic and serious. His heroes' personalities are undivided, heart-whole in thought and action. Repentance does not make them querulous; success does not make them complacent. On the other hand, neither are they mere representations, in human form, of unhumanly ideal behavior, puppets without personality to be analyzed. The problem of Morris to a modern reader is this: his heroes are not modern, and their heroism partakes of qualities we have learned to suspect. We have seen the evil results of nineteenth-century ideals of human behavior that emphasize freedom, individualism, and self-confidence. We prefer heroes who doubt themselves, who are not always sure of their ground. In Morris we see the nineteenth-century ideal in its pure form: the hero without qualms. Morris was a Romantic in the tradition of Scott, not Byron.

Morris was the first fantasist to turn to the epic and saga literature of the far past, bypassing the lesser folklore and fairy-tale sources that fantasy had previously drawn upon, but the impact of his work is not the same as that of epic literature. It straddles the division between medieval and modern literature, because, however much Morris may have detested the contemporary world, he could not help being influenced by it. He added a dimension of intimacy to the old romances and epics, being more careful to describe the feelings and hopes of his characters. But he was curiously, formally old-fashioned. An unmistakable air of impersonality hangs over the proceedings he describes; the events seem to be happening on some other plane of existence, to be remote and distant: and so the charm of distance surrounds them, as if one were looking through the wrong end of a telescope. Everything is miniature, serene, and perfect.

Lord Dunsany was a different sort of miniaturist. The Pre-Raphaelites were out of fashion when Dunsany began to write, and he, like the American James Branch Cabell, was permanently marked by the Aestheticism of the Nineties. Since Dunsany was Irish, he was also strongly influenced by Yeats; he even wrote plays for the Abbey Theatre. But his real bent was for the exotic; hence, he made more of an impact on adventurous, ironic, and horrific fantasy than on heroic fantasy, and his output was mainly in short-story form. Only two of his four novels were heroic, *The Charwoman's Shadow* (1926) set in chivalric Spain, and *The King of Elfland's Daughter* (1924). The former book is Cabellian, philosophical and arch, while the latter is extremely repetitious, but beautifully written. The contribution of Dunsany to fantasy is style. He may surfeit, but he does not irritate. He brought an Oriental sound into fantasy, not confining himself to European sources. And yet, he made very little impact on heroic fantasy; almost all of his successors and imitators write straight adventure fantasy. It is difficult to admire Dunsany's heroes. Too much of the sickly and perverse air of the Nineties infects them. They may fascinate, but they do not inspire awe or esteem, for Dunsany himself views them with ironic accuracy.

A wholly different contribution is that of E. R. Eddison, whose fantasy is in the high mimetic mode, occupying a middle ground between Morris's romance and Dunsany's irony. High mimetic writing expresses itself in images of royalty and splendor, at which Eddison was a master. His language is lavish, extravagant, and grandiose, as archaic in its Elizabethan manner, as Morris's simpler prose with its faint echoes of medieval speech, but with a gorgeousness wholly foreign to Morris. At the same time, it is totally unlike the exotic lyricism of Dunsany. Dunsany reeks of incense; Eddison carries a pomander ball. Morris and Dunsany were both concerned with individuals acting alone, privately; Eddison's heroes are all public men, concerned with great matters of State, power, policy, and war, men whose private lives mold and are affected by public affairs. He portrayed Renaissance princes, not knights-errant.

He was as concerned with love as with power; his women are as important as his men, a rarity in heroic fantasy. These women are not drooping princesses or healthy Viking maids, as in Morris, but great court ladies, the wives and mistresses of the powerful, as intelligent and as subtle as the men. They too take part in the intrigues and necessities of government; they are as capable of revenge and murder as they are of soft words and lingering glances. They are not all Messalinas: Queen Sophonisba and Lady Mevrian in *The Worm Ouroboros* (1926), Queen Antiope and Duchess Amalie in the Zimiamvia trilogy are lovable, tender, delicate, chaste, and witty; Rosalinds and Mirandas. But Eddison's heart was given to women like Queen Prezmyra in *The Worm* and the inimitable Fiorinda of Zimiamvia, who added arrogance, towering passions, rage, hauteur, cunning, and ruthlessness to milder qualities.

Everything, characters, plot, setting, and philosophy, in Eddison is larger than life. The climax of his *A Fish Dinner in Memison* (1941) is a banquet during which the characters discuss metaphysics; the King of Zimiamvia creates our world to illustrate the argument; and Fiorinda casually destroys it with her fingernail. The climax of *The Worm* resurrects the heroes' enemies in order to give them a purpose in life; without the challenge of war, they will dwindle into squires. These books reflect Eddison's ideal of perfected action and noble behavior. He had no social conscience; he believed that the world was created to benefit the great. Even the lowliest characters in his books are gentry—younger sons of knights, and the like; Fiorinda's handmaidens are immortal nymphs. Eddison has had no imitators; his philosophy is too difficult and too repugnant for modern sensibilities. His influence has been exercised in the realms of action and description, where he is unparalleled. The magnificence, splendor, ornamentation, and hurricane-swiftness of his vision has impressed other heroic fantasists, but none have copied him.

The first genuinely modern heroic fantasy is T. H. White's *The Once and Future King* (1958). White was also something of a philosopher: he believed in intelligence and reasonableness. He was not a polemicist, nor did he display any special prejudices against the present or for the past, which meant that he was unique. Most fantasists detest the present and exalt the past. White had no special love for the present, but he knew that the answers of the past were no longer sufficient. Instead of imitating or re-creating older forms, White retold old stories from a modern perspective.

He did this to Malory's *Morte d'Arthur* with a calculated use of anachronism that no lesser writer could succeed with, because few writers have been as sensitive to emotional tone as White was. To have portrayed Sir Ector as a kindly Victorian country squire, Sir Gawaine as a touchy rustic in a kilt and with a brogue, King Pellinore as a huntin', fishin', shootin', sportin' old lunatic, and Mordred as the leader of an organization of thirteen-century storm troopers, White had to have perceived the underlying emotional reality and unity of the Arthurian material that made such treatment poetically right. *The Once and Future King* is one of the few fantasies that succeeds both as a fantasy, a type of romance, and as a realistic novel. His Secondary World is enchanting; his characters are real people as well as dialectical figures of good and evil. It is the fantasy—the humorously accurate anachronisms, including Merlyn, a version of White himself—that makes the novel work. Arthurian material is notoriously difficult to work with because of its mixture of history, legend, and magic. The most successful modern attempts to make it valid for us have been strictly realistic, like Rosemary Sutcliff's *Sword at Sunset*—except for *The Once and Future King*, because it captures the blend of history, legend, and magic in twentieth-century terms.

J. R. R. Tolkien's *The Lord of the Rings* (1954–56) is also a fully modern work, but not because Tolkien meant it as one. Like most other fantasists, he was a worshipper of the past and of history. He did not invent his Middle-Earth in order to provide background for a story, but made up stories—histories—to fit the world he had made, a world that he obviously preferred to this one. This world was linguistic in inspiration, for Tolkien was a philologist, a scholar of Anglo-Saxon, Icelandic, medieval German, and Welsh. Not satisfied with these languages, he made up his own, probably beginning with Elvish, since the first stories he wrote were set in the Elf kingdoms of Middle-Earth's First Age. He never thought that any of this work would be published; it was a hobby, done for his private amusement. His reputation as the creator of the hobbits is ironic, because the hobbits were not part of his original creation at all; he stumbled over them by accident.

One day in the late 1920's Tolkien suddenly, impulsively, wrote the first line of *The Hobbit* (1937) on the back of an examination paper; from then on his history of Middle-Earth took on new and unexpected directions. The hobbits added a human dimension to the remote epic history of the Three Ages of Middle-Earth. Bilbo Baggins began as an almost purely comic character, but as the tale began to show unforeseen ramifications, the hobbits developed from amusing little fat people to courageous and capable heroes in their own right. This almost subconscious development was something Tolkien never planned; it happened in spite of his original plans and proved to be the means by which Tolkien could communicate with his contemporaries.

What the hobbits offered to Tolkien was a modern way to deal with his immense creation. The hobbits were low mimetic heroes in a world of epic romance, whose point of view became all-important; it is not accidental that the story of the War of the Ring is told "as seen by the hobbits." Tolkien must have subconsciously realized that they, with their modest abilities, self-doubts, and preference for the practical over the "heroic," provided him with the means to make his heroic characters and events plausible beyond the confines of the narrative.

A substantial change in *The Hobbit* had to be made later because of this. In the original story, the Ring was a handy bit of magic that aided Bilbo in escaping from goblins, spiders, Elves, the dragon, and the battle, but had no further importance. The composition of *The Lord of the Rings* changed all that: the Ring was now the chief justification of Bilbo's adventures, all else being incidental. So Chapter Five, "Riddles in the Dark," was altered to make it consistent with the adult book. The Ring was now a dangerous object of power which had bad effects on Bilbo's personality and behavior. But the overall emphasis of *The Hobbit*, despite the change, remained the same, and the more serious implications of Bilbo's lucky find were not explored elsewhere in the book.

The primary adverse criticism of *The Hobbit* has been its shift in emphasis from Bilbo's funny adventures to the great battle in the last few chapters. Bard, not Bilbo, kills the dragon; Beorn and the Eagles, not Bilbo, bring victory in the battle. Some have felt that this destroys the book's coherence. However, given Bilbo's stated abilities, desires, and importance, this is not a tenable objection. He is not a hero, but a burglar; battles and dragons are not his responsibility. Indeed, no battle hinges on the actions of one person, or hobbit, however courageous. If anything, the shift enhances the story's credibility: we may be interested in Bilbo's adventures, but this does not oblige him to behave like James Bond. The story may have begun as a bedtime story for children—the first chapters seem to indicate this—but it quickly took on far more importance to Tolkien. With the miraculous afterthought of *hobbits*, he gained a perspective on the main history of Middle-Earth, which enabled others to enter it. *The Hobbit*, meanwhile, gains in significance as part of a greater story, as does any historical incident, rather than as an isolated book that suddenly seems to change its mind. The hobbits made the whole of Middle-Earth come to life, because they were so very lively themselves.

And yet, even though the hobbits are at the center of the book's action, and even though they represent qualities that Tolkien emphatically favored, the real imaginative center of Middle-Earth is the Elves, its elder children, Tolkien's first love. The hobbits arose because Tolkien wanted to communicate his creation to others, but the Elves were the heart of the creation. They named and ennobled everything; they taught trees and men to talk; they lived in dream and memory as much as in waking; and their destiny was not that of men. More important, they could be deceived, but they could not be corrupted. Men and hobbits could go bad; dwarves succumb to greed; Ents, or Tree-Herds, could surrender to hatred and rage; the worst that could happen to Elves was that they might become a little over-suspicious of strangers. The Elves of Middle-Earth are not like the fairies or Good People of European folklore. They are not mischievous; they are not even particularly "magical," as Galadriel tells Samwise, not "conjurors." What magic they have is used to make their environment pure and safe from evil things and to give rest and peace to themselves and their visitors. They are not given to gorgeousness and exotica, but to simplicity and naturalness: their most typical emblems are stars and trees. In describing them, their names, and their languages, Tolkien is most characteristically himself, far more so than with the hobbits' rustic jollity and vigor. All his names are beautiful and fitting, but none more so than the Elf-names: Tinúviel, Celebrant, Silmariën, Arwen, Valinor, Belfalas, Lothlórien.

The key to *The Lord of the Rings* lies in Tolkien's oft-repeated statement that he "would rather have written in Elvish." The story came long after the world was invented, and the world came after the languages, which Tolkien began to invent in his youth. Tolkien was a philologist; Middle-Earth was an expression of philology. Most people who are obsessed by language become writers of high style; Tolkien invented languages, each with its own style, instead. His English prose style is competent and readable at best, over-formal and "forsoothly" at worst, and his most fervent defenders have never claimed that he was a great stylist. But he had an instinctive feel for the possibilities of language as an instrument of naming that has never been equalled. Not just his Elvish and Dwarvish names—Lúthien, Elrond, Gandalf, Khazad-dûm, Dol Amroth, Grimbeorn—but his English names are perfect: Sackville-Baggins, the Chetwood, Rivendell, Mirkwood, Freddy Bolger, Sam Gamgee. One of the characteristics of magic, or enchantment, is that names are all-important, and Tolkien was a magician with names. The internal consistency of Middle-Earth is what makes it great, and that consistency is based upon linguistic considerations. The plot is intriguing, the characters credible, if not always distinctive, the versification pleasant, if not particularly good as poetry; but these things are not what makes the fantasy come to life. Nor does the fact that Middle-Earth is so extensive, so large, contribute to the book's success in any important way. What is important is Tolkien's ability to make the world seem like a real place because it is described with real names.

Heroic fantasy before Tolkien had always been more concerned with deeds than with the world they were acted in; Tolkien infused a new awareness of the background into heroic writing. Heroism without a genuine setting is mere adventurousness, while a magnificent setting without heroism is mere exotica. Tolkien demonstrated that consistency is everything in fantasy. No other fantasy world is as fully developed and as satisfying as his, thanks to the imaginative consistency of his languages and histories. It is true that when he tries to depict certain aspects of his creation, he sometimes fails, especially in his portraits of women, and in his attempts at formal, elegant speech, which are too often stilted and awkward. But these are failures of execution, not of conception. Likewise, his attempts to depict the War of the Ring as a cosmic struggle between good and evil sometimes fail. His identification of beauty with goodness is often simplistic, his characters are often clichés, and his evils are anti-climactic. The Orcs who kidnap Merry and Pippin, for instance, are ugly, brutal, filthy, and foul-mouthed, but they are charming compared to the horrors of modern terrorism. Still, Tolkien is the first fantasist who has tried, and, on the whole, succeeded, to add the power and profundity of mythopoeic fantasy to the courage and strength of heroic fantasy.

The inspiration of Middle-Earth has prompted many other writers to create fully developed Secondary Worlds of their own: worlds as diverse as Ursula Le Guin's Earthsea, Lloyd Alexander's Prydain, Richard Adams's Beklan Empire, Joy Chant's Kendrinh, Katherine Kurtz's Gwynedd, and Alan Garner's Alderley Edge owe a debt to Tolkien, a debt repaid by the excellence of their conception. But the inspiration of his moral concern on other writers has not always been so beneficial. Several have repeated his errors of oversimplification without approaching the grandeur of his vision. It is not enough for a writer to set up an Evil and pit his characters against it; it must have credible motives and history, and the battle must be a real one. Susan Cooper's otherwise excellent *The Dark is Rising* is an example of this tendency. In it, a boy of eleven, Will Stanton, finds that he is one of the Old Ones, superhuman guardians of the human race against the Dark. The Dark's outwardly innocent supporters and captains seem to have inexhaustible resources and the time to use them. But the contest is unequal, because Old Ones, including Will, *cannot be hurt* by the Dark. What is the point of this—that the human race will always succumb to ultimate evil without the help of literally invulnerable outsiders? The Dark's henchmen are sitting ducks. When violent attack and blackmail fail, the Dark tries to tempt Will, but he knows that its temptations are evil, so they pose no real moral dilemma.

However, Tolkien, however much he may have erred, is not to blame for the errors of his followers. We should instead be grateful that his interest in a cosmic moral struggle has saved heroic fantasy from degenerating into mere adventure fiction. His immense popularity has given all of fantasy a new impetus; his success is responsible not only for the huge upsurge in fantasy writing today, but for the reappearance of older works that were previously known to only a few readers. Much of the controversy over Tolkien has centered around the question of whether he is appropriate reading for cultivated adults, or mere "juvenile trash"—a question that only exposes the neuroses of the culturally defensive. He has already entered the small class of books that are enjoyed by both children and adults, along with *Gulliver's Travels, Huckleberry Finn,* and *The Wind in the Willows*. And it is important to remember that Tolkien's published work is still incomplete. No true judgment of his worth can be made until the First and Second Age materials, the *Silmarillion* and *Akallabeth,* are published. Let us hope that their publication will not be subject to the difficulties that surrounded the publication of *The Lord of the Rings*.

The first edition of *The Lord of the Rings* was not copyrighted in the United States, because the U.S. was not signatory to the Geneva Convention under which it was copyrighted by Tolkien's British publishers. A paperback house, Ace Books, photocopied the hardcover edition and published the three volumes in the U.S. without either notifying Tolkien or offering to pay him compensation. In so doing, Ace was within its rights, but a storm of controversy erupted, which caused Ballantine Books, another paperback publisher, to put out the second, copyrighted, "Authorized Edition." It was this edition that took advantage of—indeed, may have caused—the great Tolkien craze of the mid-1960s. It may well have been the controversy over this unfortunate situation, in which Tolkien was victimized, that was the initial source of his great success, and of the subsequent fantasy revival to which the present work bears witness.

The Lord of the Rings is not a trilogy; its three volumes were published in that form for reasons of convenience. It is a single book— what used to be called a "three-decker"—in six parts with several appendices. These appendices offer background material on the early history of Middle-Earth, its geography, chronology, calendars, languages, and peoples: all the varied paraphernalia of Tolkien's creative genius, condensed, to support the history of the War of the Ring and the end of the Third Age. When the histories of the First and Second Ages are published, there may well be a temporary reaction against him, if only for the inane reason that these books will probably not mention hobbits. But any such reaction will only be temporary. If any fantasy is likely to survive, it will probably be Tolkien's.

Among the many writers influenced by Tolkien, three are of special interest: Ursula Le Guin, Alan Garner, and Richard Adams. Le Guin, whose childhood was strongly marked by her family's friendships with American Indians, displays a major concern with the unification of man and nature and with the development of a sense of spiritual balance. *A Wizard of Earthsea* (1968) and *The Lathe of Heaven* (1971) deal with the evil effects of pride; *The Farthest Shore* (1973), which won the National Book Award, shows that denying death is more deadly than death itself. Le Guin has a sense of humor, but she is never comic; on the other hand, her seriousness never descends into ponderousness. Her work possesses a graceful and sensitive gravity. Alan Garner began, in *The Weirdstone of Brisingamen* (1960) and its sequel, *The Moon of Gomrath*, by combining and developing elements of British mythology and folklore to an extent equalled only by Tolkien himself. His later books have almost gone beyond fantasy into the study of sexual, personal, and class conflicts; the Carnegie Medal-winning *The Owl Service* (1967) re-enacts the ancient Welsh myth of the woman turned into an owl as punishment for her treachery. Garner has a violent imagination, and the potential to develop it to its maximum extent. Richard Adam's two books, *Watership Down* (1972) and *Shardik* (1975), have both been best-sellers and have suffered accordingly from perverse and shoddy criticism. *The New Yorker,* for example, castigated *Shardik* for its "odd names like Santil-ke-Erketlis, Gel-Ethlin, Mollo, and Rantzay." [8] Worse than this, however, is the persistent, and wholly unwarranted, assumption of popular critics that the books are "novels" in a strict realistic sense. Nothing could be less true. *Watership Down* is a reworking of the *Aeneid* from the perspective of rabbits, while *Shardik* combines elements from the history of Mohammed and from the medieval romance of *Sir Gawain and the Green Knight.* The books can be justly criticized on other grounds, notably the leader-worship of the first book and the anti-climactic resolution of the second. But Adams's potential is enormous and, probably, almost untapped as yet. His future work may use the potential hinted at in these books, or he may degenerate into mere best-selling adventure fantasy. Too much fame has broken better authors. But if he can live up to his potential, he will be a major figure.

Since Lin Carter has so thoroughly covered the field of adventure fantasy in his *Imaginary Worlds,* it will not be necessary to give a complete history of the field here. But some observations may be in order. The amazing and thrilling advances in geographical and paleological knowledge during the last half of the nineteenth century led many writers to set their tales in remote parts of the globe, filling them with ridiculous combinations of prehistoric creatures and magical people. Jules Verne's *Journey to the Center of the Earth* and Rider Haggard's *She* (1886) are the most respectable early examples. In books like Conan Doyle's *The Lost World* and William Bradshaw's *Goddess of Atvatabar* (1892), which imitated such stories, absurdity and a sad lack of ingenuity came to the forefront.

Another common characteristic of early adventure fantasy was a compulsive reliance on "science," not to explain, but to justify the actions of the characters. The figure of the eccentric scientist with his lovely daughter, so familiar from a million "B" movies, came out of adventure fantasy. An unpleasant corollary of this was racism. Not only were the villains and "savages" non-white (or, at most, "Levantine"), but all sorts of pseudo-scientific muck was raked up to justify

8. *The New Yorker,* May 5, 1975, pp. 142–3.

the heroes' destruction of them. A typical example is W. H. Hudson's *Green Mansions* (1904), in which Rima's "grandfather," himself a murderer, thief, and brigand, condemns the local Indians as a bunch of superstitious, bloodthirsty savages. Theories of "Aryan superiority," which were beginning to appear in the real world, found receptive audiences through some adventure fantasy.

But adventure fantasy has some good points, chief among which are exciting action and exotic settings. Soon, too, adventure writers grew tired of merely earthly backgrounds and began inventing other worlds, heavily influenced by science fiction, or setting their tales in the prehistoric past. Atlantis and Mu began to be popular, as in C. J. Cutliffe Hyne's *The Lost Continent* (1899). But all other writers were cast into the shade by the rise of the most popular adventure fantasist of all time, Edgar Rice Burroughs. In 1912 Burroughs began his rise to fame with two stories published within three months of each other: "Under the Moons of Mars," which introduced John Carter and Dejah Thoris of Barsoom, and *Tarzan of the Apes*. Burroughs' work had all the virtues and faults of adventure fantasy—exciting action, wooden characters, pseudo-scientific gimcrackery, exotic backgrounds, and a rather pathetic reliance on the moral code of the British aristocracy, as expressed in the *Boys' Own Paper*. Not only is Tarzan preternaturally intelligent and unhumanly strong; he is a baron, descendant of a line of feudal lords. No hero in Burroughs' pulp fiction ever let down the old school, kicked a man when he was down, lost a stiff upper lip, or shot a fox, even when about to be tortured by sinister witch doctors or when saving the heroine from a fate Worse than Death. The more wild, weird, and exotic the fantasy became, the stiffer became the moral code. John Carter was a perfect Southern gentleman through thick and thin, even on Mars.

Pulp fantasy eventually discarded the obsolete moral code of Raffles and his ilk in favor of a more elemental set of standards, thanks to Robert Howard's Conan stories (c. 1930–36). Conan is a prehistoric barbarian rover of the mythical Hyborian Age, searching for, and getting, adventure, power, excitement, sex, and magic. He is amoral, brutal, violent, ruthless, tough and warlike but has a sort of barbaric nobility based on the brotherhood of the sword. He is no *preux chevalier:* when he rescues a woman he expects compensation. This is not difficult for the women, who are are only half-clad to begin with, and whose diaphanous gowns are artistically torn in convenient places. Howard's stories hold up remarkably well, in spite of his racism and *machismo,* because his fantastic settings are intriguing; he mixed everything connoting "barbarism" into a world of glamorous, nightmare beauty—Egyptian magicians, Scandinavian berserkers, Arab robbers, Greek pirates, Celtic slave girls, caravans, galleys, temples, markets, fortresses, ruins, palaces. All rose out of his perfervid and psychotic imagination from sources impossible to guess; perhaps his upbringing on the dry Texas plains forced him to compensate for their silent loneliness by creating a teeming world of savage vitality. He died a suicide. Few adventure writers have written as well as he did, but all since have imitated him.

Most of these imitations have been weak hackwork, like Lin Carter's Thongor of Lemuria series, although a few writers, notably Fritz Leiber in his Grey Mouser and Fahfrd stories, have achieved creditable work. But the newest and most promising trend in adventure fantasy has come from women writers. Women's adventure writing tends to be more ingenious and more interesting psychologically. The leading writer in adventure fantasy (and adventure science fiction) is Andre Norton, one of the most prolific of modern writers, publishing five or six full-length novels a year. This speed does not work to her advantage; most of her work is badly executed, and has all the well-known faults of first drafts, written in haste, unpolished, inconsistent, and cliché-ridden. Even at her best, her writing is hackneyed, mannered, and full of moral pretentiousness. For example, in one of her most popular books, *Witch World* (1963), a wise older character advises the hero: "Think now upon this one between whom and you has been the trial of power, or the tie of blood."

Norton's Secondary Worlds, however different in detail, all seem the same, because every story centers around her simplistic philosophical notions on the evils of technology and the necessity of returning to a simpler way of life. Interchangeable puppets for characters, vaguely feudal backgrounds, and incoherent plotting do nothing to improve matters. For a writer so prolific, her inventiveness and imagination are surprisingly limited. The wisdom of Gorth is exactly like the wisdom of Avalon; the feudal society of Clio is exactly like the feudal society of the Dales. It may be that Norton wishes to state that good and evil are much the same everywhere, a laudable idea. But her efforts look weak beside those of a writer like Ursula Le Guin, who is capable of depicting not only different societies, but different philosophies. And the result of showing that good and evil are always the same is that they are both, always, deadly dull. Wisdom in Norton is not spoken, but intoned; nothing could be more soporific. Worst of all, she relies heavily on mysterious psi powers and even more mysterious supernatural beings who make solemn, delphic pronouncements at every turn of the action; and she commits the really unforgivable sin of writing sequels that cannot stand on their own.

In spite of all this, however, Norton's work is still often well worth reading, since she displays far more imagination than most adventure fantasists; her female and animal characters are originally and sensitively portrayed; and the occasional book that seems to have been more carefully written, like *Ice Crown* (1970), *Star Gate* (1958), or *Lavender-Green Magic* (1974), is rewarding, its new world developed with imagination and empathy. She can write unhackneyed and worthwile books when she takes the trouble; but a writer who puts out five or six novels every year simply does not have the time to take trouble.

Two other adventure fantasies by women indicate where the field is likely to go in the future. Jane Gaskell's Atlan trilogy (*The Serpent*, 1963; *Atlan*, 1965; *The City*, 1966) and Tanith Lee's *The Birthgrave* (1975) both deal with the adventures of lone women in violent, barbaric worlds. Because of women's greater physical vulnerability, Cija's and Karrakaz's adventures show them enduring many more abrupt and shocking changes of fortune than any male hero has ever undergone. Cija goes from princess and goddess to hostage, maidservant, refugee, cook, soldier's mistress, Empress, scrubwoman, slave, ape-man's concubine, back to princess again; Karrakaz, who is immortal and unkillable, suffers precisely because she cannot escape her self-hate in death. Male adventure heroes see their world from the outside, from positions of freedom and power; women see it from the inside, which means that their world must be far better developed and more consistent. *The Birthgrave*, except for an unfortunate conclusion, is so good that it rises beyond the limitations of adventure fantasy and verges on the heroic. If more adventure fantasies could achieve such heights, both heroic and adventure fantasy would be better off: heroic fantasy would become even more vigorous, while adventure fantasy would become intellectually respectable.

3. *Ironic fantasy*

Ironic fantasy is another variation on heroic fantasy. It is as grand in conception as heroic fantasy, but lacks the moral certainty of its model. Like all fantasy, it assumes a supernatural reality behind the physical reality of a universe, but unlike other forms it does not assume that this supernatural power is good: rather, it is ambiguous, and probably capricious. Such fantasies do not celebrate heroism; they laugh at it, with the bitter undertone that characterizes irony.

Authors with this outlook—the ability to create a new world and sneer at it—are rare, and rarer still are the writers who can succeed with it. Too little bitterness implies that the writer does not care enough about his world; too much, that he is not interested in another world at all, but in satirizing this one. Mark Twain's *The Mysterious Stranger* (1916) and *A Connecticut Yankee in King Arthur's Court* (1889) suffer from too much anger, not enough irony. Both succeed as art, neither as fantasy; they bear the same relationship to fantasy that Swift's *Modest Proposal* bears to his *Gulliver's Travels*. The overall impression they give is not of irony, but of unmitigated loathing and horror. Fantasy cannot sustain such emotions for long; hatred, even hatred of evil, cannot create. Twain's Secondary World is only ours with all its redeeming qualities left out.

What ironic fantasy really requires is detachment, the philosophy of someone who is willing to be amused, but not intimately concerned with matters of moral seriousness. It is a form made for skeptics. The two writers who have made the most of it are James Branch Cabell and Charles G. Finney. Cabell's is the textbook case of a meteoric career: a little-known dabbler for many years who achieved sudden notoriety at the center of a censorship dispute, vindication, fame, and critical praise, followed by an abrupt and permanent eclipse in both popularity and esteem. The eighteen volumes of his fantasy, the *Biography of Manuel* (1928), burned him out; the end of that effort coincided with the great reaction against him, and, although he wrote many more novels, essays, and plays, he never again reached a wide public. In 1957, Edmund Wilson wrote a long rehabilitation in *The New Yorker*,[9] which recognized his many good points, but acknowledged that his audience would always be limited.

Ironic fantasy is essentially a protest against Babbitry and Philistinism, against convention and the status quo, against moral and emotional blindness; Cabell's popularity in the 1920s stemmed from this aspect of his work. H. L. Mencken himself considered Cabell a leader in the struggle of art against the mob. But today, Cabell seems to lean too far in the other direction, as a patronizing champion of elitism, an aesthete convinced that he alone understands life, a Pharisee; a snob. His style and his philosophy are arch, supercilious, and cynical; his cynicism has not even the merit of sincerity, but is affected. He is a poseur. His protest against Philistinism seems far more like denigration of ordinary people than like a noble blow in the cause of the artist.

Other aspects of Cabell's work are equally exasperating: garrulity, repetitiousness, coyness, ostentation, bad taste, and sexism can all be found abundantly in his books—especially sexism. Woman is a goddess and a whore, dedicated to making man miserable with or without her.

9. Edmund Wilson, "The James Branch Cabell Case Reopened," *The New Yorker*, April 21, 1956, pp. 140–168.

There is no thought that women too may dream dreams and see visions; on the contrary, no woman, Cabell says, has ever journeyed to Antan, the paradise of thinkers, gods, and poets. Men long for greatness; women exist to prevent it. Men are individuals; women all the same. Man is the prey of woman, who is barely sentient. The role-playing that Cabell forces on men and women would be funny if it were not so offensive; what is really dreadful about it is that here Cabell is not satirizing. He really believes that this is the ultimate wisdom about woman's place in the universe. Satire and irony are lavished on the male characters: Jurgen's concupiscence; Manuel's artistic pretensions; Gerald's belief that he is chosen of mankind. There are no female characters, there is only Woman under different names.

The qualities that make Cabell's ironic fantasy work in spite of these deficiencies are oddly attractive. He revels in invention; he has a sly sense of humor and enjoys bawdry; he plays tricks upon his characters and upon the reader, which (despite his cynicism) are not cruel tricks. He has a healthy respect for Dame Fortune and likes to join in her practical jokes on us. Ultimately, he is rather good-humored, willing to admit that his posturing and cynicism are of no more or less merit than any other kind of behavior, although they are congenial to his temperament. He is detached, yet involved.

Likewise, Charles Finney, author of *The Circus of Dr. Lao* (1935), detaches himself. His jest on Babbitry is more successful than any of Cabell's work, because Finney lacks Cabell's snobbery and condescension. He writes like a reporter, straight-faced and innocent; he offers no opinions. If the good people of Abalone, Arizona, can't tell or don't care what the difference is between the fake and the real, it's none of his business. He just tells the story. If you don't believe in magic, then magic itself can't convince you that it is real, and certainly Finney can't, either—so he doesn't. This tone is what makes ironic fantasy work, because the ironic outlook clashes with the desire to subcreate if it is too strong. An ironist, unlike most fantasists, cannot surrender to the mythic spirit, cannot allow it to summon the deepest elements of the subconscious mind. He must control it, dominate it, far more than any other fantasy writer, but he cannot completely dominate it. He must balance precariously between a subcreation that distorts irony into parody, and a universe that is not a subcreation at all. It is no wonder that ironic fantasy is the most difficult and least popular kind of fantasy.

4. Comic fantasy

Humor in fantasy usually derives from a display of the contradictions between the powers of magic and human understanding of them.

The fact that fantasy has rules implies that misunderstandings are bound to arise. The work of E. Nesbit and her American disciple, Edward Eager, demonstrates how such humor works. One of the basic rules is that one always gets exactly what one wishes for; so when the children in Nesbit's *Five Children and It* (1902) wish to become as beautiful as the day, they must cope with the consequences: no one recognizes them, they get no dinner, and their baby brother is kidnapped by a woman who cannot resist his beauty. In Eager's *Half Magic* (1954), four children find a magic charm that grants wishes by halves. When Katharine tells Morgan le Fay to go jump in a lake, she falls into a pond; when she wishes to defeat Sir Lancelot in a joust, Katharine forgets to wish that she knew the rules of jousting, which puts her into the untenable position of winning without knowing how. Other rules guide the characters in and out of such situations: the magic may end at sunset; magical beings may assist the wishes; wishes may only come in threes, or on every third day; adults may not notice the effects of the magic; magic words may cut an adventure short; the characters may have to perform a good deed in order to earn more wishes; and the like.

But humor itself is not the end of comic fantasy. The rules and restrictions on the magic exist in order to force the characters to earn what they get from it; they cannot merely ask for whatever they want. Magic does not come into a character's life, in any good fantasy, to give him a good time, but to help him achieve some purpose. The object of most comic fantasy is the achievement of a heart's desire, which rests on good deeds rather than good intentions, and good intentions rather than whims. Humor arises from the character's fumbling attempts, not from the object of desire, which may be happiness, the return of a beloved parent or friend, the restoration of another's rights, the reconciliation of enemies—anything restoring harmony to a situation. Unlike ironic fantasy, comic fantasy laughs with, not at, its actors.

Many writers seem to think that absurdity and whimsy, rather than affection and restoration, are the keys to comic fantasy, which is not at all the case. This attitude may be called "Whangdoodlery," after a book by Julie Edwards entitled *The Last of the Really Great Whangdoodles* (1973). The Whangdoodle is a magical creature apparently made up out of the leftover parts of other animals, with a fatuous and gullible personality, who is surrounded by such wish-fulfilling artifacts as a machine that makes magic banana splits. Such books cater to those who think that magic, like money, would exist solely to satisfy the whims of those lucky enough to get hold of it. But magic is not whimsy, as Eleanor Cameron points out: "You could not call black magic black whimsy. . . ." [10]

The Edwards book is far from being the worst example of the Whangdoodle effect, a somewhat dubious honor which is held by Roald Dahl's execrable *Charlie and the Chocolate Factory* (1964). Charlie, a poor-but-noble boy without discernible personality, is one of five children selected by Mr. Willy Wonka to tour his wonderful chocolate factory. Dahl disposes of the other four children, each of whom represents some trait Dahl dislikes such as gum-chewing, so Charlie inherits the factory and will live happily ever after, eating as much as he likes. Aside from the cruelty and bad taste displayed in eliminating the other children, whose worst faults are annoying rather than evil, and the racism displayed in Dahl's creation of the pygmy Oompa-Loompas who run the factory, the fantasy has no coherence and no reference to any Primary reality other than children's greed for candy. The reader knows that Charlie is deserving and noble because Dahl tells him so, not because he can see Charlie behaving in a noble manner; Charlie, in fact, plays almost no part in the story. The magic has no rules or restrictions beyond Willy Wonka's caprice; Charlie's heart's desire—to get enough to eat—might be pathetic and noble if he were a real victim of starvation, but as he is a stick figure straight out of bedtime-story fantasy, he does not need sympathy. In any case, someone whose heart's desire is fulfilled by getting a factory full of candy has a heart of marshmallow—totally lacking in substance.

The horrible example of *Charlie* illustrates the worst pitfall of fantasy, comic fantasy, and children's fantasy for the inexperienced writer: the temptation to patronize his audience. If fantasy is mere escapism, then anyone (especially a successful adult novelist) can write it; if his own children love his bedtime stories (because they love him), then all children will; if he is the hit of every cocktail party, his humor will certainly knock 'em out in a book. But fantasy is not whimsical escapism. Telling bedtime stories to one's children is a fine practice, but it does not necessarily imply that the stories have any artistic value, even if the children enjoy them. Humor not rooted in a serious and loving purpose is just a gag. Not every writer can be a Lewis Carroll or a Kenneth Grahame.

Some whimsicality, properly employed, can enhance comic fantasy, as shown by the work of L. Frank Baum, whose work is full of extravagant inventions. Nothing was impossible in Baum—talking tin men, a sawhorse who came to life, entire countries populated by paper dolls, insects magnified into Professors, clockwork men who were always

10. Eleanor Cameron, *The Green and Burning Tree: on the Writing and Enjoyment of Children's Books*, Boston, Little, Brown, 1969, p. 87.

running down, witches who melted when water was thrown on them, people with flat heads, pointed heads, and no heads, people who were scissors or cookies, people with feet made out of rolling pins—the list is endless. Somehow Baum made it all live, even in his later and weaker books. As Roger Sale has observed, Baum's imagination was characteristically American—cheerful, optimistic, practical, enthusiastic, and tolerant.[11] The magic of Oz is not the nostalgic and mysterious enchantment of Faerie, but the magic of discovery, practicality, and miraculous technology.

But this whimsical, wildly inventive magic is the servant, not the master, of Baum's stories (although in the many sequels, mere inventiveness tended to dominate the emotional themes). In *The Wonderful Wizard of Oz* (1900), Baum achieved a classic statement of the theme of magic encouraging, rather than enabling, characters to accomplish results that aided both themselves and others. The themes of *The Wizard* are the themes of any good literary work: resourcefulness, loyalty, friendship, perseverance, fortitude, and reconciliation. Magic is a means to an end defined by these virtues; enchantment is produced because they are valid even in the crazily inventive world of Oz. One can laugh at the comical situations the magic gets the characters into, but only the ordinary virtues are required, as in the Primary World, to get them out.

Besides contradiction, restoration, and whimsy, a fourth type of humor characterizes comic fantasy: emphasis on an attitude of conscious reasonableness and eccentric dignity, which is expressed in humorous delineation of character. Hugh Lofting's Doctor Dolittle books (1920–47) and Kenneth Grahame's *The Wind in the Willows* (1908) best illustrate this trait. Strictly speaking, there is no magic in either the Dolittle tales or the story of Toad, Rat, Mole, and Badger: they are animal fantasies, in which animals talk like men, but no magic is actually exercised in them. The Doctor speaks all the languages of animals, taught to him by Polynesia the parrot, which naturally makes him the best animal doctor in the world. His early adventures center around the famed Dolittle Circus, noted for its marvelous animal acts, the Canary Opera and the Puddleby Pantomime; his later ones concentrate on the immense knowledge of natural history given him by the animals. In every situation, the Doctor is kind, hardworking, ingenious, intelligent, sensible, reasonable, amiable, dedicated, good-humored, modest, and calm. The only things that rouse him to righteous anger are cruelty and stupidity, and yet he is never sanctimonious. He is

11. Roger Sale, "L. Frank Baum, and Oz," *Hudson Review*, Vol. 25 No. 4 (Winter 1972–1973), p. 576, p. 578.

perfectly happy whether he is directing a pelican chorus, mixing cough
medicine for giant turtles, conversing with Lunar talking flowers, living
on sixpence a week and hard-boiled eggs, or enjoying the peace and
quiet of a sojourn in jail. The Doctor is exquisitely funny not in spite
of these qualities, but because of them. It is delightful to watch him
being affable to thousands of crocodiles, hushing Polynesia when her
bad temper gets out of hand, pretending that a seal is his wife in order
to help her escape from a circus, or telling a wicked ruler that his jail
is most unsanitary.[12]

The masterpiece of humorous fantasy, *The Wind in the Willows*,
contains all four of the traits we have discussed: controlled whimsicality, contradiction between expectation and actuality, restoration of
harmony, and dignified eccentricity. In Grahame, humor is ennobled
to comedy by being played against a sincere sense of the beauty and
wonder of Nature, which is more profound for being written with a
light hand. Added to this is a wholly English sense of coziness, which
focuses our attention on the material of the story by concentrating it
and irradiating it with warm lights. When Grahame is romantic, his
prose is sheer poetry; when he is comic, he is irresistibly funny. The
misdeeds of Mr. Toad and the serenity of the Piper at the Gates of
Dawn complement each other as well as Bottom does Titania. It is not
enough for Toad to wreck one motor-car; no, he wrecks seven, while
dressed in the height of Edwardian motoring fashion. Given twenty
years for "cheeking" the police, he is flung into a medieval dungeon,
complete with halberdiers and a sympathetic gaoler's daughter. Meanwhile, his friends are engaged in the homely rustic pursuits that fill
their hearts with satisfaction; the Water-Rat's poetry compensates him
for his unfulfilled wanderlust, the Mole returns to his little house and

12. Unfortunately, four of the Dolittle books are badly hurt by the inclusion
of racial slurs that would never be published today, and that are essentially irrelevant to the stories. *The Story of Doctor Dolittle*, *The Voyages of Doctor Dolittle*, *Doctor Dolittle's Post Office*, and *Doctor Dolittle's Return* all contain slighting
references to blacks, both in Africa and England. Prince Bumpo of Jolliginki goes
to Oxford, but refuses to wear shoes and misuses all the big words he has learned
there; his father, the King, uses a lollipop for a scepter and has a cousin who runs
a shoeshine parlor in Alabama; the Jolliginkians are stupid, lazy, and obstructive—
even the animals look down on them; the illustrations are caricatures. The Doctor
himself never says anything to denigrate blacks, but as he is portrayed as their
benefactor, bestowing the blessings of white civilization on them, his kindness is
patronizing. It is certain that Lofting did not consciously mean to insult and
patronize blacks; he was merely repeating commonplace jokes. Nonetheless, these
attitudes are unforgivable today. Similar attitudes and remarks in Pamela Travers's
Mary Poppins (1934) were removed from the second edition without doing any
harm to the book; removal of these comments from the Dolittle books would be
beneficial to children, regardless of race. The originals would not be destroyed, but
supplanted. It would be a shame to condemn one of the greatest characters in
children's literature for faults so easily eliminated and so inessential to the stories.

gives a party for the Christmas carolers, the Badger roams the Wild Wood. The taking of Toad Hall from the usurping stoats restores harmony to a small, perfect, lovable world; since the characters' happiness has increased, the restoration is also an augmentation.

5. *Nostalgic fantasy and sentimental fantasy*

Nostalgic fantasy is the other face of comic fantasy, expressing the fulfillment of the heart's desire through tenderness and melancholy rather than through humor. Humor appears, but it tends to be wry humor. Most people think of nostalgic fantasy as the true center of fantasy, since it emphasizes mood, wonder, mystery, enchantment, ethereality, regret, and sweetness. Events are not important in nostalgic fantasy; character and emotion are. In sentimental fantasy, on the other hand, contriving both mood and action so that they dovetail into a complete, pat statement is the author's central concern. Nostalgic fantasy awakens that longing which is better than any satisfaction; sentimental fantasy purports, falsely, to satisfy it. Sentimental fantasy is a debased, wish-fulfilling form of nostalgic fantasy.

A typical example of sentimental fantasy is Robert Nathan's *Portrait of Jennie* (1939). The book deals with the relationship of a young artist (starving in the proverbial garret) and a girl who inspires him. But the relationship is phony, because the girl's personality is unimportant: what inspires the artist is the fact that she appears to him out of the past. Her effect on him is based on the charm of her old-fashioned quaintness, the fact that she is an adolescent on the verge of womanhood, and the "Providential" nature of her appearance, not on her personality, which is colorless. The artist himself is a combination of every possible cliché. He is unknown, poor, but talented; he derides "modernity" in his peers; and he needs only one great experience to be able to fulfill his potential—presumably the supernatural one provided by Jennie. Rembrandt had less favor from the Muse. The worst thing about Nathan's book is that the fantasy actually detracts from the story. Without it, he might have written a real novel about an artist and his inspiration; with it, he created a story with all the enchantment of a shampoo commercial about young lovers running on a beach.

Another type of sentimental fantasy exploits comic rather than nostalgic fantasy, with results surpassed only by Saturday morning kiddie cartoons. An example is Paul Gallico's *Manxmouse* (1968), the story of a tailless blue china mouse who comes to life. The reader is embarrassed to read, and Gallico should have been embarrassed to write, the climactic scene, in which the Manxmouse's defiance of the

Manx Cat leads the Cat to cry out "Bully, old fellow!" and announce that he never wanted to fight, anyway. After a narrative during which the mouse is chased by a fox hunt straight out of P. G. Wodehouse and adopted as a mascot by a dashing, tall, dark, handsome RAF pilot, the reader can hardly help wishing Gallico had restrained his urge to banality. This is, however, something sentimental fantasists never do.

But where sentimental fantasy is saccharine, nostalgic fantasy is ambrosial: it really does delight the heart and enchant the fancy. Sentimental fantasy beats the reader over the head with its message; nostalgic fantasy shows him the way into a Secondary World of sweet refreshment. Unlike sentimental fantasy, nostalgic fantasy does not fear an unhappy ending, or contrive to avoid one, or paper it over with pompous banalities about time healing all wounds; on the other hand, a happy result, when it comes about, occurs because it is the only genuine conclusion to the activities of the characters. In nostalgic fantasy, emotion and sentiment are honestly and clearly delineated. And yet, sincerity is not enough to make a work succeed. What is necessary is an acute sense of tragedy and suffering and a conviction that love redeems all sorrow; an awareness of time, loss, and death; and a profound sensitivity to emotional tone.

Among the many writers who have produced excellent nostalgic fantasy, five are worthy of special note. Hans Christian Andersen's fairy tales rank among the great works of world literature: his humor is sharp, his sweetness is piercing, but both are infinitely kind. "The Emperor's New Clothes" and "The Princess and the Pea" are justly famous examples of Andersen's pungent humor, which he directed at snobbery and pomposity. But the most memorable Andersen tales center around the theme of cruelty and suffering redeemed by love's power and beauty. He shows us enormous pain: "The Girl Who Trod on a Loaf" sinks into a slimy pit; "The Little Mermaid" gets the human feet she desired, but every step is agony; "The Ugly Duckling" is cast out to starve; "The Nightingale" alone remains with the dying Chinese Emperor; "The Little Match-Girl" dies of hunger and cold. But love and hope give even the darkest Andersen tales an unalterable sunniness.

Oscar Wilde's fairy tales (*The Happy Prince and Other Stories*, 1889) interest us because they succeed in spite of Wilde's characteristic exaggeration and melodrama. "The Happy Prince" and "The Selfish Giant" balance between joy and anguish as well as Andersen's tales do, and "The Remarkable Rocket" summons up Wilde's noted wit at its peak; but they are not typical of Wilde's stories. The air of intellectual, aesthetic, and spiritual bravado that we associate with Wilde's tragic downfall is evident in the majority of his fairy tales; the religious emotion that emerged in his final years is first found in them. But Wilde's religiosity, except in the tales of the Prince and the Giant, emphasized despair, sin, corruption, and damnation rather than hope. In his darkest stories, "The Fisherman and His Soul" and "The Birthday of the Infanta," we see the Wilde of legend, the decadent, dissolute, embittered aesthete of the sinful Nineties. Neither of these stories is "sick" in the modern sense of bad taste and black humor, nor are they "perverted" in the Victorian sense that caused Wilde's persecution. Instead, they are full of self-conscious despair, a sort of posed depravity. When the priest refuses to bless the corpses of the fisherman and his beloved, it is not enough that the reader know that God has absolved their sins; no, Wilde makes the "strange perfume" of the flowers on their grave hypnotize the priest into blessing them. When the little dwarf has died of shame and grief because the Infanta he loves has mocked his ugliness, Wilde makes the Infanta almost inhumanly heartless. In these stories, Wilde is deliberately trying to shock conventional piety and sensibility by wallowing in exotic evils.

And yet, in spite of their melodrama, their bathos, their extravagance, and their bravado, these stories succeed as nostalgic fantasy because Wilde's sense of tragedy was real, even though his effects were often forced. The overheated style that exercised a bad influence on many lesser writers (notably Dunsany and Cabell, in fantasy) is the perfect expression of Wilde's essentially Victorian rebellion against Victorianism, his tormented awareness that life is made up of insoluble problems and painful conflicts. To read his stories is to join with him in the longing that is nostalgic fantasy's characteristic mood.

Eleanor Farjeon, the greatest of twentieth-century nostalgic fantasists, preferred to express joy and laughter rather than pain and tragedy; tragedy is an undercurrent in her work, never overstated, never ignored, giving it a gentle melancholy, but always subordinate to an essential optimism. Her stories are full of merriment, singing, and dancing; her characters cheerful, contented, and charitable. Her retelling of "Cinderella," *The Glass Slipper* (1955), is miraculously right, from the hilarious description of Ella's stepsisters—Araminta, skinny, peevish, sly, and untidy; Arethusa, sloppy, fat, greedy, and vain—to the entrancing game of Hide and Seek during which Ella and the Prince fall in love, while Ella's meek father and the Prince's mute, childlike zany conspire to pilfer sugarplums. Farjeon's celebration of the natural beauty of the English countryside transmutes Sussex and the West Country into provinces of Faerie, especially in the Martin Pippin books and *Kaleidoscope* (1929). Farjeon's masterpiece (from *Martin Pippin in the Daisy Field,* 1937) is the long story "Elsie Piddock Skips in Her

Sleep," with its enchanting skipping-rhyme refrain. Elsie at three, trying to skip with her father's braces, and Elsie at one hundred and ten,
saving the villagers' rights and repaying Andy Spandy for teaching her
to skip like a fairy, are equally lovable and equally genuine.

Similar to Farjeon in many ways is the novelist Elizabeth Goudge,
whose skill with names and love of Nature are the foundations of her
fantasies. Surrounding the core of each of her stories is a lyrical description of its setting, which lends it the enchanted aura of a stained-glass
window without the stiffness associated with stained glass. Goudge has
less of the tragic view that characterizes Andersen, Wilde, and Farjeon;
she concentrates on the strength of love and forgiveness. In her Carnegie Medal-winning *The Little White Horse* (1946), Maria Merryweather's courage enables her to save the outcast Sir Wrolf by ending
the feud between her family and his; in *Linnets and Valerians* (1964),
the Linnet children's solidarity helps them destroy the curse that has
broken up the Valerian family. Her stories do not possess the delicate,
timeless grace of Farjeon's, but are cozier, warmer, more tied to a
single moment: the long Edwardian afternoon of Goudge's childhood,
the lost paradise of the English countryside. Farjeon was almost Ar-
cadian; Goudge is superbly British.

Lucy Maria Boston's moving Green Knowe books (1954–1964)
celebrate the beauty of Nature, but focus far more on the bonds between individuals, especially those between past and present. The
beauty of the physical surroundings derives from their association with
the many people, dead and living, who have loved them and loved one
another in them. Telling a story at Green Knowe is like tracing a single
strand of colored wool through a closely-knit design, of which the tale,
the teller, and the hearer are integral components. Time and love are a
seamless web undamageable by grief, hate, and death, and every person
and object is given its proper valuation in the scheme. In Boston, hate
and fear may cause heartbreak, but not despair. In *A Stranger at Green
Knowe*, Ping learns to live with the necessity for the death of the
gorilla he loves, after learning to love the animal in the first place; in
An Enemy at Green Knowe, Tolly and Ping fight to overcome the
witch who threatens them, but never give in to hatred themselves, for
the sake of their love for Mrs. Oldknow and what she represents. From
these five nostalgic fantasists, more than any others, we receive the essential elements of the form: simplicity and directness from Andersen;
longing and heartbreak from Wilde; mirth and sweetness from Farjeon;
celebration and warmth from Goudge; and from Boston, the content-
ment of a heart and mind at peace.

6. Horrific fantasy

Horrific fantasy displays many affinities to adventure fantasy, largely because of the influence of Lord Dunsany, who had absorbed all the most obvious notions of the Aesthetic Nineties: the studied decadence, the ornamentation of style, the interest in exotica, especially Oriental exotica out of the *Arabian Nights*, the wallowing in bizarre sins and deliberately shocking behavior, and the elitist, gnostic view of both life and art. Very little difference is perceptible between the fantasies and the straight horror stories of most horrific fantasists, because the aura of the Aesthetes hangs over both sorts. A writer like Arthur Machen writes both types together: his *The Three Impostors* (1923) is a horror story that includes several shorter narratives; one of them, "The Novel of the Black Seal," is a horror fantasy centered around the existence of fairies, whom Machen thought to be a brutish, wicked, primitive race of revolting habits. But most of Machen's work was unadulterated horror fiction, rather than fantasy.

A horrific fantasy does establish a Secondary World, but the author's interest focuses on the creatures of horror who inhabit it and in description of an atmosphere of terror and dread. Naturally, bizarrerie makes the writer's job easier; the trouble is, it makes it too easy. As in adventure fantasy, the bizarre and the exotic take over the story. Still, horrific fantasy is capable of some attractive effects. Dunsany's "The Exiles' Club," in which deposed kings and emperors are only the waiters—the members are beings of greater distinction—begins in the clubby atmosphere of late Victorian London, but concludes in a far less cozy universe. His *The Blessing of Pan* (1927) described how the god Pan entrapped a village, converting it to an outpost of his worship, even, finally, suborning the vicar, whose attempt to conquer the god ended in his becoming Pan's priest. The horrific effect arises out of the reversal of normal expectations. In comic and ironic fantasy, such a reversal leads to laughter and reconciliation; in horrific, to death, damnation, or madness.

The few fantastic stories of H. P. Lovecraft exemplify this rule. Lovecraft was an extreme neurotic, a recluse who hated the modern world, lived in an unhealthy and morbid emotional atmosphere at home, and thought that literature had reached its zenith in the Nineties. As a result his fantasies are nearly unreadable, although he had a real talent for lovely names—Celephais, the Tanarian Hills, the Cerenarian Sea, Oukranos, Akariel, Thran, Inquanok, Kadath. The short story "Celephais" is a transparently autobiographical tale. A writer, whose ethereally strange stories arouse only ridicule in the mundane-minded critics who reject them, seeks, finds, and eventually rules the lovely city of Celephais in his dreams, which are real. On the morning of his triumphant entry into the city, the ordinary folk who scorned him find his dead body in this world. Here both madness and morbidity are celebrated and justified; the reader is invited to scorn the unimaginative philistines who rejected the hero, rather than to be horrified by his delusions and his death. The fact that his delusions are true visions is irrelevant, because they represent a flight from life, rather than an affirmation of it. Compare this with Andersen's "The Little Match Girl," who wants to live, and dreams of realities which are unattainable because of circumstance. The dreamer of "Celephais" is selfishly unhappy because others do not take him at his own valuation or live up to his expectations, so he invents another world to retreat to. Both surrender to a reality that is too harsh for them, but the Match Girl cannot help herself more than she already has. The dreamer has made no such effort to live in reality.

An entirely different attitude characterizes Mervyn Peake's famous Gormenghast trilogy (1946–1959). Here are no shimmering Oriental splendors and miasmas of evil, no Swinburnian affectations, no dream-palaces; instead, we are in a grim, dismal world of monumental inflexibility, drabness, and misery. The Gormenghast trilogy is a celebration of the Victorian Gothic sensibility, deliberately echoing Dickens at his most melodramatic—Dickens when he invented Mr. Murdstone, Madame Defarge, and Uriah Heep. The atmosphere of Gormenghast is copied from the "dark satanic mills" of the English Midlands and the deadly, polluted fogs of Whitechapel; the people are sly, wretched, ratty, treacherous, venal, haughty, or crabbed; the story revolves around a conspiracy aimed at destroying the supremacy of the Groans, lords of Gormenghast. Oddly enough, the trilogy ends on an optimistic note: young Titus Groan, the hero, attempts to break out of the pattern set by his ancestors by leaving the stifling airs of Gormenghast for the unknown world outside it. The books approach heroic fantasy in their grandeur of conception. But their attraction is in their grotesquerie, their monstrous and strangely thrilling world of moldering walls, suffocating customs, and furtive characters. Peake's overripe, convoluted, discursive style enhances the grotesque ambience, making the story a masterpiece of fear and loathing. The reader, no less than Titus himself, is repelled and fascinated by Peake's unique creation. It exists, in fact, to be negated. It is a word-maze, an exploration into the darkest recesses of the mind, not a living world, and thus does not really belong in the fantasy tradition. Instead, it is part of a tradition in English literature distinguished by its eccentricity: Ossian, Christopher Smart,

De Quincey, Carroll, and Beardsley were some of its perpetuators. Gormenghast is only the most recent expression of this quintessentially English tradition of literary oddness.

The potential of horrific fantasy has been best realized in the work of Ray Bradbury, who balances the conflicting demands of subcreation and horrification with remarkable skill and simplicity. Reversal of expectations in Bradbury leads not to disgust or loathing, but to shock, pain, and grief; but these, in turn, are assuaged by hope. In Bradbury, horror is what it should be: a means, rather than an end. In his greatest fantasy, *Something Wicked This Way Comes,* he can dwell on things of horror, even enjoy them, yet he makes it clear that he, no less than the characters, abhors them, and he shows that love can triumph over them. Perhaps the greatest fault of most horrific fantasies is that their authors revel in horrors, even prefer them, while paying lip service to the idea that horrors ought to be destroyed. Bradbury loves to show us his evil creations, and is (justly) proud of the imagination and inventiveness that went into them; but he does not love them. Bradbury's errors—relying too much on his mannerisms, and self-plagiarism —are sometimes obtrusive, especially in his later work, but they are minor compared to the depth and breadth of his basic conception: a world where it is always an enchanted Halloween and terror is always deliciously thrilling.

Where is fantasy heading? No one can say; the very nature of the form is such that originality and unpredictability are inherent in it. Any new book may open up possibilities previously undreamed-of. One trend that is becoming more important, which covers the entire field, is the reconciliation of adult and children's fantasy. Adult readers are overcoming their fears of "childishness," becoming more willing to appreciate books they might previously have ignored. Contributing to this change is the fact that the paperback revolution has finally reached children's publishing. Good children's fantasies, like other good children's books, are now available both cheaply and widely; people who would never go to the children's room of a library for a book will buy it in paper covers. An example of this is Ursula Le Guin's *A Wizard of Earthsea* trilogy, recently published in a major paperback house's adult line with advertising aimed at adults. Perhaps even more pertinent is the example of Richard Adams' *Watership Down,* published with great success as a children's book in England, then published with even greater success as an adult book in America.

An unfortunate corollary of this reconciliation, however, is the air of didactic pomposity that has infected many recent books. Children's writers, ever mindful of the example of Tolkien, have expended huge amounts of energy trying to infuse moral seriousness into their work, a process doomed to failure: moral seriousness must be inherent in, not inserted into, a story; evil must be genuinely motivated, not set up as a straw man to be knocked over by invincibly wise heroes. Preachy moralizing has less place in fantasy than in any other kind of literature. A scene like the one in Sheila Moon's *Knee-Deep in Thunder* (1967) where Maris, suddenly trapped in solidifying fog, realizes that the fog consists of her own uncharitable and doubting thoughts, is repulsive. Characters like Susan Cooper's Old Ones, who are always wise, tolerant, and good, who talk like Hollywood versions of the Delphic Oracle, and who are invulnerable to hurt, detract from fantasy, because they are wish-fulfilling authority figures without referents in the Primary World. In a fantasy whose moral seriousness is inherent, authority figures may exist, but they are not omniscient; they do not always have an answer to every problem. Tolkien's Gandalf, Le Guin's Ogion, T. H. White's Merlyn, Lloyd Alexander's Dallben, Boston's Mrs. Oldknow, even C. S. Lewis's lion-Christ, Aslan, cannot solve every difficulty with portentous, wise-sounding talk. Even the divine Aslan has to die, to be tortured and murdered, before he can redeem Narnia. Likewise, figures of evil do not exist merely to give the good characters something to chew on, but have motives and desires of their own. It is an artistic mistake to invent an evil being who exists purely to do, and to represent, "evil"; it puts the subcreator in the position of a God who deliberately creates the Devil in order to make things more interesting. Fantasists who find themselves writing this kind of thing should give serious consideration to rethinking their intentions.

A similar difficulty affects adult books, which, however, seem not to be morally pompous so much as literarily pompous. The fact that fantasy is finally beginning to receive serious critical attention has gone to some writers' heads: they think that introducing some anthropological or linguistic material into their work will (somehow) make it more respectable. An instance is Michael Moorcock's long and complicated Elric of Melniboné adventure-fantasy series, into which Moorcock has dragged all sorts of pseudo-intellectual baggage. In the later volumes he reworks the entire corpus of Welsh and Irish mythology, wrenching it ruthlessly around to serve his purposes, but demonstrating no interest whatsoever in the mythic material itself. The mythic material does not inspire him as it has Alan Garner, Evangeline Walton, Katherine Kurtz, Lloyd Alexander, and many other writers who have drawn upon it to create their own worlds; it merely provides him with grist that he mills out, lavishly but inattentively. This in itself is not so terrible; writers have to eat. What is offensive is the grandiose way in which Moorcock presents his butchery, as if the mythic material were somehow ennobled by his deigning to make use of it, when he has drained all the sap out of it; as if knowing the names of the Celtic gods makes him a great mythopoeic fantasist. As a matter of fact, Moorcock is capable of much better writing than the hack sword-and-sorcery stuff he grinds out and has written sensitive and imaginative science fiction. But, as with Roald Dahl, H. P. Lovecraft, C. S. Forester, and many other writers, skill and success in other types of literature does not ensure success in fantasy, where the least misstep can spoil an entire world.

But we can hope that these problems will remain the faults of individual writers, and that they will not spread to a majority in the field of fantasy. What is much more hopeful in fantasy today is an emphasis on subjects and persons who have previously been ignored, such as women and girls, non-European backgrounds, and worlds relevant to a future of depersonalization, technological gimmickry, and mass culture. Andre Norton's *Lavender-Green Magic* (1974) has a heroine who is a black child in an all-white community; Ursula K. Le Guin's Earthsea is populated by civilized dark-skinned people and blond barbarians; Tanith Lee's *The Birthgrave* is only one book of many in which female characters are becoming more independent and more aware of their abilities; Penelope Lively's *The House in Norham Gardens* is only one book of many in which future shock is central to the story's design. Outside of the novel and the short story, groups like the Firesign Theatre and Monty Python's Flying Circus are creating fantasy worlds that are wholly contemporary. Fantasy seems to be becoming more humane, more aware of the potential of all kinds of human creations, more willing to consider significant changes in the human condition, less willing to rely on formulas and obsolete materials. Fantasy has always extended the range of human possibilities; as it begins its second century, it seems to be more aware of its own potential in so doing than ever before.

A Timeline of Fantasy
1858-1975

1858—MacDonald, George. *Phantastes*.
1871—MacDonald, George. *At the Back of the North Wind*.
1872—MacDonald, George. *The Princess and the Goblin*.
1882—Anstey, F. "Vice Versa."
    MacDonald, George. *The Princess and Curdie*.
1886—Haggard, Rider. *She*.
1889—Twain, Mark. *A Connecticut Yankee in King Arthur's Court*.
    Wilde, Oscar. *The Happy Prince and Other Stories*.
1894—Morris, William. *The Wood Beyond the World*.
1895—MacDonald, George. *Lilith*.
    Morris, William. *The Well at the World's End*.
1900—Baum, L. Frank. *The Wonderful Wizard of Oz*.
1902—Nesbit, E. *Five Children and It*.
1906—Kipling, Rudyard. *Puck of Pook's Hill*.
1908—Chesterton, G. K. *The Man Who Was Thursday*.
    Grahame, Kenneth. *The Wind in the Willows*.
1911—Barrie, James. *Peter Pan*.
1912—Burroughs, Edgar Rice. "Under the Moons of Mars"; *Tarzan of the Apes*.
1917—Milne, A. A. *Once on a Time*.
1919—Cabell, James Branch. *Jurgen*.
1920—Lindsay, David. *A Voyage to Arcturus*.
1922—Lofting, Hugh. *The Voyages of Doctor Dolittle*.
1924—Stephens, James. *The Crock of Gold*.
1926—Eddison, E. R. *The Worm Ouroboros*.
    Milne, A. A. *Winnie-the-Pooh*.
    Mirrlees, Hope. *Lud-in-the-Mist*.

1927—Masefield, John. *The Midnight Folk.*

1928—Woolf, Virginia. *Orlando.*

1930—Williams, Charles. *War in Heaven.*

1933—Hilton, James. *Lost Horizon.*

1934—Smith, Thorne. *The Night Life of the Gods.*

1935—Finney, Charles G. *The Circus of Dr. Lao.*

1936—Walton, Evangeline. *The Virgin and the Swine* (also titled *The Island of the Mighty*).

1937—Tolkien, J. R. R. *The Hobbit.*

1939—White, T. H. *The Sword in the Stone.*

1941—De Camp, L. Sprague, & Pratt, Fletcher. *The Incomplete Enchanter.*

1942—Wright, Austin Tappan. *Islandia.*

1946—Goudge, Elizabeth. *The Little White Horse.*
    Lewis, C. S. *That Hideous Strength.*
    Peake, Mervyn. *Titus Groan.*

1949—Myers, John Myers. *Silverlock.*
    Tolkien, J. R. R. *Farmer Giles of Ham.*

1950—Bradbury, Ray. *The Martian Chronicles.*
    Lewis, C. S. *The Lion, the Witch, and the Wardrobe.*

1954—Eager, Edward. *Half Magic.*
    Tolkien, J. R. R. *The Fellowship of the Ring* (Vol. 1 of *The Lord of the Rings*).

1955—Farjeon, Eleanor. *The Glass Slipper.*
    Tolkien, J. R. R. *The Two Towers* (Vol. 2 of *The Lord of the Rings*).

1956—Tolkien, J. R. R. *The Return of the King* (Vol. 3 of *The Lord of the Rings*).

1958—White, T. H. *The Once and Future King* (revised editions of *The Sword in the Stone*, *The Witch in the Wood*, and *The Ill-Made Knight*, with a fourth novel, *The Candle in the Wind*, added).

1959—Kendall, Carol. *The Gammage Cup.*
    Pearce, Philippa. *Tom's Midnight Garden.*

1960—Garner, Alan. *The Weirdstone of Brisingamen.*

1962—L'Engle, Madeleine. *A Wrinkle in Time.*

1964—Alexander, Lloyd. *The Book of Three.*
    Goudge, Elizabeth. *Linnets and Valerians.*

1966—Gaskell, Jane. *The City.*
    Mayne, William. *Earthfasts.*
    Schmitz, James H. *The Witches of Karres.*

1967—Garner, Alan. *The Owl Service.*

1968—Beagle, Peter S. *The Last Unicorn.*
    Le Guin, Ursula K. *A Wizard of Earthsea.*
1970—Amis, Kingsley. *The Green Man.*
    Chant, Joy. *Red Moon and Black Mountain.*
1971—Le Guin, Ursula K. *The Lathe of Heaven.*
1972—Farmer, Penelope. *A Castle of Bone.*
    Adams, Richard. *Watership Down.*
1973—Le Guin, Ursula K. *The Farthest Shore.*
1975—Adams, Richard. *Shardik.*
    Lee, Tanith. *The Birthgrave.*

Some Fantasy Award-Winners

The Hans Christian Andersen Award
Eleanor Farjeon, 1956
Tove Jansson, 1966

The Boston Globe-Horn Book Award
John Lawson, *The Spring Rider*, 1968
Ursula K. Le Guin, *A Wizard of Earthsea*, 1969
Susan Cooper, *The Dark is Rising*, 1973

The Caldecott Medal
James Thurber, author; Louis Slobodkin, illustrator, *Many Moons*, 1944.

The Carnegie Medal
Elizabeth Goudge, *The Little White Horse*, 1946.
Walter de la Mare, *Collected Stories*, 1948
Mary Norton, *The Borrowers*, 1953
Eleanor Farjeon, *The Little Bookroom*, 1956
C. S. Lewis, *The Last Battle*, 1957
Philippa Pearce, *Tom's Midnight Garden*, 1959
Lucy Maria Boston, *A Stranger at Green Knowe*, 1962
Pauline Clarke, *The Twelve and the Genii*, 1963 (also titled *The Return of the Twelves*)
Alan Garner, *The Owl Service*, 1968
Rosemary Harris, *The Moon in the Cloud*, 1969
Richard Adams, *Watership Down*, 1973
Penelope Lively, *The Ghost of Thomas Kempe*, 1974

The National Book Award
Lloyd Alexander, *The Marvelous Misadventures of Sebastian*, 1971
Ursula K. Le Guin, *The Farthest Shore*, 1973
Eleanor Cameron, *The Court of the Stone Children*, 1974

The Newbery Medal
Hugh Lofting, *The Voyages of Doctor Dolittle*, 1923
Robert Lawson, *Rabbit Hill*, 1945
Carolyn Sherwin Bailey, *Miss Hickory*, 1947
William Pène Du Bois, *The Twenty-One Balloons*, 1948
Madeleine L'Engle, *A Wrinkle in Time*, 1963
Lloyd Alexander, *The High King*, 1969
Robert C. O'Brien, *Mrs. Frisby and the Rats of NIMH*, 1972

The Regina Medal
Eleanor Farjeon, 1959
Padraic Colum, 1961

The Laura Ingalls Wilder Award
E. B. White, 1970

The Hugo Award
James Blish, *A Case of Conscience*, 1959

APPENDIX C

Fantasy Illustration

FANTASY ART and fantasy illustration are not the same thing—often, they are not even similar. Fantasy art is untroubled by considerations of internal logic and includes work as diverse as the horrific paintings of Bosch, the charming pastel-colored pictures of Paul Klee, the folk-tale and nursery-rhyme illustrations of Arthur Rackham, Randolph Caldecott, Walt Disney, Kay Nielsen, Kate Greenaway, and many others, the strange tesselations of M. C. Escher, the work of the Sur-realists—the list is endless. Fantasy illustration is, or should be, the servant of literary fantasy and should conform to the same rules of logic and order that the narrative does. Illustrations and text should be interdependent, but text ought always to be supreme. If mood and enchantment are the keynotes of the narrative, then illustrations ought to feature dreaminess; if action or character is the center of a book, its illustrations ought to reflect this. A work of violent adventure fantasy should not have delicate pictures; illustrations for nostalgic fairy tales should not be boldly striking. Beyond such obvious considerations, only the good taste of the artist need be consulted. However, a few trends in illustration are worthy of note.

Fantasy illustration derives primarily from two sources: the pulp magazines of the first half of this century, and children's book illustration. Pulp writing and illustration were almost always wild and exaggerated, as their descendants, today's adventure comic books, demonstrate; bold, garish, oversimplified, extravagantly inventive drawings accompanied the texts. Today, the pulp legacy to fantasy is largely confined to the covers of paperback editions of adventure fantasies, since adult fantasies, like other adult novels, are rarely illustrated now. Sometimes the cover drawings are wildly inappropriate, as shown by the cover of De Camp and Pratt's *The Incomplete Enchanter*, reprinted by Pyramid Books, which shows a muscular, steatopygous girl, clad in a lot of hair and a G-string, standing atop a half snail, half serpent monster that appears to be gnashing its teeth at a small sailing ship in the background. What this picture has to do with the adventures of Harold Shea in the worlds of Norse myth and the *Faerie Queene* is a mystery whose solution may not even be known to the artist. In other cases, the pulp style is more than suitable; Gino d'Achille's cover drawing of Burroughs's A *Princess of Mars* for Ballantine has all necessary elements—sex and swordplay—although it is not really specific enough to be a fine illustration. Illustrations like these are not meant to be specific to the story they illustrate; they are a signal to the reader that the book is fantasy, nothing more.

The other major source, children's book illustration, has been far more productive for both children's and adult fantasies. The fantasy revival of the 1960s and 1970s has borrowed a sort of medieval *ambiance* from children's fantasy to denote the presence of adult fantasy, especially heroic fantasy. At first this borrowing was extremely clumsy. The 1965 paperback edition of Tolkien's *Lord of the Rings*, for example, made Hobbiton look more like the Mushroom Planet, complete with flamingos, than like the Shire; the Ballantine cover of Eddison's A *Fish Dinner in Memison* shows a fish flying through the air above a medieval castle and a woman on horseback wearing a hennin. The picture is surrounded by the dragon-swallowing-its-own-tail emblem of Eddison's *Worm Ouroboros*. None of this has anything to do with Eddison's story, which is set in a period like the Renaissance rather than the Middle Ages in any case. But soon covers began to improve, thanks mostly to Ballantine's Adult Fantasy series, edited by Lin Carter, who tried to emphasize work of high quality. The dreamy, surreal quality of the earlier illustrations remained; the clumsy execution and careless ignorance of text disappeared. Of all the striking Ballantine covers, including David Johnston's stylized, powerful picture for Walton's *The Children of Llyr*, and Gervasio Gallardo's quaint, enameled, primitive cover of Mirrlees's *Lud-in-the-Mist*, perhaps the loveliest is Ian Miller's drawing for Ernest Bramah's *Kai-Lung's Golden Hours*, which combines vivid color, traditional Chinese themes, the mosaic effect of some early Chinese paintings, and the misty, surreal mood of fantasy.

These developments in paperback publishing eventually returned to their source, children's book illustration, to influence it; today, fantasy illustration is becoming more homogeneous, with little distinction between drawings for adult and children's works. Still, there are some surprising gaps in fantasy illustration. The rising costs of book publishing are forcing many publishers to issue books with no more than three or four pictures, or with none at all. The cover (by Peter Schaumann) of Patricia McKillip's magnificent *The Forgotten Beasts of Eld* is superb, but the text is not illustrated; nor were the texts of Penelope Lively's *The Ghost of Thomas Kempe,* Andre Norton's *The Jargoon Pard,* Josephine Poole's *The Visitor,* and many other recent books. Another surprising omission is the lack of first-rate illustration of J. R. R. Tolkien's work. Pauline Baynes, who also illustrated C. S. Lewis's Narnia series, did some wonderfully drawn pictures for Tolkien's *Farmer Giles* and *Adventures of Tom Bombadil;* Tolkien himself drew the pictures for the first edition of *The Hobbit.* But *Lord of the Rings* has never been illustrated as its many readers would like it to be. Ballantine's annual Tolkien Calendar for 1975 featured illustrations of notable scenes by Tim Kirk, an artist who came out of science fiction fandom, which were disappointingly amateurish, especially in depicting the Elves; the 1976 and 1977 calendars featured similar drawings by the Brothers Hildebrand, more or less in the style of N. C. Wyeth, but lacking Wyeth's artistic skill. So far, these are the only published attempts at a definitive illustration of Tolkien's great work. It would be a pity if the illustration of *Lord of the Rings* were to remain indefinitely in the hands of amateurs and hack painters.

However, there is much to be hopeful and gratified about in fantasy illustration today; just as the literary quality of fantasy seems to be generally improving, so too does illustration, as readers become more aware of the potentials of the form, less willing to accept hack work. The work of Gail Garraty, Maurice Sendak, Richard Cuffari, N. M. Bodecker, Lillian Hoban, Ian Miller, Trina Schart Hyman, Peter Schaumann, and Garth Williams, among many others, is proof that the great days of fantasy illustration are not over, and that H. R. Millar, Ernest Shepard, Arthur Rackham, Fritz Eichenberg, Howard Pyle, Pauline Baynes, Edward Ardizzone, James Thurber, and many other great illustrators have found worthy successors.

J.R.R. TOLKIEN

THE
Fellowship
OF THE
Ring

An adventurous trip into

the looking-glass landscape of the hobbits

The cover of the first American edition of *The Lord of the Rings* was charming and mystical, but a little vague.

The "Authorized Edition" cover of 1965 confused the fantastic
with the exotic, introducing flamingoes and leprechaun-like igloos
to the homely Shire.

The hill : hobbiton~across~the Water

Tolkien's own conception of Hobbiton, from *The Hobbit*: fruitful fields, neatly trimmed hedges, well-kept burrow-houses, and a whitewashed, rustic mill.

Pauline Baynes used a stylized medieval look for Tolkien's nursery poem "The Man in the Moon Came Down Too Soon."

The Last Shore

Tim Kirk's misty "The Last Shore" shows Frodo's farewell to
Middle-Earth. From *The Tolkien Calendar 1973*.

Pauline Baynes's use of medieval Persian models exactly suits this picture of a Calormene nobleman from C. S. Lewis's *The Horse and His Boy*.

Peter Schaumann's cover painting for McKillip's *The Forgotten Beasts of Eld* is strongly reminiscent of Maxfield Parrish.

The captives' rage, despair, and exhaustion contrast
forcefully with the hinted serenity of the starry sky in
Gail Garraty's "Magelight" illustration for LeGuin's
The Farthest Shore.

The wicked Attorney General gets his comeuppance.
A humorous sidelight on the triumphant climax of
MacDonald's *The Princess and Curdie,* drawn by
Helen Stratton.

Mr. Toad's last, private exhibition of vainglory, drawn by Ernest Shepard, accompanies the boasting song "When the Toad—Came—Home!" from *The Wind in the Willows.*

Maurice Sendak used comic exaggeration to match the sly humor
of Frank Stockton's "The Bee-Man of Orn".

E. Nesbit's Psammead or Sand-Fairy—a "fairy" very different from the usual gauzy-winged sprites—drawn in all its bad-tempered glory by H. R. Millar for *Five Children and It*.

Ann and Eliza's toy city, built around the toy castle of Ivanhoe, comes to life with surprising results in Edward Eager's *Knight's Castle*, drawn by N. M. Bodecker.

Maria and the Professor inspect a Lilliputian woman in T. H.
White's *Mistress Masham's Repose*, drawn by Fritz Eichenberg.

BB Ballantine

LUD-in-the-Mist

Hope Mirrlees

Introduction by Lin Carter

BB LUD-in-the-Mist   Hope Mirrlees

A child reaches for fairy fruit floating in the River Dapple. Cover by: Gervasio Gallardo for Hope Mirrlees's *Lud-in-the-Mist*.

THE WOOD BEYOND THE WORLD
Chapter I. Of Golden Walter and his
father ✤ ✤

WHILE AGO THERE WAS A YOUNG MAN DWELLING IN A GREAT AND goodly city by the sea which had to name Langton on Holm. He was but of five and twenty winters, a fair-faced man, yellow-haired, tall and strong; rather wiser than foolisher than young men are mostly wont; a valiant youth, & a kind; not of many words but courteous of speech; no roisterer, nought masterful, but peaceable and knowing how to forbear: in a fray a perilous foe, & a trusty war-fellow. His father, with whom he was dwelling when this tale begins, was a great merchant, richer than a baron of the land, a head-man of the greatest of the Lineages of Langton, and a captain of the Porte; he was of the Lineage of the Goldings, therefore was he called

William Morris's lovely, pure, and ruthless heroine, the Maid, from his *The Wood Beyond the World.*

PAN/BALLANTINE

A FISH DINNER IN MEMISON

E. R. EDDISON

AUTHOR OF "THE WORM OUROBOROS"

This paperback cover painting for E. R. Eddison's *A Fish Dinner in Memison* incorrectly implies a medieval setting for the story and links it with *The Worm Ouroboros*.

"Swords of Mars," a cover painting by Frank Frazetta, a leading
exponent of the thunder and guts school of fantasy illustration.
From The Frank Frazetta Calendar 1978.

J. Jones's cover for De Camp and Pratt's *The Incomplete Enchanter*, in the style of Frank Frazetta, gives no hint of the story's true setting or development.

Bert Tanner's *Magazine of Fantasy and Science Fiction* cover, illustrating Swann's "The Manor of Roses," summarizes the story's theme rather than illustrating an event.

$1.25

ORIGINAL
ADULT FANTASY

Kai Lung's Golden Hours
Ernest Bramah
Introduction by Lin Carter

Ballantine Books 02574·1·125

Ernest Bramah's enchanted medieval China appears like a vision in
Ian Miller's cover painting for *Kai-Lung's Golden Hours*.

Subgenres of Fantasy

AS WE SAW in Chapter Two, fantasy can be divided into sub-groupings according to the mood, or general emotional tone, of the individual works considered. Thus mythopoeic fantasy is religious in mood, heroic fantasy emphasizes courage and achievement, adventure fantasy concentrates on action and exotic effects, and ironic, comic, nostalgic, sentimental, and horrific fantasies attempt to create moods appropriate to their types. But other methods of subdividing fantasy can be found; the following list is an attempt at such a system of sub-classification. Each book listed by author and title here will be found in the Bibliographic Guide, which is arranged alphabetically by author, with a complete bibliographic citation and an annotation.

The operation of magic, or Enchantment, in a fantasy may be active or passive. In the first type of work, magic, or magical beings, actively operate on the lives of people living in a Secondary World which is otherwise like our own. Humans living in what E. R. Eddison called "natural present" are affected by magic—by experience of the powers of human magicians, magical objects, gods, devils, or supernatural spirits, creatures of Faerie, ghosts, and so forth; or by magically induced time travel; or by magically induced travel through dimensions or space to other worlds; or by experience of magic in the guise of science. In the second type, individual characters may have magical powers, but the story is not taking place because of them. Instead, the story is set in a Secondary World, which is based on the existence of a numinous, but passive, power: worlds in which toys and animals talk; worlds of fairy-tale; worlds whose history diverges from our own at some crucial point; worlds whose geography differs in some specific way from our own; and, finally, worlds wholly different from our own, worlds not connected in any way to natural present. These two types of fantasy (speaking broadly) may be called "magic in operation" and "magic of situation."

MAGIC IN OPERATION

I. Magic in Operation in Natural Present

A. MAGIC

This category is divided into two parts. The first deals with stories in which a human with magical powers—magician, wizard, or witch—affects the life of ordinary people. Such stories range from tales about little witch-girls who want to go to school like other people, to frightening stories of malignant and power-hungry people who attack the innocent.

026 Amis, Kingsley. *The Green Man.*
123 Bellairs, John. *The House With a Clock in Its Walls.*
124 ———. *The Figure in the Shadows.*
125 Benary-Isbert, Margot. *The Wicked Enchantment.*
126 Bennett, Anna E. *Little Witch.*
153 Boston, L. M. *An Enemy at Green Knowe.*
262 Chichester, Imogen. *The Witch Child.*
291 Curry, Jane Louise. *Mindy's Mysterious Miniature.*
292 ———. *The Lost Farm.*
325 Dickinson, Peter. *The Weathermonger.*
326 ———. *Heartsease.*
327 ———. *The Devil's Children.*
364 Estes, Eleanor. *The Witch Family.*
387 Finney, Charles G. *The Circus of Dr. Lao.*
429 Goudge, Elizabeth. *Linnets and Valerians.*
491 Hunter, Mollie. *Thomas and the Warlock.*
502 Ish-Kishor, Shulamith. *The Master of Miracle.*
541 Langton, Jane. *The Diamond in the Window.*
542 ———. *The Swing in the Summerhouse.*
543 ———. *The Astonishing Stereoscope.*
565 Leiber, Fritz. *Conjure Wife.*
608 Little, Jane. *Sneaker Hill.*
613 Lively, Penelope. *The Ghost of Thomas Kempe.*
663 Masefield, John. *The Midnight Folk.*

The second section of the Magic category deals with adventures brought about by magical objects: tokens, charms, dolls, automobiles, furniture, even swimming pools—anything one can think of.

B. MYTHIC FANTASY

Mythic fantasy is generally, but not always, mythopoeic: it implies magical powers which are generally more intense than those of magic or Faerie, powers which affect the soul. We find fantasy based on religious inspirations here. This means, however, that Santa Claus may be found in mythic fantasy, as well as God and his angels; the Devil may be a gentleman, or the epitome of horror. It all depends on the point of view. The first section here following includes more serious works.

025   Allen, Judy. *The Spring on the Mountain.*
256   Chesterton, G. K. *The Man Who Was Thursday.*
406   Garner, Alan. *The Owl Service.*
407   ———. *Red Shift.*
545   Laubenthal, Sanders Anne. *Excalibur.*
572   L'Engle, Madeleine. *A Wrinkle in Time.*
573   ———. *A Wind in the Door.*
577   Lewis, C. S. *Out of the Silent Planet.*
578   ———. *Perelandra.*
579   ———. *That Hideous Strength.*
610   Lively, Penelope. *Astercote.*
653   Machen, Arthur. "The Great Return."
747   North, Joan. *The Whirling Shapes.*
748   ———. *The Light Maze.*
788   Phipson, Joan. *The Way Home.*
813   Rayner, William. *Stag Boy.*
930   Walton, Evangeline. *The Island of the Mighty (The Virgin and the Swine).*
931   ———. *The Children of Llyr.*
932   ———. *The Song of Rhiannon.*
933   ———. *Prince of Annwn.*
963   Williams, Charles. *War in Heaven.*
964   ———. *Many Dimensions.*
965   ———. *The Place of the Lion.*
966   ———. *Shadows of Ecstasy.*
967   ———. *The Greater Trumps.*
968   ———. *Descent Into Hell.*
969   ———. *All Hallows' Eve.*

The second part of this category includes lighter treatments of mythic and religious ideas.

047   Babbitt, Natalie. *The Devil's Storybook.*
301   Davies, Valentine. *Miracle on 34th Street.*
323   Dickens, Charles. *A Christmas Carol.*

324   ———. *The Chimes.*
329   Druon, Maurice. *Tistou of the Green Thumbs.*
361   Eliot, Ethel Cook. *The Wind Boy.*
380   Farmer, Penelope. *The Summer Birds.*
381   ———. *Emma in Winter.*
410   Garnett, David. *Two by Two.*
428   Goudge, Elizabeth. *The Valley of Song.*
451   Harris, Rosemary. *The Moon in the Cloud.*
452   ———. *The Shadow on the Sun.*
453   ———. *The Bright and Morning Star.*
786   Pearson, Edward. *Chamiel.*
929   Wallop, D. *The Year the Yankees Lost the Pennant.*
945   White, T. H. *The Elephant and the Kangaroo.*

C. FAERIE

Stories in this category center on the presence of creatures of Faerie, the realm of fairies and of many other types of beings. Fairies themselves are rather out of fashion nowadays; the children in Edward Eager's *Half Magic* turned away with loathing, as most modern children would, from the sweet old neighbor lady who told them that a "dear little fairy . . . lived in the biggest purple foxglove." But all kinds of other creatures inhabit Faerie: werewolves, elves, giants, silkies, brownies, goblins, trolls, dragons, griffins, mantichores, genies, changelings, monsters, kelpies, dryads, fauns, centaurs; the Sidhe; Arthur and his court, Ogier the Dane, Roland and Oliver, and many other heroes; dwarfs, banshees, poltergeists, boggarts, minotaurs; the Four Winds; the gods of Greece and Rome, Egypt and Persia, China and Australia; and many other such. All these creatures come from folk tale, fairy-story, legend, or mythology; the first section of this category lists stories involving them.

We can also use a division by time. "Present" means that the story is supposed to be taking place in the modern era, from about 1870 to today; "past" means any period before 1870, from pre-history to the early Victorians; and "future" means after next week.

1. Present
159   Boucher, Anthony. *The Compleat Werewolf and Other Stories.*
236   Calhoun, Mary. *Ownself.*
245   Carryl, Charles E. *Davy and the Goblin.*

264 Clarke, Pauline. *The Two Faces of Silenus.*
272 Collier, John. *Fancies and Goodnights.*
277 Cooper, Susan. *Over Sea, Under Stone.*
278 ———. *The Dark is Rising.*
279 ———. *Greenwitch.*
286 Curry, Jane Louise. *Beneath the Hill.*
290 ———. *The Sleepers.*
315 De Camp, L. Sprague, and Pratt, Fletcher. *Land of Unreason.*
333 Du Bois, William Pène. *The Giant.*
395 Fritz, Jean. *Magic to Burn.*
400 Gannett, Ruth Stiles. *My Father's Dragon.*
454 Harris, Rosemary. *The Seal-Singing.*
490 Hunter, Mollie. *The Kelpie's Pearls.*
493 ———. *The Walking Stones.*
497 Ingelow, Jean. *Mopsa the Fairy.*
636 Lynch, Patricia. *Brogeen Follows the Magic Tune.*
637 ———. *Brogeen and the Bronze Lizard.*
650 MacDonald, Greville. *Billy Barnicoat.*
651 McGowen, Tom. *Sir Machinery.*
668 Mayne, William. *Earthfasts.*
686 Molesworth, Mary. *The Cuckoo Clock.*
733 Nesbit, E. *Wet Magic.*
777 Ormondroyd, Edward. *David and the Phoenix.*
825 Selden, George. *The Genie of Sutton Place.*
848 Smith, Thorne. *The Night Life of the Gods.*
878 Tarn, W. W. *The Treasure of the Isle of Mist.*

2. Past
033 Anderson, Poul. *The Broken Sword.*
053 Baker, Michael. *The Mountain and the Summer Stars.*
280 Craik, Dinah M. M. *The Adventures of a Brownie.*
287 Curry, Jane Louise. *The Change-Child.*
330 Druon, Maurice, *Memoirs of Zeus.*
396 Fry, Rosalie. *The Mountain Door.*
401 Gard, Joyce. *Talargain.*
402 Gardner, John. *Grendel.*
426 Goudge, Elizabeth. *Smoky House.*
427 ———. *The Little White Horse.*
438 Greaves, Margaret. *The Dagger and the Bird.*
489 Hunter, Mollie. *The Smartest Man in Ireland.*
492 ———. *The Ferlie.*
494 ———. *The Haunted Mountain.*

But there are creatures in Faerie besides the ones from folk and fairy-stories: they have been invented by modern authors. The creatures themselves need not have magic powers, any more than King Arthur has. Their existence alone is enough.

1. Present

770   Norton, Mary. *The Borrowers.*
771   ———. *The Borrowers Afield.*
772   ———. *The Borrowers Afloat.*
773   ———. *The Borrowers Aloft.*
774   ———. *Poor Stainless.*
851   Snyder, Zilpha Keatley. *Season of Ponies.*
916   Travers, Pamela. *Mary Poppins.*
917   ———. *Mary Poppins Comes Back.*
918   ———. *Mary Poppins Opens the Door.*
919   ———. *Mary Poppins in the Park.*
944   White, T. H. *Mistress Masham's Repose.*
982   Winterfeld, Henry. *Castaways in Lilliput.*
987   Wrightson, Patricia. *An Older Kind of Magic.*
988   ———. *The Nargun and the Stars.*

2. Past
521   Kingsley, Charles. *The Water-Babies.*
862   Stewart, Mary. *Ludo and the Star Horse.*
868   Swann, Thomas Burnett. *Day of the Minotaur.*
869   ———. *The Forest of Forever.*
870   ———. *The Weirwoods.*
871   ———. *The Dolphin and the Deep.*
872   ———. *Moondust.*
873   ———. *Where is the Bird of Fire?*
874   ———. *The Goat Without Horns.*
875   ———. *How Are the Mighty Fallen.*
876   ———. *The Not-World.*

3. Future
116   Beatty, Jerome, Jr. *Matthew Looney's Voyage to the Earth.*
117   ———. *Matthew Looney's Invasion of the Earth.*
118   ———. *Matthew Looney in the Outback.*
119   ———. *Matthew Looney and the Space Pirates.*

D. GHOST FANTASY

The ghost fantasies presented in the list below are a different sort of tale, with a different sort of operation, than the ghost story. The ghost story means to frighten the reader or, sometimes, to convince him that ghosts may really exist. The ghost is an intruder into the

Primary World. But in a ghost fantasy, we are in a Secondary World; ghosts there are characters interacting with the ordinary human characters. In many cases the humans do not discover that the ghosts are ghosts until well into the story. Ghost fantasies are usually either comic or nostalgic.

054   Barber, Antonia. *The Ghosts.*

114   Beagle, Peter S. *A Fine and Private Place.*

149   Boston, L. M. *The Children of Green Knowe.*

150   ———. *The Treasure of Green Knowe.*

243   Cameron, Eleanor. *The Court of the Stone Children.*

267   Coles, Manning. *Brief Candles.*

268   ———. *Happy Returns.*

269   ———. *Come and Go.*

270   ———. *The Far Traveller.*

334   Du Maurier, George. *Peter Ibbetson.*

363   Erwin, Betty K. *Who Is Victoria?*

391   Finney, Jack. *Marion's Wall.*

549   Lawson, John. *The Spring Rider.*

631   Love, Edmund. *An End to Bugling.*

655   MacKellar, William. *Alfie and Me and the Ghost of Peter Stuyvesant.*

658   McKillip, Patricia A. *The House on Parchment Street.*

779   Ormondroyd, Edward. *Castaways on Long Ago.*

787   Peeples, Edwin A., Jr. *A Hole in the Hill.*

796   Pope, Elizabeth Marie. *The Sherwood Ring.*

826   Severn, David. *The Girl in the Grove.*

843   Smith, Thorne. *Topper.*

844   ———. *Topper Takes a Trip.*

854   Stahl, Ben. *Blackbeard's Ghost.*

855   ———. *The Secret of Red Skull.*

921   Turkle, Brinton. *Mooncoin Castle.*

979   Williams, Ursula Moray. *Castle Merlin.*

E. HORROR FANTASY

The purpose of the horror fantasy, like the horror story, is to scare the living daylights out of the reader. It uses all the effects of the ordinary horror story, along with various twists out of the lore of Faerie, to do so. The only necessity is that some magical character or creature must embody the spirit of horror; no "Things from the Unknown" or mysterious miasmas of evil are permitted.

162 Bradbury, Ray. *The October Country.*
163 ———. *Something Wicked This Way Comes.*
252 Chambers, Robert. *The King in Yellow.*
339 Dunsany, Lord. *Gods, Men, and Ghosts.*
344 ———. *The Blessing of Pan.*
409 Garnett, David. *Lady Into Fox.*
425 Gordon, John. *The House on the Brink.*
611 Lively, Penelope. *The Wild Hunt of the Ghost Hounds.*
632 Lovecraft, H. P. *The Dream-Quest of Unknown Kadath.*
653 Machen, Arthur. *Tales of Horror and the Supernatural.*
746 North, Joan. *The Cloud Forest.*
782 Peake, Mervyn. *Titus Groan.*
783 ———. *Gormenghast.*
784 ———. *Titus Alone.*
794 Poole, Josephine. *Moon Eyes.*
795 ———. *The Visitor.*
819 Sarban. *Ringstones.*
958 Wilde, Oscar. *The Picture of Dorian Gray.*
989 Wylie, Elinor. *The Venetian Glass Nephew.*

F. SENTIMENTAL FANTASY

Books in this category might be placed in others—time travel, science fantasy, and ghost fantasy might be suitable for many titles—were it not for the sickly, vapid air which permeates them. In the long run, their tone is more important than the details of how their magic works. *Caveat lector.*

302 Davies, Valentine. *It Happens Every Spring.*
397 Gallico, Paul. *The Abandoned.*
398 ———. *Thomasina.*
399 ———. *Manxmouse.*
667 Matheson, Richard. *Bid Time Return.*
720 Nathan, Robert. *Portrait of Jennie.*
721 ———. *The Devil With Love.*
722 ———. *The Fair.*
723 ———. *Mia.*
724 ———. *The Summer Meadows.*

811 Quiller-Couch, Arthur, and Du Maurier, Daphne. *Castle Dor.*
815 Rios, Tere. *The Fifteenth Pelican.*
834 Sherburne, Zoa. *Why Have the Birds Stopped Singing?*
879 Terrot, C. *The Angel Who Pawned Her Harp.*
950 Wibberley, Leonard. *Mrs. Searwood's Secret Weapon.*
955 ———. *McGillicuddy McGotham.*
956 ———. *The Quest of Excalibur.*

II. Magic Time Travel

Time travel fantasies appeal to the historian in us, the part of us that longs to see Henry VIII in all his massive flesh, shake hands with Lincoln, or bow to Sargon of Akkad; to see, to participate in, even to change the course of history. The traveler's destination may be any-when, although most stories confine themselves to Western European and English history. But Jane Curry's *The Daybreakers* takes us back to the days of the Mound Builder Indians; L. Sprague De Camp's *Lest Darkness Fall* is set in Gothic Rome; and Virginia Woolf's *Orlando* does not travel backward, but forward in time to the present from Elizabethan England. The criterion of a time-travel fantasy is the desire to experience a vanished culture through the adventures of a modern hero or heroine. The trip, of course, must be made by magic, not by machine.

A. TIME TRAVEL THROUGH INDIRECT MAGIC

In these stories the time traveler has no control over his method of travel; the magic just happens. At most, the traveler may have expressed a wish to travel through time, without expecting it to be granted. Bolts of lightning and knocks on the head are favored means of embarking on this kind of trip!

036 Andrews, J. S. *The Green Hill of Nendrum.*
170 Brandel, Marc. *The Mine of Lost Days.*
173 Burford, Lolah. *The Vision of Stephen, an elegy.*
284 Cresswell, Helen. *Up the Pier.*
288 Curry, Jane Louise. *The Daybreakers.*
289 ———. *Over the Sea's Edge.*
305 De Camp, L. Sprague. *Lest Darkness Fall.*

359 Edmondson, Garry C. *The Ship that Sailed the Time Stream.*
382 Farmer, Penelope. *Charlotte Sometimes.*
460 Holm, Anne. *Peter.*
612 Lively, Penelope. *The Driftway.*
614 ———. *The House in Norham Gardens.*
669 Mayne, William. *The Hill Road.*
780 Parker, Richard. *The Old Powder Line.*
785 Pearce, Philippa. *Tom's Midnight Garden.*
839 Sleigh, Barbara. *Jessamy.*
924 Twain, Mark. *A Connecticut Yankee in King Arthur's Court.*
926 Uttley, Alison. *A Traveller in Time.*
983 Woolf, Virginia. *Orlando.*

B. TIME TRAVEL THROUGH DIRECT MAGIC

In these stories the traveler makes his journey through the interference of magic exercised by a character or an object. In Section 1, this someone or something is of human origin—a wizard, a talisman. In Section 2, the being or object is of Faerie. In both cases, some measure of control over the process is possible, even if the characters do not at first know how to use it.

1. HUMAN MAGIC

041 Arnold, Edwin L. *The Wonderful Adventures of Phra the Phoenician.*
293 Curry, Jane Louise. *Parsley Sage, Rosemary, and Time.*
303 Dawson, Carley. *Mr. Wicker's Window.*
304 ———. *The Sign of the Seven Seas.*
442 Grosser, Morton. *The Snake Horn.*
450 Hamley, Dennis. *Pageants of Despair.*
499 Ingram, Tom. *The Night Rider.*
609 Little, Jane. *The Philosopher's Stone.*
673 Merritt, Abe. *The Ship of Ishtar.*
740 Netherclift, Beryl. *The Snowstorm.*
759 Norton, Andre. *Octagon Magic.*
763 ———. *Dragon Magic.*
766 ———. *Lavender-Green Magic.*
778 Ormondroyd, Edward. *Time at the Top.*
852 Snyder, Zilpha Keatley. *The Truth About Stone Hollow.*

877 Sykes, Pamela. *Mirror of Danger.*
923 Turton, Godfrey. *The Festival of Flora.*

2. FAERIE MAGIC

021 Alexander, Lloyd. *Time Cat.*
049 Bacon, Martha. *The Third Road.*
164 Bradbury, Ray. *The Halloween Tree.*
294 Cutt, W. Towrie. *Seven for the Sea.*
350 Eager, Edward. *Knight's Castle.*
352 ———. *The Time Garden.*
535 Kuttner, Henry. *The Mask of Circe.*
574 Levin, Betty. *The Sword of Culann.*
575 ———. *A Griffon's Nest.*
605 Lewis, Hilda. *The Ship That Flew.*
730 Nesbit, E. *The House of Arden.*
731 ———. *Harding's Luck.*
760 Norton, Andre. *Fur Magic.*

III. *Travel from Our Universe to Another*

Science fiction (and, of recent years, the nightly news) tells us of travel from our world of natural present to other worlds within our universe. As C. S. Lewis pointed out, only distance lies between us and them. But traveling to another universe, one with different natural laws, is fantasy. The major difference between our universe and the other, of course, is the presence of magical or supernatural powers; the journey comes about with the aid of these powers. Sometimes the trip is voluntary; more often, it is not. A clever twist on this idea is in De Camp and Pratt's *The Incomplete Enchanter*: the heroes think themselves into new worlds by reciting logical formulas designed to change the basic assumptions binding us to this universe. This is magic in the cloak of philosophy.

A. JOURNEYS FOR FUN OR ADVENTURE

The magic operating on the characters of these stories gives them adventure for its own sake; if it teaches them a lesson, it does so in the vernacular sense of that phrase, not any philosophical sense.

043 Arnold, Edwin Lester. *Lieutenant Gulliver Jones.*
063 Baum, L. Frank. *The Wonderful Wizard of Oz.*
064–100, Thirty-nine sequels by Baum and other writers.
  102–103
104 ———. *The Enchanted Island of Yew.*
106 ———. *The Magical Monarch of Mo.*
107 ———. *Queen Zixi of Ix.*
108 ———. *The Sea Fairies.*
109 ———. *Sky Island.*
160 Brackett, Leigh. *The Sword of Rhiannon.*
166 Bradley, Marion Zimmer. *Falcons of Narabedla.*
174 Burroughs, Edgar Rice. *A Princess of Mars.*
175–183 Nine sequels.
312 De Camp, L. Sprague, and Pratt, Fletcher. *The Incomplete Enchanter.*
313 ———. *The Castle of Iron.*
314 ———. *Wall of Serpents.*
316 ———. *The Carnelian Cube.*
348 Durrell, Gerald. *The Talking Parcel.*
360 Edwards, Julie. *The Last of the Really Great Whangdoodles.*
389 Finney, Jack. *The Woodrow Wilson Dime.*
517 Juster, Norton. *The Phantom Tollbooth.*
719 Myers, John Myers. *Silverlock.*
938 Wheeler, Thomas G. *Loose Chippings.*
993 Zelazny, Roger. *Nine Princes in Amber.*
994 ———. *The Guns of Avalon.*
995 ———. *Sign of the Unicorn.*

B. JOURNEYS WITH SERIOUS MOTIVES AND RESULTS

032 Anderson, Poul. *Three Hearts and Three Lions.*
253 Chant, Joy. *Red Moon and Black Mountain.*
355 Eddison, E. R. *Mistress of Mistresses.*
356 ———. *A Fish Dinner in Memison.*
357 ———. *The Mezentian Gate.*
405 Garner, Alan. *Elidor.*
513 Johnston, Thomas. *The Fight for Arkenvald.*
514 Jones, Adrienne. *The Mural Master.*
580 Lewis, C. S. *The Lion, the Witch, and the Wardrobe.*
581 ———. *Prince Caspian.*
582 ———. *The Voyage of the "Dawn Treader."*

583 ———. *The Silver Chair.*
584 ———. *The Horse and His Boy.*
585 ———. *The Magician's Nephew.*
586 ———. *The Last Battle.*
606 Lindsay, David. *A Voyage to Arcturus.*
638 MacDonald, George. *Phantastes.*
642 ———. *Lilith.*
657 McKenzie, Ellen Kindt. *Drujienna's Harp.*
661 McNeill, Janet. *Tom's Tower.*
687 Moon, Sheila. *Knee-Deep in Thunder.*
688 ———. *Hunt Down the Prize.*
743 Nichols, Ruth. *A Walk Out of the World.*
744 ———. *The Marrow of the World.*
758 Norton, Andre. *Steel Magic.*
765 ———. *Here Abide Monsters.*
781 Parker, Richard. *A Time to Choose.*
937 Wheeler, Thomas Gerald. *Lost Threshold.*
974 Williams, Jay. *The Hero from Otherwhere.*

IV. *Science Fantasy*

Stories of science fantasy occupy a border country between fantasy and science fiction, dressing up magic in scientific terms—or science in magical terms. Science fiction deals with farfetched possibilities; science fantasy with plausible impossibilities. For example, a science fiction story might show a boy who was raising a dinosaur which had hatched after millions of years—but not a dinosaur that had come out of a hen's egg (Butterworth's *The Enormous Egg*). Labeling magic "science" only gives magic a new label, not a new meaning.

132 Blish, James. *A Case of Conscience.*
133 ———. *Black Easter.*
161 Bradbury, Ray. *The Martian Chronicles.*
220 Butterworth, Oliver. *The Enormous Egg.*
221 ———. *The Narrow Passage.*
237 Cameron, Eleanor. *The Wonderful Flight to the Mushroom Planet.*
238 ———. *Stowaway to the Mushroom Planet.*
239 ———. *Mr. Bass's Planetoid.*
240 ———. *A Mystery for Mr. Bass.*

MAGIC OF SITUATION

We will now turn to the second major type of fantasy: the story set in a world that exists only because of enchantment, or in which magical happenings are natural. This is "magic of situation" rather than "magic in operation" because, although magic may exist within the new world, the emphasis of the story is on the new world's existence. Many such stories lack "magic," as a procedure, entirely. A world may exist simply in order to allow animals and toys to talk; it may be a fairy-tale world, vaguely situated "long ago and far away"; it may be our own world with an altered history or geography; or, finally, it may be a wholly new, subcreated universe. The first two types lean toward fairy-story, the third and fourth toward myth and romance.

I. *Fairy-story Fantasy*

A. FAIRY TALES

1. *Hausmärchen.* These stories are modern imitations of the folk tale, simple, short, and profound.

008   Aiken, Joan. *Armitage, Armitage, Fly Away Home.*
009   ———. *A Necklace of Raindrops.*
010   ———. *Smoke from Cromwell's Time.*
011   ———. *More Than You Bargained For.*
012   ———. *Not What You Expected.*
027   Andersen, Hans Christian. *Complete Fairy Tales and Stories.*
136   Bomans, Godfried. *The Wily Wizard and the Wicked Witch.*
318   De la Mare, Walter. *The Magic Jacket.*
319   ———. *Broomsticks.*
320   ———. *A Penny a Day.*
322   De Regniers, Beatrice Schenk. *The Enchanted Forest.*
365   Farjeon, Eleanor. *Martin Pippin in the Apple Orchard.*
366   ———. *Martin Pippin in the Daisy Field.*
367   ———. *Italian Peepshow.*
368   ———. *Kaleidoscope.*
369   ———. *The Old Nurse's Stocking-Basket.*
370   ———. *Jim at the Corner.*
373   ———. *The Little Bookroom.*
394   Forester, C. S. *Poo-Poo and the Dragons.*
436   Gray, Nicholas Stuart. *Mainly in Moonlight.*
462   Housman, Laurence. *Cotton-Woolleena.*
463   ———. *The Field of Clover.*
464   ———. *The Rat-Catcher's Daughter.*
511   Jarrell, Randall. *The Bat-Poet.*
518   Juster, Norton. *Alberich the Wise and Other Journeys.*
666   Mason, Arthur. *The Wee Men of Ballywooden.*
683   Milne, A. A. *Prince Rabbit.*
735   Nesbit, E. *Oswald Bastable and Others.*
761   Norton, Andre. *High Sorcery.*
789   Picard, Barbara Leonie. *The Mermaid and the Simpleton.*
790   ———. *The Faun and the Woodcutter's Daughter.*
791   ———. *The Lady of the Linden Tree.*

792   ———. *The Goldfinch Garden.*
806   Pyle, Howard. *Pepper and Salt.*
807   ———. *The Wonder Clock.*
808   ———. *The Twilight Land.*
817   Ruskin, John. *The King of the Golden River.*
840   Sleigh, Barbara. *Stirabout Stories.*
863   Stockton, Frank R. *The Griffin and the Minor Canon.*
864   ———. *The Bee-Man of Orn.*
865   ———. *The Storyteller's Pack.*
881   Thurber, James. *Many Moons.*
882   ———. *The Great Quillow.*
883   ———. *The White Deer.*
884   ———. *The Thirteen Clocks.*
885   ———. *The Wonderful O.*
927   Uttley, Alison. *Magic in My Pocket.*
957   Wilde, Oscar. *The Happy Prince and Other Stories.*
990   Yolen, Jane. *The Girl Who Cried Flowers and Other Tales.*

2. Novelized fairy tales. These stories are fairy tales, but their development is more elaborate and their characters are more realistic. Section (a) contains light-hearted, humorous, or folklike stories; section (b) contains more serious and philosophical works.

(a)
014   Aiken, Joan. *The Kingdom and the Cave.*
022   Alexander, Lloyd. *The Marvelous Misadventures of Sebastian.*
023   ———. *The Cat Who Wished to Be a Man.*
024   ———. *The Wizard in the Tree.*
045   Babbitt, Natalie. *The Search for Delicious.*
046   ———. *Knee-Knock Rise.*
121   Beeks, Graydon. *Hosea Globe and the Fantastical Peg-legged Chu.*
122   Bellairs, John. *The Face in the Frost.*
130   Biegel, Paul. *The King of the Copper Mountains.*
274   Colum, Padraic. *The Boy Apprenticed to an Enchanter.*
281   Craik, Dinah Maria M. *The Little Lame Prince.*
295   Dahl, Roald. *James and the Giant Peach.*
296   ———. *Charlie and the Chocolate Factory.*
332   Du Bois, William Pène. *The Twenty-One Balloons.*
362   Enright, Elizabeth. *Tatsinda.*
371   Farjeon, Eleanor. *The Silver Curlew.*
372   ———. *The Glass Slipper.*

385   Fenton, Edward. *The Nine Questions.*

435   Gray, Nicholas Stuart. *Grimbold's Other World.*

539   Lang, Andrew. *Prince Prigio and Prince Ricardo.*

547   Lawrence, Ann. *Tom Ass.*

559   Lee, Tanith. *The Dragon Hoard.*

628   Lofting, Hugh. *The Twilight of Magic.*

630   Longman, Harold. *Andron and the Magician.*

679   Milne, A. A. *Once on a Time.*

835   Shura, Mary F. *The Nearsighted Knight.*

867   Stone, Ann. *The Balloon People.*

880   Thackeray, William M. *The Rose and the Ring.*

935   Watson, Sally. *Magic at Wychwood.*

936   Wersba, Barbara. *A Song for Clowns.*

962   Williams, Anne S. *Secret of the Round Tower.*

977   Williams, Ursula Moray. *The Three Toymakers.*

978   ———. *Malkin's Mountain.*

(b).

115   Beagle, Peter S. *The Last Unicorn.*

151   Boston, L. M. *The River at Green Knowe.*

152   ———. *A Stranger at Green Knowe.*

317   De la Mare, Walter. *The Three Royal Monkeys.*

342   Dunsany, Lord. *The King of Elfland's Daughter.*

393   Follett, Barbara. *The House Without Windows.*

440   Gripe, Maria. *The Glassblower's Children.*

441   ———. *The Land Beyond.*

487   Hudson, W. H. *Green Mansions.*

488   ———. *Little Boy Lost.*

512   Jarrell, Randall. *The Animal Family.*

536   La Motte Fouqué, Friedrich de. *Undine.*

548   Lawson, John. *You Better Come Home With Me.*

643   MacDonald, George. *The Golden Key.*

644   ———. *The Light Princess.*

640   ———. *The Princess and the Goblin.*

641   ———. *The Princess and Curdie.*

659   McKillip, Patricia A. *The Throme of the Erril of Sherill.*

818   St.-Exupery, Antoine de. *The Little Prince.*

890   Tolkien, J. R. R. "Leaf by Niggle" (in *Tree and Leaf*).

893   ———. *Smith of Wootton Major.*

934   Warburg, Sandol Stoddard. *On the Way Home.*

961   Willard, Nancy. *Sailing to Cythera.*

991   Yolen, Jane. *The Magic Three of Solatia.*

B. TOY TALES

Stories of talking or magical toys are not as common as one might think, above the picture-book level; yet among them are three of fantasy's greatest classics: *Pinocchio, Winnie-the-Pooh,* and *The Velveteen Rabbit.* Generally, the toys themselves cannot work magic. It is their ability to talk that makes them creatures of an enchanted Secondary World.

051   Bailey, Carolyn Sherwin. *Miss Hickory.*
254   Chase, Mary. *Loretta Mason Potts.*
262   Clarke, Pauline. *The Return of the Twelves.*
273   Collodi, Carlo. *The Adventures of Pinocchio.*
417   Godden, Rumer. *Impunity Jane.*
418   ———. *The Fairy Doll.*
419   ———. *Miss Happiness and Miss Flower.*
420   ———. *Little Plum.*
421   ———. *The Doll's House.*
422   ———. *Home is the Sailor.*
439   Greenwald, Sheila. *The Secret Museum.*
458   Hoban, Russell. *The Mouse and His Child.*
680   Milne, A. A. *Winnie-the-Pooh.*
681   ———. *The House at Pooh Corner.*
975   Williams, Margery. *The Velveteen Rabbit.*

C. ANIMAL FANTASY

The desire to "talk to the animals," as Rex Harrison sang in the movie of "Doctor Dolittle," is as old as man himself: it seems impossible that creatures of such distinctive personality should be unable to speak to us. The kind of fantasy in this category is not merely a story in which an animal happens to speak to a character, as in many folk and fairy tales, but one in which the animals are the focus of the story. Section 1 will list stories in which the animals can speak, but are not otherwise magical; Section 2 will list those in which the animals themselves have magic powers.

1. Talking animals
001   Adams, Richard. *Watership Down.*
052   Baker, Margaret. *Porterhouse Major.*

137   Bond, Michael. *A Bear Called Paddington.*
138–146   Nine sequels.
147   ———. *The Tales of Olga da Polga.*
148   Boshinski, Blanche. *Aha and the Jewel of Mystery.*
171   Brooks, Walter. *To and Again.*
172   Buchwald, Emilie. *Gildaen.*
271   Collier, John. *His Monkey Wife.*
331   Du Bois, William Pène. *The Great Geppy.*
431   Grahame, Kenneth. *The Wind in the Willows.*
523   Kipling, Rudyard. *The Jungle Book.*
524   ———. *Just-So Stories.*
537   Lampman, Evelyn Sibley. *The Shy Stegosaurus of Cricket Creek.*
538   ———. *The Shy Stegosaurus of Indian Springs.*
544   Lanier, Sterling E. *The War for the Lot.*
550   Lawson, Robert. *Ben and Me.*
551   ———. *I Discover Columbus.*
552   ———. *Rabbit Hill.*
553   ———. *The Tough Winter.*
554   ———. *The Fabulous Flight.*
555   ———. *Robbut.*
556   ———. *Mr. Revere and I.*
557   ———. *Captain Kidd's Cat.*
615   Lofting, Hugh. *The Story of Doctor Dolittle.*
616–627   Twelve sequels.
798   Potter, Beatrix. *The Fairy Caravan.*
816   Robertson, Keith. *Tales of Myrtle the Turtle.*
821   Selden, George. *Oscar Lobster's Fair Exchange.*
822   ———. *The Cricket in Times Square.*
823   ———. *Tucker's Countryside.*
824   ———. *Harry Cat's Pet Puppy.*
827   Sharp, Margery. *The Rescuers.*
828–833   Six sequels.
841   Smith, Dodie. *The Hundred and One Dalmatians.*
842   ———. *The Starlight Barking.*
928   Van Leeuwen, Jean. *The Great Cheese Conspiracy.*
939   White, E. B. *Stuart Little.*
940   ———. *Charlotte's Web.*
941   ———. *The Trumpet of the Swan.*
981   Wilson, Gahan. *Harry, the Fat Bear Spy.*

2. Magical or supernatural animals
048   Bach, Richard. *Jonathan Livingston Seagull.*

050 Bacon, Peggy. *The Ghost of Opalina.*
242 Cameron, Eleanor. *The Terrible Churnadryne.*
394 Forester, C. S. *Poo-Poo and the Dragons.*
400 Gannett, Ruth S. *My Father's Dragon.*
432 Grahame, Kenneth. *The Reluctant Dragon.*
465 Howard, Joan. *The Thirteenth is Magic.*
495 Hyers, Conrad. *The Chickadees.*
662 Manning, Rosemary. *Dragon in Danger.*
725 Nesbit, E. *The Complete Book of Dragons.*
776 O'Brien, Robert C. *Mrs. Frisby and the Rats of NIMH.*
814 Reit, Seymour. *Benvenuto.*
837 Sleigh, Barbara. *Carbonel, the King of the Cats.*
838 ———. *The Kingdom of Carbonel.*
856 Steig, William. *Dominic.*

II. Worlds of Enchantment

In this category are three divisions: A—New Geographies, stories about, or set in, lands which are supposed to be in this universe which never existed. Burroughs's Africa, Bramah's China, the "lost continents" of Atlantis and Mu, and many other such countries will be found here. B—New Histories, stories set in alternate versions of Primary history. Here are worlds in which the Plantagenets still rule England; worlds in which duchies five miles square can defeat the United States; worlds in which King Arthur ruled at Camelot. C—New Universes, stories set in worlds which are not at all related to ours. Tolkien's *The Lord of the Rings*, although theoretically set in the far past of our Earth, is so remote from our world as to constitute a separate universe and is entered here, along with Le Guin's Earthsea, Alexander's Prydain, Leiber's Nehwon, and others.

A. NEW GEOGRAPHIES

1. Primitive civilizations; the far past and future; hollow-earth tales
127 Benoit, Pierre. *Atlantida.*
167 Bradshaw, William R. *Goddess of Atvatabar.*
246 Carter, Lin. *The Wizard of Lemuria.*
247–251 Five sequels.
276 Cooper, Louise. *The Book of Paradox.*

300 Davidson, Avram. *Ursus of Ultima Thule.*
307 De Camp, L. Sprague. *The Tritonian Ring.*
311 ———. *Warlocks and Warriors.*
336 Dunsany, Lord. *A Dreamer's Tales and Other Stories.*
337 ———. *At the Edge of the World.*
338 ———. *Beyond the Fields We Know.*
412 Gaskell, Jane. *The Serpent.*
413 ———. *Atlan.*
414 ———. *The City.*
459 Hodgson, William Hope. *The House on the Borderland.*
466 Howard, Robert. *Conan the Conqueror.*
467–482 Sixteen sequels by Howard and other writers.
496 Hyne, C. J. Cutliffe. *The Lost Continent.*
674 Merritt, Abe. *Dwellers in the Mirage.*
672 ———. *The Moon Pool.*
689 Moorcock, Michael. *Stormbringer.*
690–705 Sixteen sequels.
920 Trevino, Elizabeth Borton de. *Beyond the Gates of Hercules.*
996 Zelazny, Roger. *Jack of Shadows.*

2. Oriental lands
120 Beckford, William. *Vathek.*
168 Bramah, Ernest. *Kai-Lung's Golden Hours.*
169 ———. *Kai-Lung Unrolls His Mat.*
282 Crawford, F. Marion. *Khaled.*
457 Hilton, James. *Lost Horizon.*
670 Meredith, George. *The Shaving of Shagpat.*

3. Uncharted Africa
184 Burroughs, Edgar Rice. *Tarzan of the Apes.*
185–210 Twenty-six sequels.
443 Haggard, Rider. *She.*
444 ———. *Ayesha.*
445 ———. *The People of the Mist.*

4. Unexplored America
675 Merritt, Abe. *The Face in the Abyss.*

5. New countries in the modern world
984 Wright, Austin Tappan. *Islandia.*
985 Saxton, Mark. *The Islar.*

B. NEW HISTORIES

003 Aiken, Joan. *The Wolves of Willoughby Chase.*
004 ———. *Black Hearts in Battersea.*
005 ———. *Nightbirds on Nantucket.*
006 ———. *The Whispering Mountain.*
007 ———. *The Cuckoo Tree.*
034 Anderson, Poul. *Operation Chaos.*
035 ———. *A Midsummer Tempest.*
039 Ariosto, Ludovico. *Orlando Furioso: the Ring of Angelica.*
062 Barringer, Leslie. *Gerfalcon.*
222 Cabell, James Branch. *The Biography of Manuel.* (18 vols.)
298 Davidson, Avram. *The Phoenix and the Mirror.*
299 ———. *Peregrine: Primus.*
341 Dunsany, Lord. *Don Rodriguez.*
343 ———. *The Charwoman's Shadow.*
411 Garrett, Randall. *Too Many Magicians.*
448 Haggard, Rider, and Lang, Andrew. *The World's Desire.*
455 Heinlein, Robert. "Magic, Inc."
532 Kurtz, Katherine. *Deryni Rising.*
533 ———. *Deryni Checkmate.*
534 ———. *High Deryni.*
546 Lawrence, Ann. *The Half Brothers.*
718 Munn, H. Warner. *Merlin's Ring.*
859 Stewart, Mary. *The Crystal Cave.*
860 ———. *The Hollow Hills.*
942 White, T. H. *The Sword in the Stone.*
943 ———. *The Once and Future King.*
951 Wibberley, Leonard. *The Mouse That Roared.*
952 ———. *Beware of the Mouse.*
953 ———. *The Mouse on the Moon.*
954 ———. *The Mouse on Wall Street.*
960 Wilkins, Vaughan. *The City of Frozen Fire.*
980 Williamson, Jack. *The Reign of Wizardry.*

C. NEW UNIVERSES

002 Adams, Richard. *Shardik.*
015 Alexander, Lloyd. *The Book of Three.*

016 ———. *The Black Cauldron.*

017 ———. *The Castle of Llyr.*

018 ———. *Taran Wanderer.*

019 ———. *The High King.*

020 ———. *The Foundling and Other Tales of Prydain.*

308 De Camp, L. Sprague. *The Goblin Tower.*

309 ———. *The Clocks of Iraz.*

310 ———. *The Fallible Fiend.*

353 Eddison, E. R. *The Worm Ouroboros.*

498 Ingram, Tom. *Garranane.*

500 Ipcar, Dahlov. *The Warlock of Night.*

519 Kendall, Carol. *The Gammage Cup.*

520 ———. *The Whisper of Glocken.*

560 Lee, Tanith. *The Birthgrave.*

561 Le Guin, Ursula K. *A Wizard of Earthsea.*

562 ———. *The Tombs of Atuan.*

563 ———. *The Farthest Shore.*

566 Leiber, Fritz. *Swords and Deviltry.*

567 ———. *Swords Against Death.*

568 ———. *Swords in the Mist.*

569 ———. *Swords Against Wizardry.*

570 ———. *The Swords of Lankhmar.*

656 McKenzie, Ellen Kindt. *Taash and the Jesters.*

660 McKillip, Patricia A. *The Forgotten Beasts of Eld.*

685 Mirrlees, Hope. *Lud-in-the-Mist.*

706 Morris, William. "The Hollow Land."

707 ———. *The Story of the Glittering Plain.*

708 ———. *The Wood Beyond the World.*

709 ———. *The Water of the Wondrous Isles.*

710 ———. *The Well at the World's End.*

711 ———. *The Sundering Flood.*

750 Norton, Andre. *Witch World.*

751–757 Seven sequels.

804 Pratt, Fletcher. *The Well of the Unicorn.*

805 ———. *The Blue Star.*

888 Tolkien, J. R. R. *The Hobbit.*

889 ———. *The Lord of the Rings.*

SOURCES

BOOKS

1. Aldiss, Brian. *Billion Year Spree: the True History of Science Fiction.* Garden City, N.Y., Doubleday, 1973. 339 p.
2. Allen, Richard Stanley, comp. *Science Fiction: the Future.* New York, Harcourt, 1971. 345 p.
   A textbook anthology of science fiction as the literature of "future shock," including essays, articles, poems, and stories.
3. Amis, Kingsley. *New Maps of Hell: a Survey of Science Fiction.* New York, Harcourt, 1960. 161 p.
4. Atheling, William (pseudonym of James Blish). *More Issues at Hand: Critical Studies in Contemporary Science Fiction.* Ed. and with an introduction by James Blish. Chicago, Advent, 1970. 154 p.
5. Birkhead, Edith. *The Tale of Terror.* New York, Russell & Russell, 1963 (1921). xi, 241 p.
6. Bleiler, Everett F., ed. *The Checklist of Fantastic Literature: a Bibliography of Fantasy, Weird, and Science Fiction Books Published in the English Language.* Chicago, Shasta, 1948. xiv, 455 p.
   An excellent source of titles, though none are annotated.
7. Briney, Robert E. and Wood, Edward. *Science Fiction Bibliographies: an Annotated Bibliography of Bibliographical Works on Science Fiction and Fantasy Fiction.* Chicago, Advent, 1972. ix, 49 p.
8. Cameron, Alastair G. W. *Fantasy Classification System.* St. Vital, Manitoba, Canadian Science Fiction Assoc., 1952.
9. Cameron, Eleanor. *The Green and Burning Tree: on the Writing and Enjoyment of Children's Books.* Boston, Little, Brown, 1969. xiv, 377 p.
   The title essay is especially helpful.
10. Carter, Lin. *Imaginary Worlds: the Art of Fantasy.* New York, Ballantine, 1971. 278 p.

A detailed and informative history of heroic and adventure fantasy which is vitiated by poor theoretical backing, incredible carelessness about details, and Carter's tendency to blow his own horn.

11. Clareson, Thomas D. *Science Fiction Criticism: an Annotated Checklist*. Kent, Ohio, Kent State University Press, 1972. xiii, 225 p.

12. Clareson, Thomas D., ed. *Science Fiction: the Other Side of Realism*. Bowling Green, Ohio, Bowling Green University Popular Press, 1971. xvi, 365 p.

Twenty-five essays, including some reprinted from the Modern Language Association newsletter, *Extrapolation*.

13. Crawford, Joseph H., Jr., Donahue, James J., and Grant, Donald M. *333: A Bibliography of the Science-Fantasy Novel*. Providence, R.I., Grandon, 1953. 80 p.

A well-annotated bibliography of science fiction, fantasy, horror, and Gothic stories (about 300 entries).

14. Crouch, Marcus. *Treasure Seekers and Borrowers*. London, Library Association, 1962. 160 p.

15. Crouch, Marcus. *The Nesbit Tradition: the Children's Novel in England, 1945–1970*. London, Benn, 1972.

16. Cullinan, Bernice E. *Literature for Children: its Discipline and Content*. Dubuque, Iowa, W. C. Brown, 1971. 108 p.

17. De Camp, L. Sprague. *Science Fiction Handbook: the Writing of Imaginative Fiction*. New York, Hermitage House, 1953. 328 p.

18. Eshbach, Lloyd A. ed. *Of Worlds Beyond: the Science of Science Fiction*. Reading, Pa., Fantasy Press, 1947. 104 p.

Includes essays by Jack Williamson, Robert Heinlein, and L. Sprague De Camp.

19. Eyre, Frank. *British Children's Books in the Twentieth Century*. New York, Dutton, 1971. 208 p.

20. Frye, Northrop. *Anatomy of Criticism: Four Essays*. Princeton, N.J., Princeton University Press, 1957. x, 383 p.

Expounds Frye's theory of literary modes ranging from myth to irony.

21. Goodknight, Glen, ed. *Mythcon I: Proceedings*. Los Angeles, Mythopoeic Society, 1972.

22. Gove, Philip Babcock. *The Imaginary Voyage in Prose Fiction: a History of Its Criticism and a Guide for Its Study, with an Annotated Check List of 215 Imaginary Voyages from 1700 to 1800.* (Columbia University Studies in English and Comparative Literature, No. 152). New York, Columbia University Press, 1941. xiii, 445 p.

23. Green, Roger Lancelyn. *Into Other Worlds: Space Flight in Fiction from Lucian to Lewis*. London, Abelard-Schuman, 1957. 184 p.

24. Hall, H. W., ed. *Science Fiction Book Review Index, 1923–1973.* Detroit, Gale, 1975. 450 p.

Contains citations to 14,500 reviews of 6,900 books.

25. Haviland, Virginia. *Children's Literature—Guide to Reference Sources.* Washington, D.C., Library of Congress, 1966. x, 341 p.

26. Higgins, James E. *Beyond Words: Mystical Fancy in Children's Literature.* New York, Teachers College Press, 1970. 112 p.

27. Ketterer, David. *New Worlds for Old: the Apocalyptic Imagination, Science Fiction, and American Literature.* Garden City, N.Y., Anchor Books/Doubleday, 1974. xii, 346 p.

Considers apocalyptic American writing from Poe and Melville to Vonnegut and Le Guin.

28. Lanes, Selma G. *Down the Rabbit Hole: Adventures and Misadventures in the Realm of Children's Literature.* New York, Atheneum, 1971. xv, 239 p.

29. Lewis, C. S. *Selected Literary Essays.* Ed. by Walter Hooper. Cambridge, England, Cambridge University Press, 1969. xx, 330 p.

Noteworthy are essays on "William Morris," "Kipling's World," "High and Low Brows," and "The Anthropological Approach."

30. Lovecraft, H. P. *Supernatural Horror in Literature.* Introduction by August Derleth. New York, Ben Abramson, 1945. 106 p.

31. Mundhenk, Rosemary. *Another World: the Mode of Fantasy in the Fiction of Selected Nineteenth-Century Authors.* Los Angeles, UCLA Department of English, 1972. ix, 323 p. (Ph.D. dissertation).

32. Negus, Kenneth. *E.T.A. Hoffman's Other World: the Romantic Author and his "New Mythology."* Philadelphia, University of Pennsylvania Press, 1965. 183 p.

33. Nye, Russel. *The Unembarrassed Muse: the Popular Arts in America.* New York, Dial, 1970.

34. Pfeiffer, John R. *Fantasy and Science Fiction, a Critical Guide.* Palmer Lake, Colo., Filter Press, 1971. iv, 64 p.

Each entry is competently annotated, but no distinction is made between fantasy and science fiction titles.

35. Philmus, Robert M. *Into the Unknown: The Evolution of Science Fiction from Francis Godwin to H. G. Wells.* Berkeley, University of California Press, 1970. xii, 174 p.

Considers science fiction in the light of its "rhetorical strategy" of causing the reader to suspend disbelief by calling upon "science."

36. Scholes, Robert. *The Fabulators.* New York, Oxford University Press, 1967. x, 180 p.

37. Sewell, Elizabeth. *The Field of Nonsense.* London, Chatto and Windus, 1952. 198 p.

38. Slochower, Harry. *Mythopoesis: Mythic Patterns in the Literary Classics*. Detroit, Wayne State University Press, 1970. 362 p.

39. Thalmann, Marianne. *The Romantic Fairy Tale: Seeds of Surrealism*. Translated by Mary B. Corcoran. Ann Arbor, University of Michigan Press, 1964. vii, 133 p.

40. Tuck, Donald M., comp. *The Encyclopedia of Science Fiction and Fantasy Through 1968: a Bibliographic Survey of the Fields of Science Fiction, Fantasy, and Weird Fiction Through 1968*. Vol. I: Who's Who, A-L. Chicago, Advent, 1974. xii, 286 p.

Includes many fantasists, from Edwin L. Arnold to H. P. Lovecraft. Commentary is not always scrupulously accurate, but bibliographical details are.

41. Welland, D. S. R. *The Pre-Raphaelites in Literature and Art*. London, Harrap, 1953. 215 p.

42. Wertham, Frederic. *The World of Fanzines: A Special Form of Communication*. Carbondale, Ill., Southern Illinois University Press, 1973. 144 p.

A definitive work on fanzines, especially those in the fields of science fiction and fantasy. Many excellent illustrations, a glossary, and addresses of all fanzines mentioned are given.

43. Young Adult Reviewers of Southern California. *Fantasy for Young Adults*. Temple City, Calif., Public Library, n.d. 40 p.

ARTICLES

1. Alexander, Lloyd. "The Flat-Heeled Muse," in *Horn Book Reflections, on Children's Books and Reading, Selected from Eighteen Years of the Horn Book Magazine—1949–1966*, ed. by Elinor Whitney Field. Boston, The Horn Book. 1969, pp. 242–247.

2. Alexander, Lloyd. "High Fantasy and Heroic Romance." *Horn Book*, Vol. 47 No. 6 (December 1971), pp. 577–584.

3. Barnes, Myra Jean Edwards. "Linguistics and Languages in Science Fiction-Fantasy." *Dissertation Abstracts Index*, Vol. 32 No. 9 (March 1972), pp. 5210A–5211A.

4. Cornwell, Charles Landrum. "From Self to the Shire: Studies in Victorian Fantasy." *Dissertation Abstracts Index*, Vol. 33 No. 3 (Sept. 1972), p. 1163A.

5. Drury, Roger. "Realism and Fantasy-Magic." *Horn Book*, Vol. 48 No. 2 (April 1972), pp. 113–119.

6. Eager, Edward. "Daily Magic," in *Horn Book Reflections* . . . , pp. 211–217.

7. Fowler, Helen. "C. S. Lewis: Sputnik or Dinosaur?" *Approach*, No. 32 (Summer 1959), pp. 8–14.

8. Heinlein, Robert A. "Ray Guns and Rocket Ships." *Library Journal*, Vol. 78 (July 1953), pp. 1188–1191.

9. Helson, Ravenna. "Through the Pages of Children's Books." *Psychology Today*, Vol. 7 No. 6 (November 1973), pp. 107–117.

10. Helson, Ravenna. "Fantasy and Self-Discovery." *Horn Book*, Vol. 46 No. 2 (April 1970), pp. 121–134.

11. Kuyk, Dirk A., Jr. "Strategies of Unreason." *Dissertation Abstracts Index*, Vol. 32 No. 1 (July 1971), p. 440A.

12. Langton, Jane. "The Weak Place in the Cloth: A Study of Fantasy for Children." *Horn Book*, Vol. 49: Part I, No. 5 (October 1973), pp. 433–441; Part II, No. 6 (December 1973), pp. 570–578.

Considers fantasy "waking dreams" set in a "surreal landscape," and includes ghost stories and science fiction in fantasy.

13. Lewis, C. S. "On Three Ways of Writing for Children," in *Only Connect: Readings on Children's Literature*, ed. by Sheila Egoff, G. T. Stubbs, and L. F. Ashley. New York, Oxford University Press, 1969, pp. 207–220.

14. Lourie, Helen. "Where is Fancy Bred?", in *Only Connect* . . . , pp. 106–110.

15. McHargue, Georgess. "A Ride Across the Mystic Bridge, or Occult Books: What, Why, and Who Needs Them?" *School Library Journal*, Vol. 19 No. 9 (May 1973), pp. 25–30.

16. Merla, Patrick. " 'What is REAL?' Asked the Rabbit One Day." *Saturday Review*, Vol. LV No. 45 (November 1972), pp. 43–50.

17. Sanders, Joseph L. "Fantasy in the Twentieth Century British Novel." *Dissertation Abstracts Index*, Vol. 33 No. 2 (August 1972), p. 764A.

18. Tolkien, J. R. R. "On Fairy-Stories," in his *Tree and Leaf*. Boston, Houghton Mifflin, 1965, pp. 3–84.

19. Wilson, George R., Jr. "The Quest Romance in Contemporary Fiction." *Dissertation Abstracts Index*, Vol. 30 No. 2 (August 1969), p. 741A.

20. Young Adult Services Division Media Selection and Usage Committee, American Library Association. "Trekking Science Fiction's Stars." *ALA Top of the News*, Vol. 31 No. 2 (January 1975), pp. 210–217.

FANZINES

1. *Fantasiae*. Published by the Fantasy Association, P.O. Box 24560, Los Angeles, Calif. 90024.
2. *Mythlore*. Published by the Mythopoeic Society, P.O. Box 24150, Los Angeles, Calif. 90024. Incorporates the *Tolkien Journal*.
3. *Amra*. Published by the Hyborian Legion, Box 8243, Philadelphia, Pa., 19101.

A Bibliographic Guide
to Fantasy

THE FOLLOWING list of fantasies includes novels, novellas, collections of short stories, and a few individual short stories that are expected to be of interest to adult readers. This does not exclude "children's" books; many fantasies written for children may be read by adults with enjoyment, just as children may read some "adult" fantasies with pleasure. But since the list is primarily meant for adults, it does exclude books that may be characterized as "easy books" or picture books. The great majority of the books listed were originally written in English, by British, American, Canadian, or Australian authors, but a few translations from other languages have been included if they have become part of the English fantasy tradition—books like *Pinocchio* or the Moomintroll series.

The list is arranged alphabetically by author. However, works of criticism, biography, and bibliography are listed under the name of their subject, rather than under the name of their author. The fantasies are listed chronologically by the date of their first publication; sequels are listed directly after their predecessors, even if strict chronological order is upset. I have preferred to list editions which are readily available in American bookstores and libraries whenever possible. The date of the work's original composition or publication is given in parentheses after the date of the particular edition cited.

Each fantasy is followed by complete bibliographical information and a critical annotation. Critical and biographical works may, or may not, be annotated, and are arranged in the following order:

1. Books about the author;
2. Articles or short essays about the author;
3. Books about the author and other writers;

4. Articles or short essays about the author and other writers. Each title has been assigned a unique number, by which it may be found in the index.

ADAMS, RICHARD, 1920– .

001   *Watership Down.* New York, Macmillan, 1973. ix, 429 p.

A band of rabbits, led by the modest but courageous Hazel and his prophet brother Fiver, leave their warren on an epic migration that leads them to a new home on Watership Down. The rabbits' behavior is credibly rabbity, the narrative exciting and engrossing, and the rabbit myths and legends recounted during the course of the story lend depth to the tale.

002   *Shardik.* New York, Simon and Schuster, 1975. 604 p.

Kelderek, believing Shardik, a gigantic bear, to be the reincarnation of their god, persuades his people to follow the bear to conquest of the Beklan Empire. During a subsequent rebellion, Kelderek comes to a new understanding of the meaning of Shardik's appearance. Adams's great gift is his ability to make animals convincing both as animals and as sentient beings; his humans are less convincing, but the way in which he describes their reactions to the bear is masterful.

AIKEN, JOAN, 1924– .

003   *The Wolves of Willoughby Chase.* Illus. by Pat Marriott. Garden City, N.Y., Doubleday, 1962. 168 p.

First of a series of novels set in an alternate universe, where England is ruled by King James III, wolves infest the railway lines, and wicked Hanoverians constantly plot to seize the throne. Bonnie and Sylvia escape from their wicked governess and make their way to London with the help of Simon, a kind shepherd boy. Followed by

004   *Black Hearts in Battersea.* Illus. by Pat Marriott. Garden City, N.Y., Doubleday, 1965. 240 p.

Kidnapped by Hanoverians, Simon and Dr. Field are rescued by eight-year-old Dido Twite, and Simon learns that he is the long-lost heir of the Duke of Battersea just in time to save the Duke and King Jamie from being blown up. Followed by

005   *Nightbirds on Nantucket.* Illus. by Robin Jacques. Garden City, N.Y., Doubleday, 1966. 216 p.

Dido, rescued from drowning by a whaler, goes to Nantucket and defeats another Hanoverian plot, which involves a gigantic cannon aimed at the heart of London. Followed by

oo6   *The Whispering Mountain*. Illus. by Frank Bozzo. Garden City, N.Y., Doubleday, 1968. 237 p.

A convoluted plot introduces Owen Hughes, whose naval-officer father is missing. Owen and his friends, Tom and Arabis Dando, defeat the wicked Marquess, find the lost Harp of Teirtu, restore a lost tribe of gold-workers to their Seljuk, save Prince Davie from being murdered, and win the acceptance of Owen's strict grandfather after a hair-raising chase through the caves of the Whispering Mountain. Followed by

oo7   *The Cuckoo Tree*. Illus. by Susan Obrant. Garden City, N.Y., Doubleday, 1971. 314 p.

Dido returns from Nantucket with Captain Hughes, carrying a dispatch warning of yet another Hanoverian plot: to roll St. Paul's Cathedral into the Thames during the coronation of the new king. Waylaid by Hanoverians, Dido is forced to call on smugglers, who meet at the Cuckoo Tree, for help.

All of the Willoughby Chase books are charming, and Aiken is a witty stylist, although she tends to overdo the comic Scots, Welsh, and Cockney accents, and to introduce confusing subplots.

oo8   *Armitage, Armitage, Fly Away Home*. Illus. by Betty Fraser. Garden City, N.Y., Doubleday, 1968. 214 p.

A series of connected short stories about the Armitage family, who have unusual experiences because of Mrs. Armitage's wish, on her honeymoon, for two children who would never be bored.

oo9   *A Necklace of Raindrops*. Illus. by Jan Pienkowski. Garden City, N.Y., Doubleday, 1968. 109 p.

Fairy tales suitable for younger children.

o10   *Smoke from Cromwell's Time and other stories*. Garden City, N.Y., Doubleday, 1970. 163 p.

o11   *More Than You Bargained For*. Garden City, N.Y., Doubleday, 1974.

o12   *Not What You Expected*. Garden City, N.Y., Doubleday, 1974. 320 p.

Three collections of witty and imaginative fairy tales with some unexpected twists. Typical stories are "A Small Pinch of Weather," in which a Scottish weather-witch, who keeps an embroidery-wool shop, is rescued from a gang by a retired bishop, and "The Parrot Pirate Princess," who was turned into a parrot by a bad fairy at her christening, and, when disenchanted, proves to have become a pirate with a most distressing vocabulary.

013   *Arabel's Raven.* Illus. by Quentin Blake. Garden City, N.Y., Doubleday, 1974. 118 p.

Three stories about Mortimer, a pet raven who eats escalators and croaks "Nevermore."

014   *The Kingdom and the Cave.* Illus. by Victor G. Ambrus. Garden City, N.Y., Doubleday, 1974. 160 p.

Prince Michael and his cat, Mickle, save Astalon from an invasion with the help of a wizard and a magic box containing the Ray of Truth, which turns the invaders back into their original form of fish. Not up to her usual standard.

ALEXANDER, LLOYD, 1924–   .

015   *The Book of Three.* Jacket and maps by Evaline Ness. New York, Holt, 1964. 217 p.

First of a series, the Prydain Chronicles, set in the land of Prydain, based on ancient Wales. Taran, a pigkeeper, longs for adventures and heroic deeds, but discovers that there is more to them than merely acting brave and heroic. Followed by

016   *The Black Cauldron.* New York, Holt, 1965. 224 p.

017   *The Castle of Llyr.* New York, Holt, 1966. 201 p.

Further adventures of Taran as he learns the duties and skills of a chivalric hero, with the help of his friends: Dallben, the enchanter; Coll, the farmer; Flewddur Fflam, the hyperbolic bard; Gurgi, the wildman of the forest; and the Princess Eilonwy, who can always put Taran in his place with a well-chosen word. Followed by

018   *Taran Wanderer.* New York, Holt, 1967. 256 p.

019   *The High King.* New York, Holt, 1968. 285 p.

In these last two books, matters take a darker turn. Taran goes to seek his parentage, but is horrified and repelled when the man who claims to be his father is a mere laborer. He overcomes his feelings and behaves nobly, only to discover that the man was lying. He finds new friends and useful crafts on his travels—pottery, weaving, and smithing. Then, when all Prydain is threatened by Arawn, the evil Lord of Death, Taran joins Prince Gwydion in the ghastly struggle and eventually defeats Arawn himself.

The Book of Three limps a little, and emphasizes the comical aspects of Taran's hopes, but *The High King* achieves powerful intensity without giving up humor, and without becoming pompously didactic.

020   *The Foundling and Other Tales of Prydain.* Pictures by Margot Zemach. New York, Holt, 1973. viii, 87 p.

Several rather flat short stories about characters mentioned in the five Chronicles of Prydain.

021   *Time Cat, the Remarkable Adventures of Jason and Gareth.* Drawings by Bill Sokol. New York, Holt, 1963. 191 p.

Alexander's first and weakest book. A magical cat takes a boy through several historical periods on a quest.

022   *The Marvelous Misadventures of Sebastian.* New York, Dutton, 1970. 204 p.

Sebastian, a musician, and his friends in the Gallimaufry-Theatricus, a traveling theatrical company, rescue the Princess from the evil Baron who is trying to take over the kingdom. Set in a fairy-tale world resembling eighteenth-century Germany.

023   *The Cat Who Wished to Be a Man.* Jacket by Laszlo Kubinyi. New York, Dutton, 1973. viii, 107 p.

When Lionel is turned into a man, he finds that biting, hissing, and scratching cannot protect him from the wicked townspeople; but soon he and his new friends combine to outwit the cheats.

024   *The Wizard in the Tree.* Illus. by Laszlo Kubinyi. New York, Dutton, 1975. 160 p.

Mallory, a mistreated orphan, rescues the wizard Arbican from the tree he was trapped in, and he promises to help her escape the clutches of the wicked Squire Scrupnor. But Arbican's power is unreliable, and Mallory has to do almost everything. The Dickensian setting is well developed.

ALLEN, JUDY.

025   *The Spring on the Mountain.* New York, Farrar, 1973. 153 p.

Peter, Michael, and Emma decide to look for a magic spring on Arthur's Way, but an old tramp they have met suddenly materializes as Aquarius, the spring's guardian, and forces them to realize that they will not be allowed to find it. From this realization, Peter learns that he must negate the psychic forces arising from a long-ago lynching on the Way. The conflicts and fluctuating loyalties of the three children are well drawn, but an incoherent and pointless plot spoils the book.

AMIS, KINGSLEY, 1922– .

026   *The Green Man.* New York, Harcourt, 1970. 252 p.

A Green Man, or figure made out of boughs, made by a long-dead sorcerer, comes to life and upsets the routine of a sophisticated modern innkeeper. A frightening story, in which the hero's conversation with a well-dressed God stands out as exquisite comic relief.

ANDERSEN, HANS CHRISTIAN, 1805–1875.

027   *Complete Fairy Tales and Stories of Hans Christian Andersen.* Edited by Erik Haugaard. Garden City, N.Y., Doubleday, 1974.
   A new translation by a respected Danish children's author.
028   *The Snow Queen and Other Tales.* A new selection and translation with an introduction by Pat Shaw Iversen. Illus. by Sheila Greenwald. New York, Signet/NAL, 1966. xxiii, 318 p.
   A readily available paperback edition.
029   Reumert, Edith. *Hans Andersen the Man.* Translated by Jessie Brochner. Detroit, Gale, 1971 (1927). xvi, 192 p.
030   Spink, Reginald. *Hans Christian Andersen and His World.* New York, Putnam, 1972. 128 p.
   Two biographies.

ANDERSON, CHESTER.

031   *The Butterfly Kid.* New York, Pyramid, 1967. 190 p.
   The kid appears on the streets of Greenwich Village with millions of incredible butterflies flying, newly created, from his hands. A flower-child fantasy, sadly dated now. A sequel is Michael Kurland's *The Unicorn Girl* (q.v.)

ANDERSON, POUL, 1926– .

032   *Three Hearts and Three Lions.* Garden City, N.Y., Doubleday, 1961 (1953). 156 p.
   A Danish engineer, Holger Danske, is suddenly catapulted from fighting Nazis to a world where magic really works. After many adventures with the beautiful but rustic swan-maiden, Alianora, he discovers that he is the hero Ogier the Dane from the legends of Charlemagne, thrown into our world by the enchantress Morgan le Fay, and destined to fight evil in both worlds. An excellent story with both heroic and humorous scenes, the best of which involves a stupid ogre and a riddle-game.
033   *The Broken Sword.* Rev. ed. Introduction by Lin Carter. New York, Ballantine, 1971 (1954). xvi, 207 p.

Set in Anglo-Saxon England, against a background of terrible wars between the elves and the trolls. Skafloc is a human child stolen by the elves; Valgard the changeling left in his place, who brings about the destruction of the entire family except for Skafloc's sister Freda. In the climactic battle, Skafloc and Valgard kill each other while Freda looks on. The decadent society of the elves, the horror and brutality of the trolls, and the harshness of human life in the Dark Ages are powerfully described in this saga-like story.

034   *Operation Chaos.* Garden City, N.Y., Doubleday, 1971. 232 p.

The laws of magic having been discovered after World War I, a werewolf and his girlfriend become commandos fighting Asian weretiger troops in World War II. Later, the werewolf becomes an undercover agent struggling to protect America from woolly-minded liberals who refuse to recognize the dangers of a new cult backed by collectivist enemies, who are, in turn, backed by Satan. Very cold-war.

035   *A Midsummer Tempest.* Garden City, N.Y., Doubleday, 1974. 207 p.

Set in a universe in which Shakespeare was not a playwright, but a historian. Prince Rupert of the Rhine joins Oberon and Titania to defeat Cromwell. Rupert is also aided by Holger Danske and the werewolf's daughter (from Nos. 032 and 034), who meet him in a mysterious inn that is a nexus between alternate worlds. Anderson badly distorts the real issues of the Cavalier-Puritan conflict, and writes in a remarkably poor imitation of seventeenth-century prose style.

ANDREWS, J. S., 1934– .

036   *The Green Hill of Nendrum.* New York, Hawthorn, 1969. 214 p.

Nial goes back through time and joins the monks who lived on an island off the Irish coast in the tenth century. When a Viking raid destroys the monastery, Nial not only saves a friend's life, but rescues a treasured cup, thus helping to preserve civilization. The monks have no difficulty in accepting Nial's account of himself, which is hard to believe.

ANSTEY, F., pseudonym of Thomas Anstey Guthrie, 1856–1934.

037   *Humour and Fantasy.* New York, Dutton, 1931. x, 1174 p.

A collection of novelettes and stories dating from the 1880s on. Includes the delightful "Vice Versa," in which Mr. Bultitude, a pompous banker, and his naughty schoolboy son exchange bodies.

038   Turner, Martin J. *A Bibliography of the Works of F. Anstey.*
London, privately printed, 1931. 44 p. 150 copies.

ARIOSTO, LODOVICO, 1474–1533.

039   *Orlando Furioso: The Ring of Angelica, Vol. 1.* Translated
by Richard Hodgens. Introduction by Lin Carter. New York, Ballantine,
1973 (1516). xvi, 208 p.

A fast, furious, and extremely funny prose translation of part of
Ariosto's epic about Orlando—an Italian version of the French Roland
—and the Princess Angelica of Cathay, full of lady knights, mad enchanters, kings, Saracens, and noble steeds. De Camp and Pratt drew
on the *Orlando* for their humorous *The Castle of Iron* (q.v.).

040   Gardner, Edmund G. *The King of Court Poets: A Study of the
Life, Work, and Times of Lodovico Ariosto.* London, Constable, 1906.
395 p.

ARNOLD, EDWIN LESTER, 1857–1935.

041   *The Wonderful Adventures of Phra the Phoenician.* With an
introduction by Sir Edwin Arnold. New York, A. L. Burt, 1891. 451 p.

A quasi-historical novel in which Phra, owing to the curse of a
jealous Druid, reawakes in several periods of English history, from
Caesar's invasion to the reign of Elizabeth I. The inaccurate history is
much more important to the book than is the fantasy.

042   *Lepidus the Centurion, a Roman of To-Day.* New York,
Crowell, 1901. 205 p.

043   *Lieutenant Gulliver Jones: his vacation.* London, Brown, Lang-
ham, and Co., 1905.

Having traveled to Mars by flying carpet, Jones finds it to be a
beautiful landscape of gardens and canals and has to rescue a lovely
princess from savages. This book inspired a movie entitled *Gulliver of
Mars.*

ARTHUR, RUTH M., 1905– .

044   *A Candle in Her Room.* Illus. by Margery Gill. New York,
Atheneum, 1966. 212 p.

Over many years, an evil doll causes trouble and heartbreak for three young girls, until the last of the three destroys it. Written by an author who specializes in teenage Gothics.

BABBITT, NATALIE, 1932– .

045 *The Search for Delicious.* New York, Farrar, 1969. 167 p.

Gaylen, a page, searches the kingdom in order to help the king decide what food should stand for Delicious in the new dictionary. More what educational jargon calls a "learning experience" than a quest, as the story is highly didactic.

046 *Knee-Knock Rise.* Story and pictures by Natalie Babbitt. New York, Farrar, 1970. 118 p.

Egan goes to the top of the Mammoth Mountains—mammoth only because the surrounding countryside "lay as flat as if it had been knocked unconscious"—to find out what the moaning Megrimum is. A fable on faith and credulity.

047 *The Devil's Storybook.* Stories and pictures by Natalie Babbitt. New York, Farrar, 1974. 101 p.

Ten short stories in which the Devil, suitably attired in scarlet, makes trouble for everyone, sometimes to his own advantage, sometimes not. Humorous and imaginative.

BACH, RICHARD, 1936– .

048 *Jonathan Livingston Seagull.* Photographs by Russell Munson. New York, Macmillan, 1970. 93 p.

A pretentious fable of how Jonathan dedicated his life to flight, instead of garbage, and achieved salvation. The photographs are lovely.

BACON, MARTHA.

049 *The Third Road.* Illus. by Robin Jacques. Boston, Little, Brown, 1971. 188 p.

The three Craven children travel through time and space on a unicorn's back and have adventures centering around Spain and the California missions. A confusing plot and precocious children make this a mediocre book at best.

BACON, PEGGY, 1895– .

050   *The Ghost of Opalina, or Nine Lives.* Illus. by the author. Boston, Little, Brown, 1967. 243 p.

The ghost of an eighteenth-century Persian cat tells the children, Phil, Ellen, and Jeb, about all the adventures of her nine lives—how she caught thieves, took care of various children in precarious situations, and generally ruled the roost. None of the stories are memorable, and Opalina has very little individuality.

BAILEY, CAROLYN SHERWIN, 1875–1961.

051   *Miss Hickory.* With lithographs by Ruth Gannett. New York, Viking, 1946. 123 p.

Miss Hickory, an apple-twig doll with a nut for a head, has to spend the winter outdoors because Ann has gone to Boston. Her hard head protects her from damage, but also leads her to make many mistakes, the worst of which is not going to see the Christmas miracle in the barn with the animals and birds. In the spring, she finally provokes Squirrel into eating her head; but her body is unharmed, and she returns to the apple tree, grafting herself to it, and bursting into bloom. Told in simple, direct language which revels in, but never overstates, the beauty of the New Hampshire countryside.

BAKER, MARGARET, 1918– .

052   *Porterhouse Major.* Illus. by Shirley Hughes. Englewood Cliffs, N.J., Prentice-Hall, 1967. 116 p.

In the course of "helping" Rory's father with his dental practice, Porterhouse, the giant cat, enables poor old Miss Wellcome to get a home of her own. Suitable for younger children, but not memorable.

BAKER, MICHAEL.

053   *The Mountain and the Summer Stars, an old tale newly ended.* Illus. by Erika Weihs. New York, Harcourt, 1968, 124 p.

Based on the folk tale "The Fairy Wife," this is the story of her youngest son Owain, who goes into the Fairy Mountain to find her and reconcile her with his father. Sensitively written.

BARBER, ANTONIA, pseudonym of Barbara Anthony.

054   *The Ghosts.* New York, Farrar, 1969. 190 p.
Two modern children meet the ghosts of two Victorian children, their ancestors, who point the way to a badly needed fortune, and whose story helps them find out their own identity.

BARRIE, SIR JAMES MATTHEW, 1860–1936.

055   *The Little White Bird.* Illus. by Arthur Rackham. New York, Scribner, 1912 (1902). 286 p.
In these anecdotal chapters about a man and a small boy in Kensington Gardens, the immortal Peter Pan made his first appearance. So successful was he as a character that Barrie made a play with him, *Peter and Wendy,* and later allowed the Peter Pan chapters to be collected separately in
056   *Peter Pan in Kensington Gardens.* From *The Little White Bird.* With drawings by Arthur Rackham. London, Hodder and Stoughton, 1906. xii, 126 p.
Here we see Peter as the baby who flew out the window and went to live with the fairies at Kensington. His later adventures in Never-Never Land were chronicled in the play, which was adapted into the novel *Peter Pan.*
057   *Peter Pan.* With new illustrations for this edition by Richard Kennedy. Introduction by Naomi Lewis. Harmondsworth, Penguin, 1967 (1911). 220 p.
A paperback edition of the classic story. Wendy, John, and Michael Darling fly out of the window with Peter one night and go to live with the Lost Boys in Never-Never Land. But finally, the Darlings and the Lost Boys decide they prefer a home and a mother to the delights of life with pirates and Red Indians.
058   Asquith, Lady Cynthia. *Portrait of Barrie.* London, J. Barrie, 1954. 230 p.
A memoir by Barrie's secretary of many years, who became his chief legatee and literary executor after his death.
059   Chalmers, Patrick R. *The Barrie Inspiration.* London, Peter Davies, 1938. 271 p.

A study of Barrie as a fantasist compared with F. Anstey, Max Beerbohm, Kenneth Grahame, A. A. Milne, and H. G. Wells.

060   Dunbar, Janet. *J. M. Barrie: The Man behind the Image.* Illus. with photographs. Boston, Houghton Mifflin, 1970. xvi, 413 p.

A definitive and first-class biography.

061   Green, Roger Lancelyn. *J. M. Barrie.* London, Bodley Head, 1960. "A Bodley Head Monograph." 64 p.

Study of Barrie as a children's author.

BARRINGER, LESLIE.

062   *Gerfalcon.* Garden City, N.Y., Doubleday, 1927. 310 p.

Set in the imaginary medieval kingdom of Neustria, this is more Ruritanian romance than fantasy. Raoul is an orphan, the scorned nephew of the Count of Ger. Running away from his hated uncle, Raoul saves the life of a witch-girl, Lys, and becomes page to Red Anne, the mistress of the dreaded Butcher of Campscapel. Raoul kills the Butcher on a night of horrible brutality and escapes. When his cousin's death makes him the Count, he returns to Campscapel and destroys it. A thrilling adventure story during which Raoul grows from a timid boy into a leader worth following.

BAUM, LYMAN FRANK, 1856–1919.

063   *The Wonderful Wizard of Oz.* With pictures by W. W. Denslow. Chicago, G. M. Hill, 1900. 259 p.

Also published under the title *The Wizard of Oz.* This is the classic story of how Dorothy first went to Oz and, with the help of her friends the Scarecrow, the Tin Woodman, and the Cowardly Lion, destroyed the Wicked Witch of the West. Unlike the otherwise perfect 1939 movie, the story of Dorothy's journey does not take place in a dream; Oz is a real country to which she returns several times, eventually settling down there with Uncle Henry and Aunt Em. So successful was this first Oz book that Baum was obliged to write thirteen sequels, and after his death, other authors wrote twenty-six more. Here is the complete list, all of which are available from Reilly & Lee, Chicago:

064   *The Land of Oz.* 1904. 287 p.

The first sequel introduces the boy Tip, who lives with old Mombi the witch in unpleasant servitude. Tip escapes from Mombi, and after many adventures with Jack Pumpkinhead and the Sawhorse (both brought to life by a magic powder Tip stole from the witch), he discovers that he is not a boy at all. He is the fairy princess, Ozma, the rightful ruler of Oz.

065   *Ozma of Oz.* 1907. 270 p.
066   *Dorothy and the Wizard in Oz.* 1908. 256 p.
067   *The Road to Oz.* 1909. 261 p.
068   *The Emerald City of Oz.* 1910. 295 p.
069   *The Patchwork Girl of Oz.* 1913. 340 p.
070   *Tik-Tok of Oz.* 1914. 271 p.
071   *The Scarecrow of Oz.* 1915. 288 p.
072   *Rinkitink in Oz.* 1916. 314 p.
073   *The Lost Princess of Oz.* 1917. 312 p.
074   *The Tin Woodman of Oz.* 1918. 287 p.
075   *The Magic of Oz.* 1919. 265 p.
076   *Glinda of Oz.* 1920. 279 p.
077   Thompson, Ruth Plumly. *The Royal Book of Oz.* 312 p.
078   ———. *Kabumpo in Oz.*
079   ———. *The Cowardly Lion of Oz.*
080   ———. *Grampa in Oz.*
081   ———. *The Lost King of Oz.*
082   ———. *The Hungry Tiger of Oz.*
083   ———. *The Gnome King of Oz.*
084   ———. *The Giant Horse of Oz.*
085   ———. *Jack Pumpkinhead of Oz.*
086   ———. *The Yellow Knight of Oz.*
087   ———. *Pirates in Oz.*
088   ———. *The Purple Prince of Oz.*
089   ———. *Ojo in Oz.*
090   ———. *Speedy in Oz.*
091   ———. *The Wishing Horse of Oz.*
092   ———. *Captain Salt of Oz.*
093   ———. *Handy Mandy in Oz.*
094   ———. *The Silver Princess in Oz.*
095   ———. *Ozoplaning with the Wizard of Oz.*
096   Neill, John R. *The Wonder City of Oz.*

John R. Neill is the illustrator associated with the great majority of the Oz books; having illustrated so many, he evidently decided it would be no trouble to write three of his own.

097   ———. *The Scalawagons of Oz.*
098   ———. *Lucky Bucky in Oz.*
099   Snow, Jack. *The Magical Mimics in Oz.*
100   ———. *The Shaggy Man of Oz.*

Besides these two stories, Snow also wrote a directory:

101   ———. *Who's Who in Oz*, by Jack Snow in collaboration with Professor H. M. Wogglebug, T.E., Dean of the Royal College of Oz. With over 490 of the celebrated Oz illustrations by John R. Neill, Frank Kramer, and "Dirk." Chicago, Reilly & Lee, 1954. 277 p.

Every character in the forty Oz books is listed, with complete annotations as to his or her origin, activities, and achievements. In addition, two appendices give synopses of each book and biographical sketches of each author and illustrator involved.

102   Cosgrove, Rachel. *The Hidden Valley of Oz.*

103   McGraw, Eloise J., and Wagner, Lauren McG. *Merry-Go-Round in Oz.*

In addition to the Oz books, Baum himself wrote six other fantasies of a similar type, though they do not take place in Oz.

104   *The Enchanted Island of Yew.* Illus. by Fanny Y. Cory. Indianapolis, Ind., Bobbs-Merrill, 1903. 242 p.

105   *The Master Key, An Electrical Fairy Tale.* Illus. by Fanny Y. Cory. Indianapolis, Bobbs-Merrill, 1901. 245 p.

106   *The Surprising Adventures of the Magical Monarch of Mo.* Pictures by Frank Verbeck. Indianapolis, Bobbs-Merrill, 1901. 236 p.

107   *Queen Zixi of Ix, or, The Story of the Magic Cloak.* Illus. by Frederick Richardson. New York, Century, 1905. 303 p.

108   *The Sea Fairies.* Illus. by John R. Neill. Chicago, Reilly & Britton, 1911. 239 p.

109   *Sky Island.* Illus. by John R. Neill. Chicago, Reilly & Britton, 1912. 287 p.

None of these six stories is well known, and none is as good as any of Baum's own Oz stories, though they share his never-flagging invention and his unquenchable optimism. The main interest in Baum has always been as the creator of Oz, as is shown by the following four entries:

110   *The Annotated Wizard of Oz.* Edited with an introduction, notes, and bibliography by Michael P. Hearn. Pictures by W. W. Denslow. New York, Clarkson N. Potter, Inc., 1973. 384 p.

A long introduction gives biographical data on Baum and summarizes all the major criticism, illustrated with family photographs, posters, first edition title pages and illustrations, and advertisements. The text is heavily annotated. The maps of Oz on the endpapers were drawn by Baum for *Tik-Tok of Oz.*

111   Baum, Frank Joslyn. *To Please a Child: a biography of L. Frank Baum, Royal Historian of Oz.* Chicago, Reilly & Lee, 1961. 284 p.

112   Gardiner, Martin, and Nye, Russel B. *The Wizard of Oz and Who He Was*. East Lansing, Mich., Michigan State Univ. Press, 1957.

Contains "An Appreciation," by Nye; "The Royal Historian of Oz," by Gardiner; the text of *The Wonderful Wizard of Oz*; and a bibliography.

113   Sale, Roger. "L. Frank Baum, and Oz." *Hudson Review*, Vol. 25, No. 4 (Winter 1972–73), pp. 571–592.

BEAGLE, PETER S., 1939– .

114   *A Fine and Private Place*. New York, Viking, 1960. 272 p.

The premise of this ghost fantasy is that ghosts must stay close to their bodies after death. The ghosts of a young man and woman meet and fall in love in the cemetery where they are buried. They try to maintain their relationship in the face of the certain knowledge that eventually they will lose interest in remaining conscious. A beautiful but depressing story.

115   *The Last Unicorn*. New York, Viking, 1968. 218 p.

One of the few nostalgic fantasies written for adults, *The Last Unicorn* has become a classic. The unicorn seeks her people, who have been imprisoned by grim King Haggard and his Red Bull. She is aided by Schmendrick the magician, who helps her escape from Mommy Fortuna's terrible carnival, and Molly Grue, a battered Maid Marian with no illusions. Thanks to the unicorn's pure and gentle spirit, Schmendrick achieves real power, Molly learns not to be cynical, and Haggard's son Prince Lir is freed from the shadow of his father's stern unhappiness. An outstanding book.

BEATTY, JEROME, JR., 1918– .

116   *Matthew Looney's Voyage to the Earth*. Illus. by Gahan Wilson. New York, William R. Scott, 1961. 131 p.

117   *Matthew Looney's Invasion of the Earth*. Illus. by Gahan Wilson. New York, William R. Scott, 1965. 155 p.

118   *Matthew Looney in the Outback*. Illus. by Gahan Wilson. New York, William R. Scott, 1969. 223 p.

119   *Matthew Looney and the Space Pirates*. Illus. by Gahan Wilson. New York, William R. Scott, 1972. 158 p.

A series of comic stories for children. Matthew Looney is a Moonster; he has a famous uncle, Lockhard "Lucky" Looney, an explorer;

Moonsters go to the Mooniversity in lunabiles and belong to groups like the Organization for Peace in the Universe—O.P.U. The stories themselves are pure space opera, in which Matthew makes friends with everybody in the interests of interplanetary peace. Gahan Wilson's illustrations suit the comic mood.

BECKFORD, WILLIAM, 1760–1844

120   *Vathek*. Edited with an introduction by Roger Lonsdale. London, Oxford University Press, 1970 (1782). xliii, 187 p.

One of the few survivors of the popular eighteenth-century Oriental tale, based on *The Thousand and One Nights*. Vathek is a wicked Caliph whose excessive desire to have his own way is exploited by a Giaour, or Genie, sent by Eblis the Devil to ensure Vathek's damnation. Lush, sensual, overdecorated prose appropriately expresses the perversion and sadism of Beckford's story.

BEEKS, GRAYDON.

121   *Hosea Globe and the Fantastical Peg-Legged Chu*. Illus. by Carol Nicklaus. New York, Atheneum, 1975. 170 p.

Hosea Globe is a detective from the Isle of Philomath, a land of wise philosophers; Chu is his talking dog and is far more intelligent than his inept master. Together they rescue Tobias Small, a scientist who has learned to create cyclones, and take him to Philomath so that his discoveries cannot be used for evil. An exercise in Whangdoodlery (see the Introduction, pp. 56–57).

BELLAIRS, JOHN, 1938– .

122   *The Face in the Frost*. Illus. by Marilyn Fitschen. New York, Macmillan, 1969. 174 p.

A magician named Prospero ("and not the one you are thinking of, either") and his best friend, Roger Bacon, must fight off the attacks of an unknown, evil force. After several adventures in the absurd South Kingdom, Prospero's home, they learn that an old rival of Prospero's from his schooling in sorcery is behind the attacks, and that he can only be defeated by a spell which has hitherto had no use. Bellairs makes his story rush back and forth from hilarity to grimness without ever losing its balance. A sophisticated story written for adults, but not beyond an intelligent child's comprehension.

123　*The House With a Clock in its Walls.* Pictures by Edward Gorey. New York, Dial Press, 1973. 179 p.

Set in the late 1940's in a small town in Michigan. Lewis, ten years old and newly an orphan, goes to live with his Uncle Jonathan in a huge old house full of wonderful junk. His uncle soon reveals that he is listening for the clock that the evil Isaac Izzard, a magician, left in the house when he died. With the help of their neighbor, Mrs. Zimmerman, Lewis and Jonathan manage to defeat the evil charms of Isaac and his even more malignant wife. Followed by

124　*The Figure in the Shadows.* Drawings by Mercer Mayer. New York, Dial Press, 1975.

The coin Lewis discovers is really an amulet, ruled by the ghost of an old farmer who dabbled in witchcraft before the Civil War. The farmer tries to lure Lewis to his lair and drown him, but Mrs. Zimmerman, Jonathan, and Lewis's best friend Rose Rita foil him in the nick of time. The plot is weaker, but in other respects this is a worthy sequel to the first book.

BENARY-ISBERT, MARGOT, 1889– .

125　*The Wicked Enchantment.* Illus. by Enrico Arno. New York, Harcourt, 1955. 181 p.

A fairy tale in which the ghost of a wicked magician tries to take over a small, cozy Bavarian town, but is foiled by a small girl and by the true spirit of love shared by all the people.

BENNETT, ANNA ELIZABETH, 1914– .

126　*Little Witch.* Illus. by Helen Stone. Philadelphia, Lippincott, 1953. 128 p.

A variation on the overworked theme of a small witch who wants to be like other people.

BENOIT, PIERRE.

127　*Atlantida.* Translated by Mary C. Tongue and Mary Ross. New York, Ace, c. 1920. 192 p.

Captain de Saint-Avit of the Foreign Legion, on a desert expedition, discovers a lost city ruled by the beautiful but heartless Queen

Antinea, who intends him to become one of her long line of doomed lovers. A fair example of a nearly unreadable subgenre.

BERTON, PIERRE, 1920– .

128   *The Secret World of Og.* Illus. by William Winter. Boston, Little, Brown, 1962. 146 p.

Four children and their cat, Earless Osdick, enter the secret world under their playhouse inhabited by little green men to look for their baby brother. Since the green people are highly imaginative, they believe that they are whatever type of characters they have been reading about most recently—cowboys or pirates, for instance—which causes no end of confusion. A mediocre bedtime-story attempt.

BERESFORD, ELIZABETH.

129   *The Magic World.* Pictures by Janina Domanska. Indianapolis, Bobbs-Merrill, 1964. 153 p.

A boy finds a griffin which has come to Brighton in search of its lost treasure: a complete set of china made for the Prince Regent which is now the rightful property of the boy's poverty-stricken friend Grace. The lifeless story is not enhanced by the Griffin's attempts to be as peevishly charming as E. Nesbit's Psammead.

BIEGEL, PAUL.

130   *The King of the Copper Mountains.* English version by Gillian Hume and Paul Biegel. Illus. by Babs von Wely. New York, Watts, 1969 (1965). vi, 176 p.

The king is dying, and the plot, what there is of it, centers around the Wonder Doctor's search for the Golden Speedwell which will cure him. In the meantime, the animals tell stories to keep the king interested in life. None of the stories is particularly memorable.

BLACKWOOD, ALGERNON, 1869–1951.

131   *The Fruit Stoners, Being the Adventures of Maria Among the Fruit Stoners.* London, Grayson & Grayson, 1934. 287 p.

Maria has always loved to play a game with fruit stones: she gives them names and personalities. One day she and her cat Judas find themselves in the deserted part of their house, brought there by Jack Robinson—the Man Who Winds the Clocks—to meet the Fruit Stoners, who have come to life. Unfortunately, this exciting idea gets lost in a welter of confusing philosophical ideas and even more confusing plot developments.

BLISH, JAMES, 1921–1975.

132   A *Case of Conscience*. Garden City, N.Y., Doubleday, 1958.
   A priest who is also a scientist visits a planet inhabited by kind, friendly, learned, and noble creatures of reptilian ancestry who have never had any religious ideas. From this and other indications he deduces that they have no souls and are therefore creations of the Devil, invented to make humans doubt the existence of God. This being so, he makes himself responsible for their destruction. The reasoning which leads the priest to his final action is abstruse, but the story itself is clear and involving.

133   *Black Easter, or Faust Aleph-Null*. London, Faber, 1968. 165 p.
   A companion, rather than a sequel, to A *Case of Conscience*, this novel sits directly on the borderline between science fiction and fantasy. A wealthy industrialist uses a magician to call up the power of the Devil in order to kill a political leader. Only Brother Domenico, a monk who is a scholar of witchcraft, knows enough to thwart their plans—but he fails, the Devil wins, God dies, and a nuclear war begins. Intelligently developed.

BOK, HANNES, 1914–1964.

134   *The Sorcerer's Ship*. New York, Ballantine, 1969.
135   *Beyond the Golden Stair*. New York, Ballantine, 1970.
   Two overwritten adventure fantasies in the style of A. Merritt. Bok was a well-known fantasy illustrator in Art Deco style, but neither his books nor his drawings are of interest to any but the most dedicated adventure-fantasy fans.
   See also No. 667 below.

Bomans, Godfried

136   *The Wily Wizard and the Wicked Witch and Other Weird Stories*. Translated by Patricia Crampton. Illus. by Robert Bartelt.

New York, Watts, 1969 (1965). 180 p.

A rather creepy and morbid collection of fairy tales, some of which display the kind of "sick jokes" that appeal to ten-year-olds, and some of which are genuinely frightening, like one about a rich man who refuses the Three Wise Men.

Bond, Michael, 1926–   .

137   *A Bear Called Paddington.* Illus. by Peggy Fortnum. Boston, Houghton Mifflin, 1958. 128 p.

First in a series about a bear from Darkest Peru, adopted by the Brown family in Paddington Station—hence the name. Paddington is innocent, naive, sweet, and the biggest troublemaker known in the Western Hemisphere; his well-intentioned activities spell messes, distractions, and derangement for everyone around him. Very popular with children, who enjoy Paddington's mischievous naivete, the series becomes less lively in each succeeding book.

138   *More About Paddington.* Illus. by Peggy Fortnum. Boston, Houghton Mifflin, 1959. 127 p.

139   *Paddington Helps Out.* Illus. by Peggy Fortnum. Boston, Houghton Mifflin, 1960. 127 p.

140   *Paddington At Large.* Illus. by Peggy Fortnum. Boston, Houghton Mifflin, 1962. 128 p.

141   *Paddington Marches On.* Illus. by Peggy Fortnum. Boston, Houghton Mifflin, 1964. 127 p.

142   *Paddington At Work.* Illus. by Peggy Fortnum. Boston, Houghton Mifflin, 1966. 127 p.

143   *Paddington Goes to Town.* Illus. by Peggy Fortnum. Boston, Houghton Mifflin, 1968. 125 p.

144   *Paddington Takes the Air.* Illus. by Peggy Fortnum. Boston, Houghton Mifflin, 1971. 126 p.

145   *Paddington Abroad.* Illus. by Peggy Fortnum. Boston, Houghton Mifflin, 1972. 125 p.

146   *Paddington Takes to TV.* Illus. by Ivor Wood. Boston, Houghton Mifflin, 1974. (Originally published in England under the title *Paddington's Blue Peter Story Book*). 124 p.

147   *The Tales of Olga da Polga.* Illus. by Hans Helwig. New York, Macmillan, 1971. 114 p.

Olga is a pet guinea pig who chose her own name for its exotic qualities, and who makes up tall tales to explain occurrences she can't quite understand.

BOSHINSKI, BLANCHE, 1922– .

148   *Aha and the Jewel of Mystery.* Illus. by Shirley Pulido. New York, Parents, 1968. 155 p.

Aha, the chief granary cat of all ancient Egypt, has a mysterious jeweled collar which no one knows the origin of. After plot twists too numerous to mention, the secret of Aha's collar is found: the pattern is a mnemonic for the secret of irrigation. Told by Aha in the condescending tone that seems to be the unimaginative writer's standard characterization of talking cats.

BOSTON, LUCY MARIA, 1892– .

149   *The Children of Green Knowe.* Illus. by Peter Boston. New York, Harcourt, 1954. 157 p.

First of the justly famous series set in an old English house. Tolly has come to live with his great grandmother, Mrs. Oldknow, who tells him stories of their ancestors who lived at Green Knowe. Soon Tolly notices that there are other children at Green Knowe: the ghosts of three seventeenth-century children, who befriend him and support him in his struggle with the giant in the garden. Boston sustains the mood of lyrical melancholy throughout with beautiful writing and sure sensitivity; Tolly's discovery that his friends died young is heartbreaking, but bearable. Followed by

150   *The Treasure of Green Knowe.* Drawings by Peter Boston. New York, Harcourt, 1958. 185 p. (Originally published in England under the title *The Chimneys of Green Knowe*).

Tolly, home at Green Knowe for Easter, learns that Mrs. Oldknow may have to sell all her valuables to pay the bills. He begins to search for the lost treasure of the Oldknows, Maria Oldknow's jewels, which disappeared in 1798. His search is aided by Maria's blind daughter, Susan, and her black page, Jacob, whose duties consist chiefly of protecting Susan from her mother's mistreatment. This story is as good as its predecessor. Followed by

151   *The River at Green Knowe.* Drawings by Peter Boston. New York, Harcourt, 1959. 153 p.

Two refugee boys, Ping and Oskar, and an English girl named Ida go to Green Knowe, which Ida's aunt has rented for the summer; Mrs. Oldknow and Tolly are away. The children have various magical adventures centering around the river. This is by far the weakest Green Knowe book. Followed by

152   A *Stranger at Green Knowe*. Drawing by Peter Boston. New York, Harcourt, 1961. 158 p.

Ping becomes obsessed with Hanno, a gorilla in the zoo, to whom he does a kindness. When Hanno escapes, Ping helps him with food and keeps the searchers away, until he realizes that he cannot save Hanno by hiding him. Ping's moral dilemma and love for the animal are shown with tenderness and understanding, as is Hanno's tragic fate. Followed by

153   An *Enemy at Green Knowe*. Drawings by Peter Boston. New York, Harcourt, 1964. 156 p.

Tolly, Ping, and Mrs. Oldknow are faced by a greedy witch, Miss Powers, who pretends to be a scholar but will stop at nothing to drive them away from the house. After fighting off successive plagues of vipers, maggots, and cats, they learn her real name in her demon form and exorcise her by magic; they also find the seventeenth-century book of magic that she was looking for. This last Green Knowe book is as finely written and as sensitive as the rest.

154   *The Castle of Yew*. Illus. by Margery Gill. New York, Harcourt, 1965. 57 p.

A slight story set in the garden of a house very like Green Knowe. Joseph and Robin shrink to get inside the castle, which is a yew bush trimmed into a topiary shape, and play at being knights and pages. The play becomes serious when they are attacked, first by a moorhen, then by a cat; but they fight off the animals and incidentally become friends for the first time.

155   *The Sea Egg*. Illus. by Peter Boston. New York, Harcourt, 1967. 94 p.

Two small boys, Toby and Joe, find a "sea egg" on the beach which hatches into a "triton" or baby merman. Their games with the triton culminate in a midnight swim to a nearby island, which is a maze of undersea galleries and caves. A beautiful, lyrical celebration of the sea and the shore, with realistic, engaging characters.

156   *The Guardians of the House*. Illus. by Peter Boston. New York, Atheneum, 1975. 51 p.

Tom sneaks into a historic old house in an otherwise ultra-modern factory town, and finds it occupied by many "faces"—statues, pictures, masks, paintings, and so on—which talk to him and transport him through space and time. Finally, he puts on a donkey mask which at first plays with him, but gradually is revealed as an empty horror, because he plans to steal it. The guardians, having suitably frightened him, allow him to leave, understanding that they only did so because he was an intruder. An inconclusive story, but written with all the power and beauty of Boston at her best.

157   *Memory in a House*. New York, Macmillan, 1974. 142 p.
Boston's memoirs of her life at the real Green Knowe.

158   Rose, Jasper. *Lucy Boston*. New York, Walck, 1966. 71 p.
A study of the Green Knowe books.

BOUCHER, ANTHONY, pseudonym of William Anthony Parker White, 1911–1968.

159   *The Compleat Werewolf and Other Stories of Fantasy and Science Fiction*. New York, Simon and Schuster, 1969 (1941–45). 252 p.
A delightful collection of short stories in the vein of John Collier. In the title story, a professor of Old High German discovers that he can use his lycanthropic abilities as a G-man. Another story, "Mr. Lupescu," echoes Collier's "Thus I Refute Beelzy" with an even more sardonic twist.

BRACKETT, LEIGH, 1915– .

160   *The Sword of Rhiannon*. New York, Ace, 1953. 191 p.
Matt Carse enters an ancient Martian tomb and suddenly finds himself in the Mars of a million years ago, helping the accursed god Rhiannon destroy the evil he created and expiate the curse. Barsoomian sword-and-sorcery adventure, using Welsh names, and rather better than most examples of the subgenre. See also Burroughs, Edgar Rice.

BRADBURY, RAY, 1920– .

161   *The Martian Chronicles*. Garden City, N.Y., Doubleday, 1950. 222 p.
The interrelated science fantasy stories with which Bradbury made his reputation, all based on the premise that the Martians used strange and supernatural weapons against the Earthmen who invaded their planet. Full of unforgettable images of crystal towers and alien dreams.

162   *The October Country*. New York, Ballantine, 1955. 276 p.
Nineteen stories, fifteen of which were published by Arkham House in 1947 as *Dark Carnival*. October, with its associations with

Halloween, autumn, and witchcraft, sets the mood of the tales which hover between fantasy and horror.

163   *Something Wicked This Way Comes.* New York, Simon and Schuster, 1962. 317 p.

Will Halloway and Jim Nightshade, age thirteen, are swept into the center of events when Mr. Dark's demonic carnival comes to town one October. Mr. Dark pursues them and imprisons them in the carnival's Wax Museum, but Will's father rescues them through the power of laughter and love. Though perhaps a little overwritten at times, the story grips the imagination.

164   *The Halloween Tree.* Illus. by Joseph Mugnaini. New York, Knopf, 1972. 145 p.

A group of boys are sent through time on various adventures by a mysterious being who appears on Halloween night. Bradbury plagiarizes himself in this diffuse and rambling story.

165   Nolan, William F. *The Ray Bradbury Companion.* 130 Illustrations. Detroit, Gale, 1975. xiv, 339 p.

BRADLEY, MARION ZIMMER.

166   *Falcons of Narabedla.* New York, Ace, 1964. 128 p. (Bound with *The Dark Intruder and other stories*, Ace Double, No. 22576).

Mutant Dreamers are bound in sleep to the ruling Narabedlans. One Narabedlan lord, Adric, frees his Dreamer, Narayan, and becomes enmeshed in a deadly power struggle when Narayan leads a revolt. A man from the twentieth century, Mike Kenscott, is drawn into the conflict and helps unravel the confusion that Adric's actions have brought about. An average story, not up to the standard of Bradley's science-fiction Darkover novels.

BRADSHAW, WILLIAM RICHARD, 1851–1927.

167   *The Goddess of Atvatabar, being the history of the discovery of the Interior World and the conquest of Atvatabar.* Illus. with maps by C. Durand Chapman et al. New York, Douthitt, 1892. 318 p.

Strongly influenced by Jules Verne's *Journey to the Center of the Earth* and by Rider Haggard's *She* (q.v.). A polar expedition discovers that the North Pole is an enormous gulf which leads into the center of the Earth, which is lighted by an interior sun and inhabited by races with advanced technology and primitive social organization. The expedition members travel by sacred locomotive to the chief city of the country and meet the high priestess. Thoroughly silly, with funny, dated illustrations.

BRAMAH, ERNEST, pseudonym of Ernest Bramah Smith, 1869–1942.

168   *Kai-Lung's Golden Hours.* Introduction by Lin Carter. New York, Ballantine, 1972 (1922). xiv, 242 p.

Not a novel, but an episodic plot on which Bramah strings a number of charming fairy tales. Kai-Lung is a Chinese storyteller who tells one of his tales whenever he gets into a tight spot. Bramah's China bears about the same amount of resemblance to the real China as Walter Scott's England of *Ivanhoe* bears to the real English twelfth century, and has the same kind of breathlessly romantic atmosphere. Written in an exquisitely funny, ultra-formal prose style.

169   *Kai-Lung Unrolls His Mat.* Introduction by Lin Carter. New York, Ballantine, 1974 (1927). xi, 244 p.

The same sort of construction as in the previous volume, but in this book Kai-Lung participates more in the action and tells fewer stories. When his wife IIwa-mei, the Golden Mouse, is kidnaped by the warlord Ming-shu, Kai-Lung must rescue her from his camp, which he does with the maximum amount of complication. The individual stories which Kai-Lung tells outside the main action are among the best of Bramah's work.

BRANDEL, MARC.

170   *The Mine of Lost Days.* Illus. by John Verling. Philadelphia, Lippincott, 1974. 187 p.

Henry falls into an abandoned copper mine, inside which he meets four people who are hiding from soldiers and waiting for their cousin Kevin, an Irish revolutionary. Soon Henry discovers that no time exists inside the mine, and his new friends think that it is still the time of the Irish potato famine outside. The incoherent plot has no real conflict and no resolution.

BROOKS, WALTER ROLLIN, 1886–?.

171   *To and Again.* Illus. by Adolfo Best-Maugard. New York, Knopf, 1927. (Also published under the title *Freddy Goes to Florida.*) 196 p.

First in a long and popular, though undistinguished, series about a talking pig, all published by Knopf. Typical titles are *Freddy the Detective, Freddy and the Bean Home News, Freddy Goes Camping, Freddy the Pilot, Freddy and the Baseball Team from Mars, Freddy and Simon the Dictator,* and *Freddy and the Flying Saucer Plans.* Characterized by simple-minded humor, cliché characters, and rambling plots.

BUCHWALD, EMILIE, 1935– .

172   *Gildaen, the heroic adventures of a most unusual rabbit.* Illus. by Barbara Flynn. New York, Harcourt, 1973. 189 p.

Gildaen, an adventurous rabbit, a young girl, a brave woodsman, and a good wizardess who can't remember her name thwart an evil wizard who is plotting to take over the kingdom. Gildaen is called upon to demonstrate his courage and resourcefulness in the wizard's horrible garden, infested by magic snakes, rats, and bats, in a strong climax to an otherwise undistinguished story.

BURFORD, LOLAH.

173   *The Vision of Stephen, an elegy.* Frontispiece and endpaper illus. by Bill Greer. New York, Macmillan, 1972. 192 p.

Stephen is the sensitive son of a barbaric petty king in Anglo-Saxon England. After allowing a hostage to escape he is horribly punished by his father, and in his agony of mind makes mental contact with a family in the England of 1822. Finally, given as a hostage himself, he is brought out to be killed, but instead wakes in 1822 and is adopted by the family. The author's love for and interest in both periods is evident; Stephen is a believable Dark-Age character, in spite of his sensitivity, and his escape from a life he was not meant for is a happy resolution to the plot.

BURROUGHS, EDGAR RICE, 1875–1950.

174   *A Princess of Mars.* New York, Ballantine, 1963 (1912). (Originally published as a serial under the title *Under the Moons of Mars*). 159 p.

The first of the famous Barsoom series, published only a few months before *Tarzan of the Apes.* John Carter, an ex-Confederate officer, wills himself to Mars, or Barsoom, where he meets a race of warlike six-limbed green giants, whom he impresses with his courage and fighting ability. Later, he meets and marries Dejah Thoris, a princess. Trying to repair a failing atmosphere plant, Carter overreaches himself and awakes back on Earth. Burroughs wrote nine sequels, all available from Ballantine:

175   *Warlord of Mars.* (1919).
176   *Thuvia, Maid of Mars.* (1920).
177   *Chessmen of Mars.* (1922)
178   *Master Mind of Mars.* (1928)
179   *A Fighting Man of Mars.* (1931)
180   *Swords of Mars.* (1936)
181   *The Gods of Mars.* (1940).
182   *Synthetic Men of Mars.* (1940)
183   *John Carter of Mars.* (1942)
184   *Tarzan of the Apes.* New York, Grosset, 1914 (1912).

The book that ensured Burroughs' success, introducing the inimitable ape-man in the first of twenty-seven novels. Lord and Lady Greystoke, marooned on the African coast, are killed by marauding great-apes (a species unknown to science), but their baby son is adopted by the apes. He grows into a man of incredible strength, intelligence, and nobility, who teaches himself English from the books in his parents' cabin. The story really begins when Tarzan comes to the rescue of an eccentric scientist and his lovely daughter, Jane, thus beginning the journey that reveals him to be the rightful Lord Greystoke. The twenty-six sequels are all in print, as follows:

185   *The Return of Tarzan.* New York, Ballantine, (1915).
186   *The Beasts of Tarzan.* New York, Ballantine, (1916).
187   *The Son of Tarzan.* New York, Ballantine, (1917).
188   *Tarzan and the Jewels of Opar.* New York, Ballantine, (1918).
189   *Jungle Tales of Tarzan.* New York, Ballantine, (1919).
190   *Tarzan the Untamed.* New York, Ballantine, (1920).
191   *Tarzan the Terrible.* New York, Ballantine, (1921).
192   *Tarzan and the Golden Lion.* New York, Ballantine, (1923).
193   *Tarzan and the Ant Men.* New York, Ballantine, (1924).
194   *The Eternal Lover.* New York, Ace, (1925).
195   *The Mad King.* New York, Ace, (1926).
196   *The Outlaw of Torn.* New York, Ace, (1927).

These last three are peripheral to the Tarzan series and deal with Ruritanian romances experienced by friends of the Greystokes.

197   *Tarzan, Lord of the Jungle.* New York, Ballantine, (1928).

198   *Tarzan and the Lost Empire.* New York, Ballantine, (1929).

199   *Tarzan at the Earth's Core.* New York, Ballantine, (1930).

200   *Tarzan the Invincible.* New York, Ballantine, (1931).

201   *Tarzan Triumphant.* New York, Ballantine, (1932).

202   *Tarzan and the City of Gold.* New York, Ballantine, (1933).

203   *Tarzan and the Lion Man.* New York, Ballantine, (1934).

204   *Tarzan and the Leopard Men.* New York, Ballantine, (1935).

205   *Tarzan's Quest.* New York, Ballantine, (1936).

206   *Tarzan and the Forbidden City.* New York, Ballantine, (1938).

207   *Tarzan the Magnificent.* New York, Ballantine, (1939).

208   *Tarzan and the Foreign Legion.* New York, Ballantine, (1947).

209   *Tarzan and the Madman.* New York, Ballantine, (1964).

210   *Tarzan and the Castaways.* New York, Ballantine, (1965).

Biographical works have been written about Tarzan himself as well as about his creator. The most informative and delightful work comes from the science-fiction writer Philip Jose Farmer, who has published three books about Tarzan:

211   Farmer, Philip Jose. *Tarzan Alive, a definitive biography of Lord Greystoke.* New York, Popular Library, 1972. xxii, 328 p.

A complete biography of the celebrated ape-man and English peer is followed by five appendices, in which Tarzan's genealogical connections with (among others) Sherlock Holmes, Lord Peter Wimsey, the Scarlet Pimpernel, Raffles, Nero Wolfe, and Woden are explored, the Greystoke Lineage is traced, and a chronology of Tarzan's life up to 1971 is given. An excellent bibliography and index completes the book. Farmer also has written

212   ———. *Mother Was a Lovely Beast, a Feral Man Anthology, Fiction and Fact About Humans Raised by Animals.* New York, Chilton, 1974. 246 p.

Includes some of Burroughs' *Jungle Tales of Tarzan* and extracts from the *Memoirs of "Lord Greystoke,"* edited by Farmer, and a bibliography.

213   ———. *The Adventure of the Peerless Peer,* by John H. Watson, M.D., edited by Philip Jose Farmer. Boulder, Colo., Aspen Press, 1974. 112 p.

In 1916, during the First World War, Sherlock Holmes and Tarzan join forces against the Germans in Darkest Africa.

214   Day, Bradford M. *Edgar Rice Burroughs: A Bibliography.* Woodhaven, N.Y., Day, 1962.

215   Harwood, John, comp. *The Literature of Burroughsiana: a listing of magazine articles, book commentaries, news items, book reviews,*

movie reviews, fanzines, amateur publications, and related items concerning the life and/or work of Edgar Rice Burroughs. Compiled and with commentary by John Harwood. Editor, Camille Cazedessus. Baton Rouge, La., C. Cazedessus, 1963. 105 p.

216   Lupoff, Richard. *Edgar Rice Burroughs: Master of Adventure.* New York, Canaveral Press, 1965. xxvi, 294 p.

217   Lupoff, Richard. *Barsoom: The Martian Epic of Edgar Rice Burroughs.* Baltimore, Mirage Press, 1971.

218   Moscowitz, Sam, ed. *Under the Moons of Mars, a history and anthology of "The Scientific Romance" in the Munsey Magazines, 1912–1920.* New York, Holt, 1970. 440 p.

Contains excerpts from nine pulp romances, including Burroughs's first Barsoom novel, and a history of the scientific romances in the Munsey magazines by Moscowitz (pp. 289–433). Moscowitz argues that Burroughs "turned the entire direction of science fiction from prophecy and sociology to romantic adventure" (p. 291).

219   Van Arnam, David G. et al. *The Reader's Guide to Barsoom and Amtor.* New York, Richard Lupoff, 1963. 84 p.

219.1   Porges, Irwin. *Edgar Rice Burroughs: The Man Who Created Tarzan.* 270 illustrations. Provo, Utah, Brigham Young University Press, 1975. 820 p.

BUTTERWORTH, OLIVER, 1915– .

220   *The Enormous Egg.* Illus. by Louise Darling. Boston, Little, Brown, 1956. 188 p.

A dated science fantasy about a boy in a small Vermont town whose pet hen hatches a dinosaur egg. Followed by

221   *The Narrow Passage.* Illus. by Erik Blegvad. Boston, Little, Brown, 1973. 166 p.

The hero of *The Enormous Egg* goes with a scientist friend to France to help in an archaeological dig at the famous caves of Lascaux, a site of Cro-Magnon art. He and a French boy, while exploring a passage, come upon a living caveman, whom they befriend. Both of these books emphasize "scientific facts" at the expense of plot.

CABELL, JAMES BRANCH, 1879–1958.

222   *The Works of James Branch Cabell.* Storisende Edition. New York, R. M. McBride, 1927–1930. 18 vols.

Cabell's great work, the Biography of Manuel, dealing with the lives and adventures of Manuel of Poictesme and his many descendants, both in medieval Poictesme (an imaginary province of France) and in modern-day Lichfield, Virginia (based on Cabell's own home, Richmond). The Storisende edition arranges the twenty-one separate works of the Biography, not in their order of publication or composition, but in the order in which Cabell wished them to be read. The eighteen volumes are as follows:

222a   *Beyond Life.*
222b   *Figures of Earth.*

The life of Manuel himself, from swineherd to prince: his amorous adventures, his attempts to give life and beauty to the "figures" he creates out of earth, his rule of Poictesme, and his eventual return to youth and swineherding.

222c   *The Silver Stallion.*
222d   *Domnei. The Music from Beyond the Moon.*
222e   *Chivalry.*
222f   *Jurgen.*

The novel whose banning as "libertine" was the origin of a celebrated censorship controversy and of Cabell's enormous celebrity in the 1920s.

222g   *The Line of Love.*
222h   *The High Place.*
222i   *Gallantry.*
222j   *Something About Eve.*
222k   *The Certain Hour.*
222l   *The Cords of Vanity.*
222m   *From the Hidden Way. The Jewel Merchants.*
222n   *The Rivet in Grandfather's Neck.*

Inspired by the Hans Christian Andersen story, "The Shepherdess and the Chimney Sweep."

222o   *The Eagle's Shadow.*
222p   *The Cream of the Jest. The Lineage of Lichfield.*

The Lineage is a complete genealogical chart of all the descendants of Manuel.

222q   *Straws and Prayer Books.*
222r   *Townsend of Lichfield.*

223   Brewer, Frances Joan. *James Branch Cabell: a Bibliography of His Writings, Biography, and Criticism.* With a foreword by James Branch Cabell. Charlottesville, Va., University of Virginia Press, 1957. 206 p.

Lists his books, dedications, contributions to books and magazines, biographies and criticism of his work, and bibliographies of his work.

224   Davis, Joe Lee. *James Branch Cabell.* New York, Twayne, 1962. (Twayne's U.S. Authors series, #21). 174 p.

Analyzes Cabell's work in the light of his sudden downfall after the Twenties, and discusses Cabell's idea of the "life force."

225   Klinefelter, Walter. *Books About Poictesme: an Essay in Imaginative Bibliography.* Chicago, Black Cat Press, 1937, 28 p.

By an author who specialized in imaginary bibliographies and books of bibliographical curiosa, this is a discursive bibliography of books invented by Cabell as part of the Secondary World of Poictesme. Typical titles are: *Les Gestes de Manuel; The Romaunt of Manuel Pig-tender; Les Amants de Melicent.* All are annotated, complete with spurious French quotations from imaginary scholars, and elaborately phony colophons.

226   Mecken, H. R. *James Branch Cabell: Three Essays in Criticism.* New York, R. M. McBride, 1932. 42 p.

Mencken considered Cabell a leader in the fight against philistinism, but by the time this was written, Cabell was passé.

227   Tarrant, Desmond. *James Branch Cabell: The Dream and the Reality.* Norman, Okla., University of Oklahoma Press, 1967. xii, 292 p.

Argues that Cabell created an entire mythology.

228   Van Doren, Carl. *James Branch Cabell.* 2nd ed. New York, Literary Guild, 1932.

229   Walpole, Hugh. *The Art of James Cabell.* Havertown, Pa., R. West, 1973 (1920).

230   Wells, Arvin R. *Jesting Moses: A Study in Cabellian Comedy.* Gainesville, Fla., University of Florida Press, 1962. x, 145 p.

231   *The Cabellian, a Journal of the Second American Renaissance.* Vol. I, No. 1, 1968: Inaugural issue in memory of James Branch Cabell. Published by the Cabell Society. New York, Kraus Reprint Co., 1970.

Scholarly, critical, and bibliographic essays.

232   Blish, James. "The Long Night of a Virginia Author." *Journal of Modern Literature*, Vol. 2, No. 3, pp. 393–405.

Compares Cabell's later work with *Finnegans Wake.*

233   Himelick, Raymond. "Cabell and the Modern Temper." *South Atlantic Quarterly*, Vol. 58 No. 2, (Spring 1959), pp. 176–184.

234   Wilson, Edmund. "The James Branch Cabell Case Reopened." *New Yorker*, Vol. 32 No. 9, (April 21, 1956), pp. 140–168.

A reassessment of Cabell as a writer and as a Southerner, from a modern perspective, taking account of his strengths and his weaknesses. A superior critical essay.

CALHOUN, MARY, 1926– .

235   *Magic in the Alley.* Illus. by Wendy Watson. New York, Atheneum, 1970. 167 p.

Cleery, who loves to explore alleys—they are so much more interesting than regular streets—finds a box in an alley junkshop with seven magical objects inside it, with which she proceeds to have seven Nesbitish adventures. Derivative but well-written.

236   *Ownself.* New York, Harper, 1975. 160 p.

Set in the South at the turn of the century. After a conflict with her father, who has recently converted to a hellfire religion, Laurabelle calls up a "fayry." It enters into her, but far from solving her problems, Laura finds that her father thinks she is possessed by a devil. The story really centers around the father, and Laura's relationship with him is excellently depicted through his rages and his happy moments.

CAMERON, ELEANOR, 1912– .

237   *The Wonderful Flight to the Mushroom Planet.* Illus. by Robert Henneberger. Boston, Little, Brown, 1954.

First of a series of five books. Chuck and David, having built their rocket ship out of scrap metal and lumber, find that Mr. Bass of Thallo Street not only has fuel for it, but a mission for them. They go to Basidium, the Mushroom Planet, an invisible satellite of Earth, and help the Basidiumites, or Spore People, cure the mysterious sickness which is debilitating them. A pleasant science fantasy, in which the science is never obtrusive and the fantasy is never silly. Followed by

238   *Stowaway to the Mushroom Planet.* Illus. by Robert Henneberger. Boston, Little, Brown, 1956. 226 p.

Chuck and David's rocket is stolen by a young astronomer who takes off at the wrong time, with the result that he goes through a Black Hole in the universe and comes back in physical and mental dishevelment. Followed by

239   *Mr. Bass's Planetoid.* Illus. by Louis Darling. Boston, Little, Brown, 1958. 228 p.

David and Chuck must go in their new rocket to Lepton, a tiny asteroid circling the Earth, to find Mr. Bass's cousin, Prewytt Brumblydge, before his desalinization machine, the Brumblitron, blows up. Followed by

240   *A Mystery for Mr. Bass, a Mushroom Planet Book.* Illus. by

Leonard Shortall. Boston, Little, Brown, 1960. 229 p.

Chuck, David, and Mr. Bass go to Wales in search of the missing necklace of Basidium, tracing it stone by stone, as its magic powers cause its new owners to behave irrationally. They also find an old manuscript of the Mushroom People and the ancient riddle of Mr. Bass's Elder Grandfather. This leads into the next book:

241   *Time and Mr. Bass, a Mushroom Planet Book.* Illus. by Fred Meise. Boston, Little, Brown, 1967. 247 p.

The boys and Mr. Bass return to Wales to fight against the evil spirit who murdered Elder Grandfather, who was one of King Arthur's closest advisers. Their mutual love and trust must be their only weapons, and they prove to be the right ones. This last Mushroom Planet book is a quantum jump beyond the previous books in seriousness, but it retains the qualities of good humor and reasonableness which distinguished them.

242   *The Terrible Churnadryne.* Illus. by Beth and Joe Krush. Boston, Little, Brown, 1959. 125 p.

A weak, episodic story about two children who believe in the mysterious monster of San Lorenzo. When they report seeing it, a flood of credulous tourists rushes in, who behave just as stupidly as the other adults who refuse to consider the evidence at all.

243   *The Court of the Stone Children.* New York, Dutton, 1973. 191 p.

Nina, who has only just arrived in San Francisco, loves the small French museum she has found as a refuge from other children's taunts. She meets a young girl there whose portrait she admires and realizes that her new friend is a ghost, Dominique. Dominique is determined to clear the name of her father, who was shot by Napoleon for treason, and Nina tries to help, but only when Nina puts together both what Dominique has told her and what she has learned about working in a museum does the truth appear. Nina's doubts, hopes, and relationships with others are sympathetically treated in a wonderfully satisfying story.

CARLSEN, RUTH CHRISTOFFER.

244   *Ride a Wild Horse.* Illus. by Beth and Joe Krush. Boston, Houghton Mifflin, 1970. 164 p.

A girl who has been accidentally thrown into our world from a parallel, but reverse, continuum, tries to get home by riding a magic carousel horse, which was left by a previous visitor, the great Nlocnil Maharba—Abraham Lincoln! Inane and unmemorable.

CARRYL, CHARLES EDWARD, 1841–1920.

245   *Davy and the Goblin, or What Followed Reading "Alice's Adventures in Wonderland."* Illus. by E. B. Bensell. Boston, Houghton Mifflin, 1884. 160 p.
   A delightful Victorian story of how Davy, who didn't believe in fairies, was taken for a Believing Voyage by a coal-eating goblin in a grandfather clock.

CARTER, LIN, 1930– .

246   *The Wizard of Lemuria.* New York, Ace, 1965. 127 p.
   First of a series. A straight imitation of Robert Howard's Conan books (q.v.), starring Thongor of Lemuria, a strong-thewed hero in a fur jockstrap. Followed by
247   *Thongor of Lemuria.* London, Tandem, 1974.
248   *Thongor Against the Gods.* London, Tandem, 1974.
249   *Thongor in the City of Magicians.* London, Tandem, 1974.
250   *Thongor at the End of Time.* London, Tandem, 1974.
251   *Thongor Fights the Pirates of Tarakus.* New York, Berkley, 1970. 160 p.

CHAMBERS, ROBERT W., 1865–1933.

252   *The King in Yellow and Other Horror Stories.* Selected and with an introduction by E. F. Bleiler. New York, Dover, 1970 (1895–1904). xiii, 287 p.
   Twelve Dunsany-like stories, the most famous of which, besides the title story, is "The Maker of Moons," in which horrible Chinese magic invades the good old U.S.A. Bleiler's excellent introduction gives details of Chambers's life and work.

CHANT, JOY.

253   *Red Moon and Black Mountain, the End of the House of Kendreth.* Introduction by Lin Carter. New York, Ballantine, 1971. xvi, 268 p.

Oliver, Nicholas, and Penny stumble into Kendrinh, the Starlit Land, where a great war involving men and gods is starting. The final victory over the black enchanter Fendarl ends the war but does not bring peace, because the war goddess Vir'Vachal has awakened, and will not rest until a human sacrifice is made to her. Oliver volunteers, and discovers that although he has died from Kendrinh, he and his brother and sister can return to their old life. Though the earlier part of the story is halting and awkward, the book gradually becomes more coherent and powerful, and the ending is genuinely moving.

CHASE, MARY, 1887–1973.

254   *Loretta Mason Potts.* Pictures by Harold Berson. Philadelphia, Lippincott, 1958. 221 p.

Colin discovers the reason why his older sister Loretta has been away for so long: she has made friends with magic dolls who are stupid, wicked, and selfish, and who have made her the same way. Finally Colin and a reformed Loretta save their mother and the other children from the dolls. Good characters and a suspenseful plot are spoiled by a condescending style.

255   *The Wicked Pigeon Ladies in the Garden.* Illus. by Don Bolognese. New York, Knopf, 1968. 115 p.

Maureen's problems begin when she accidentally steals a bracelet from a portrait of the pigeon ladies, and the ladies come after her to get it back. Maureen's tricky, selfish, and outspoken personality is well realized, and the story's premise is unusually interesting.

CHESTERTON, GILBERT KEITH, 1874–1936.

256   *The Man Who Was Thursday, a Nightmare.* Introduction by Garry Wills. New York, Sheed and Ward, 1975 (1908). 199 p.

Gabriel Syme, a poet, is recruited as a philosophical detective, bound to fight against a great conspiracy of anarchists. As an undercover delegate to the anarchists' central council, he finds that all the other delegates are undercover agents too, including the mysterious Sunday, who in some strange, metaphysical way is not only the chief of the detectives, but a true anarchist. When they are not engaged in wild chases across Europe, the characters' chief concern is a complicated philosophical discussion, which makes the story not to everyone's taste; but the striking plot reversals and the air of deep significance that Chesterton imparts to the book make it a memorable reading experience.

257   Barker, Dudley. *G. K. Chesterton*. New York, Stein and Day, 1973.

258   Clemens, Cyril. *Chesterton As Seen by His Contemporaries*. Introduction by E. C. Bentley. English Biographical Series, No. 31. New York, Haskell, 1969 (1938). iv, 180 p.

259   Hollis, Christopher. *The Mind of Chesterton*. Coral Gables, Fla., University of Florida Press, 1970. 303 p.

260   Montgomery, John W. *Myth, Allegory, and Gospel: an Interpretation of J. R. R. Tolkien, C. S. Lewis, G. K. Chesterton, and Charles Williams*. Minneapolis, Minn., Bethany Fellowship, n.d.

CHEW, RUTH, 1920– .

261   *What the Witch Left*. Illus. by the author. New York, Hastings House, 1973. 128 p.

An episodic witch fantasy. Kay and Louise unlock Aunt Martha's wooden chest and find a number of magical items, with which they have the usual, predictable adventures.

CHICHESTER, IMOGEN.

262   *The Witch Child*. With drawings by Robert Bartelt. New York, Coward-McCann, 1967 (1965). 189 p.

Necromancy Gumblethrush lives in the forest with her parents. Abigail and Zachary, who are teaching her to be a witch, but she wants to live in town and go to school like the other children. Eventually Zachary learns that he can make a living repairing things by magic, so the family moves into a nice modern cottage. Both the characters and the illustrations are mere comic-book caricatures.

CLARKE, ANN PAULINE, 1921– .

263   *The Return of the Twelves*. Illus. by Bernarda Bryson. New York, Coward-McCann, 1963 (1962). 253 p. (Originally published in England under the title *The Twelve and the Genii*.)

Two children living in the old home of the Brontë children discover the wooden soldiers that the Brontës used to play with. The soldiers are alive and remember the Brontës well, because they named the soldiers and gave them life, immortalizing them in the stories they wrote as children. The soldiers' return is to the Brontë Museum in Haworth, where they belong, and is a dangerous night expedition across several miles of country. A sensitive story, not in the least didactic, about the Brontë family, making them, the modern children, and the Twelves real and believable characters.

264   *The Two Faces of Silenus.* New York, Coward-McCann, 1972. 160 p.

Drusilla and Rufus and their Italian friend Luigi wish an ancient statue of Silenus to life. The police think the statue has been stolen, and Medusa, who hates Silenus, tries to kidnap Drusilla and break up Luigi's parents' marriage. The defeat of Medusa depends on a delightfully funny, and then suddenly terrifying, police search and on the reconciliation of Luigi's father and mother. Clarke is especially good at delineating and explaining sudden changes of mood, which gives the story an excited, breathless quality and makes the characters vivid and attractive.

COATSWORTH, ELIZABETH, 1893– .

265   *The Enchanted.* New York, Pantheon, 1951. 128 p.

Man meets partridge in the Maine woods. This is not the first fantasy in which a human marries a half-animal being, but the anticlimax of discovering that the heroine is actually a partridge would destroy any story, let alone this one with its more-organic-than-thou air of rural self-congratulation.

266   *The Werefox.* New York, Macmillan, 1975. (Originally published under the title *Pure Magic.*)

Johnny's friend Giles has great difficulty in getting along with his father, perhaps because Giles resembles his dead mother, from whom he inherited his ability to change into a fox. At the climax, Giles's father saves him from a hunt, and they are reconciled. In this book Coatsworth succeeded in communicating her evident love for the wild woods without being sanctimonious, and the characters' conflicts are credibly and sympathetically treated.

COLES, MANNING, pseudonym of Adelaide Manning and Cyril H. Coles.

267   *Brief Candles.* Garden City, N.Y., Doubleday, 1954. 252 p.
268   *Happy Returns.* Garden City, N.Y., Doubleday, 1955. 224 p.

269   *Come and Go.* Garden City, N.Y., Doubleday, 1958. 236 p.

Three light-hearted and lightweight ghost fantasies, in which a young couple, honeymooning in France, meet the ghosts of the husband's great-great-uncles, who were accidentally killed in the Franco-Prussian War. Pleasant recreational reading.

270   *The Far Traveller.* Garden City, N.Y., Doubleday, 1956. 224 p.

In the same vein as the three books above. A movie company, filming the story of a nineteenth-century German count on the present count's estate, unwittingly casts the dead count's ghost as himself. After numerous complications, the ghost wins his family's recognition of his commoner bride, who died with him in a boating accident, the present count and his fiancee are reconciled, and the movie comes in under budget and on time. A jaunty, satisfying story.

COLLIER, JOHN, 1901– .

271   *His Monkey Wife, or, Married to a Chimp.* In *The John Collier Reader.* Introduction by Anthony Burgess. New York, Knopf, 1972 (1931). pp. 3–157.

A deliciously arch parody of Bloomsburyian ideas about love and marriage. Emily, a chimpanzee, goes to England with her master and eventually changes places with his intended bride, who is a heartless, selfish woman. The couple return to Africa to live, disillusioned by the falsity of civilization. The straight face and air of serious philosophical consideration, which Collier got right out of Aldous Huxley, make the joke all the funnier.

272   *Fancies and Goodnights.* With a foreword by Moses Hadas. New York, Bantam, 1961 (1931–1951). xii, 418 p.

Short stories by this master of sly, absurd logic, all about young men who fall in love with department-store dummies, urbane devils, sophisticated domestic murders, gullible young ladies in gauzy undergarments, low-living but high-stepping artists in picturesque attics, and a Charon who says "Avast!" Not to be missed.

COLLODI, CARLO, pseudonym of Carlo Lorenzini, 1826–1890.

273a   *The Adventures of Pinocchio.* Translated by Carol Della Chiesa. Illus. by Naiad Einsel. Afterword by Clifton Fadiman. New York, Macmillan, 1963 (1882). vi, 192 p.

273b   *Pinocchio, the Adventures of a Little Wooden Boy.* Translated by Joseph Walker. Illus. by Richard Floethe. Introduction by May Lamberton Becker. (Rainbow Classics). Cleveland, World, 1946 (1882). 239 p.

273c   *The Adventures of Pinocchio.* With illus. by Fritz Kredel. Translated by M. A. Murray. (Illustrated Junior Library). New York, Grosset and Dunlap, 1946 (1882). ix, 255 p.

Three standard editions of the Italian classic about a wooden puppet who comes to life, behaves as naughtily as possible, but finally reforms and becomes a real boy. None of the illustrations are outstanding, and none can be compared with the beautiful Walt Disney movie, though it took many liberties with the story.

COLUM, PADRAIC, 1881–1972.

274   *The Boy Apprenticed to an Enchanter.* Illus. by Edward Leight. London, Macmillan, 1966 (1920). 150 p.

Eean, apprenticed to the fierce sorcerer Zabulun, learns that his master plans to capture the Magic Mirror of the Tower of Babylon, which protects the city from enemies; so Eean gives the Mirror to the King. Having betrayed Zabulun, Eean must flee his vengeance, so he and a young girl named Bird-of-Gold travel to each of the Three Great Enchanters—Chiron, Hermes, and Merlin—to save themselves. The writing is gorgeous, formal, and ornate, in the best tradition of Irish storytellers, and although the plot is long and episodic it is not confusing.

275   Bowen, Zack R. *Padraic Colum: a biographical-critical introduction.* With a preface by Harry T. Moore. Carbondale, Ill., Southern Illinois University Press, 1970. xii, 162 p.

One chapter (pp. 122–148) concentrates on Colum's writing for children.

COOPER, LOUISE, 1952– .

276   *The Book of Paradox.* Illus. by Barbara Nessin. New York, Delacorte, 1973. 244 p.

A man, wrongly condemned for the murder of his beloved, is sacrificed to the Death God of his primitive civilization, only to find that the Book of Paradox, which begins with blank pages, offers him an opportunity to escape death. Bloody, violent, depressing, and overwritten.

COOPER, SUSAN, 1935– .

277   *Over Sea, Under Stone.* Illus. by Margery Gill. New York, Harcourt, 1965. 252 p.

Simon, Barney, and Jane Drew go to Cornwall to their Great-Uncle Merry's house for a holiday and immediately are plunged into a struggle centered around an Arthurian relic hidden "over sea, under stone." In an exciting climax, their enemies race against the tide to retrieve the relic, only to be defeated by Great-Uncle Merry, whom the children realize may be Merlin. First of a projected series of five novels, this is an outstanding Arthurian fantasy, blessed with intelligent characters and tight plotting. Followed by

278   *The Dark is Rising.* Illus. by Alan E. Cober. New York, Atheneum, 1973. 216 p.

A boy of eleven, Will Stanton, seventh son of a seventh son, learns that he is one of the Old Ones of mankind, guardians against the powers of the Dark. Will undergoes several ordeals to prove himself, under the guidance of Merry/Merlin from the previous book, in the teeth of the Dark's opposition. The struggle between the powers of Light and Dark seems self-conscious and contrived, though the writing is powerful. Followed by

279   *Greenwitch.* New York, Atheneum, 1974. 147 p.

The self-consciousness that marred *The Dark is Rising* is also evident in its sequel. Will, Merry, and the Drews are again in Cornwall at the time when the village women make a huge wicker figure, the Greenwitch, and cast it into the sea as part of an annual folk rite. The Greenwitch herself is an incalculable creature of Old Magic; neither the Dark nor the Light can count on her, but in the end she tries to help the Light for Jane's sake. Cooper establishes an enchanted atmosphere of brooding natural violence and suspense.

CRAIK, DINAH MARIA MULOCK, 1826–1887.

280   *The Adventures of a Brownie.* Illus. by Mary Lott Seaman. New York, Macmillan, 1960 (1872). 122 p.

Six adventures of a mischievous but kind-hearted house fairy.

281   *The Little Lame Prince.* Illus. by Jon Nielsen. Introduction by May Lamberton Becker. Cleveland, World, 1948 (1875). x, 135 p.

A sweet and melancholy fairy tale about little Prince Dolor, a lame orphan whose wicked uncle sends him to live forever in a lonely tower. The Prince's fairy godmother, a brisk and sensible old dame, gives him a magic flying cloak on which he can go out to see the world, until the day when his uncle dies and the people send for him to become the new king. A beautifully balanced story.

CRAWFORD, F. MARION, 1854–1909.

282   *Khaled, a Tale of Arabia*. London, Macmillan, 1891. 258 p.

An engaging Arabian-Nights romance. Khaled, a jinni, falls in love with the beautiful Princess Zehowah, whose infidel suitor Khaled has killed. As a reward for this pious act, he is allowed to become a man, but unless he can persuade Zehowah to love him, he will never get a soul. Crawford's imitation of the characteristic Arabian-Nights atmosphere of formal piety and ornate splendors is masterfully amusing.

CRESSWELL, HELEN, 1934– .

283.   *The Night-Watchmen*. Illus. by Gareth Floyd. New York, Macmillan, 1969. 122 p.

Henry makes friends with two old tramps, soft-hearted Josh and paranoid Caleb, who are "Night-Watchmen" from "There," always traveling close to the railways so as to be able to call the Night Train from "There" at need. Henry's efforts at coping with crusty Caleb are funny, and his reward for helping them—a ride on the Night Train— gratifies both him and the reader. An excellent and well-developed fantasy idea.

284   *Up the Pier*. Illus. by Gareth Floyd. New York, Macmillan, 1971. 144 p.

On a visit to the seaside, Carrie realizes that Sam'el's longing for a family has caused the mysterious Pontifex family to be brought from 1921, which disturbs her and terrifies them. When she understands that they really want to go home to 1921, she helps them overcome old Sam'el's magic. Not as convincing as *The Night Watchmen*.

285   *The Bongleweed*. Illus. by Ann Strugnell. London, Faber, 1973. 138 p.

Becky and Jason bend all their efforts to the problem of controlling the Bongleweed, which threatens to take over Pew Gardens. When a sudden frost kills the Bongleweed, Becky realizes that she has not lost it, but has acquired the power to make other things magical.

Excellent characterizations cannot save the story, especially with its *deus-ex-machina* resolution.

CURRY, JANE LOUISE, 1932– .

286   *Beneath the Hill*. Illus. by Imero Gobbato. New York, Harcourt, 1967. 255 p.

The first book of a series centered around a common premise rather than continuous action. Four cousins learn that a mysterious boy in the woods and his family are Elves, descendants of a Welsh culture who fled to America in the sixteenth century. Their secret is a gigantic city beneath the hill, now long deserted, but which they think was built by an earlier group of fairy people. The development of the fantasy idea is only average, but the writing is superior. Followed by

287   *The Change-Child*. Illus. by Gareth Floyd. New York, Harcourt, 1969. 174 p.

In sixteenth-century Wales, a human girl who believes herself to be a changeling meets the real elves, who are about to go to America, and who help her accept her own humanity. Complicated but coherent. Followed by

288   *The Daybreakers*. Illus. by Charles Robinson. New York, Harcourt, 1970. 191 p.

A group of children, two white and two black, who do not know one another well, fall through a magic hole into the far past, and into the midst of a struggle between Mound-Builder Indians with a savage religion, and civilized people, who may be the elves who built the great city in *Beneath the Hill*. The children's job is to locate the lost elven lore before it is too late, while learning how to get along themselves. Followed by

289   *Over the Sea's Edge*. Illus. by Charles Robinson. New York, Harcourt, 1971. 182 p.

Two unhappy boys—David from the present and Dewi from the eleventh century—exchange personalities by magic. David, now Dewi, sails with his father's friend, the illegitimate Prince Madauc, to the fabled land of Antillia, where they are caught up in the struggle already outlined in the previous book, between the Indian cities of Cibotlan and the fairy people of Abaloc (or Avalon). At the end, the two Davids realize that neither has any desire to return to his old life. The stories of these two books are so complex that it becomes necessary to read both in order to understand either one, and, although the connections between them and the two earlier books are hinted at many times, the relationships are never clarified.

290   *The Sleepers.* Illus. by Gareth Floyd. New York, Harcourt, 1968. 255 p.

Four children, accompanying an uncle on an archaeological dig at Eildon in Scotland, discover not only Arthur's cave and the Treasures of Britain, but free Merlin the enchanter from the tree in which he has been shut up for centuries. With Merlin's help they waken the Sleepers, Arthur and his knights, just in time to escape from the death intended for them by Medraut and Morgan le Fay, who have also survived. Plot complications are held to a minimum in a story which blends mystery, suspense, archaeology, history, and folklore.

291   *Mindy's Mysterious Miniature.* Illus. by Charles Robinson. New York, Harcourt, 1971. 157 p.

Mindy's new dollhouse turns out to be a real house, inhabited by a group of people, which was shrunk fifty years ago by a mad professor. After the usual complications, Mindy gets the house and the people unshrunk. Followed by

292   *The Lost Farm.* Illus. by Charles Robinson. New York, Atheneum, 1974. 137 p.

How Pete McCubbin, his farm, and his Granny are shrunk by the same professor, how they lived over the years, and how one of the people Mindy rescued, who had known Pete as a small child, found Pete and unshrunk him. Both the plot and the invention are weak in this story.

293   *Parsley Sage, Rosemary, and Time.* Illus. by Charles Robinson. New York, Atheneum, 1975. 108 p.

Prim and proper Rosemary and the cat, Parsley Sage, go back in time to 1722 where they and another modern child, Baba, save Goody Cakebread from being tried as a witch. Baba turns out to be Rosemary's Aunt Sibby, and Rosemary learns not to be prim.

CUTT, W. TOWRIE.

294   *Seven for the Sea.* New York, Follett, 1974 (1972). 96 p.

Erchie and his cousin Mansie, on a trip to the Orkney Islands, find themselves in the past, where they go to live with their great-grandfather, Selkie Ward. On a terrible night of storms, Selkie breaks a promise to his wife, so she and her six eldest sons return to the seal-folk from whom she came. The story is difficult to read because it is full of thick Scottish dialect, but it is an interesting variation on the old folk motif of the Fairy Wife. See also No. 053.

DAHL, ROALD, 1916– .

295   *James and the Giant Peach*. Illus. by Nancy Ekholm Burkert. New York, Knopf, 1961. 119 p.

Beautifully drawn and colored illustrations cannot save this story of how James, mistreated by his wicked aunts, enters the giant peach and is befriended by the seven giant insects he finds inside. James and the insects travel in the peach across the ocean to New York by attaching the Silkworm's threads to a huge flock of seagulls and land on top of the Empire State Building.

296   *Charlie and the Chocolate Factory*. Illus. by Joseph Schindelman. Garden City, N.Y., Junior Deluxe Editions/Knopf, 1964. 178 p.

Poor-but-honest Charlie wins a tour of Mr. Willy Wonka's marvelous candy factory, during which the other winners prove themselves to be greedy, stupid, or rude, so Charlie wins the grand prize by default. Charlie has no personality and does nothing to deserve his good fortune except to appear good by comparison to the other children, whose "crimes" of chewing gum and watching TV are grossly over-punished. Mr. Willy Wonka's exploitation of his black pygmy slaves is unfunny and offensive, as is the story as a whole.

297   "Charlie and the Chocolate Factory: A Reply." *Horn Book*, Vol. 49, No. 1 (Feb. 1973), pp. 77–78.

Dahl's defense of his book in reply to an unfavorable article by Eleanor Cameron.

DAVIDSON, AVRAM.

298   *The Phoenix and the Mirror*. Garden City, N.Y., Doubleday, 1969. 222 p.

The medieval idea of the poet Virgil was that he was more of a sorcerer and prophet than a poet. This adventure fantasy is set in a world in which this wizard Virgil, Vergil Magus, is the real one and centers around a marvelous being he has seen in a magic mirror. A cliff-hanger ending promises a sequel which to date has not been written.

299   *Peregrine: Primus*. New York, Walker, 1971. 174 p.

Another cliff-hanger without a sequel. Peregrine, the bastard son of the King of Sapodilla, goes out to seek his fortune with the help of his servant Claud and his wizard Appledore. Written in a comic style with a lot of anachronistic wisecracking—the emperor Augustus XXV is known as "Stingy Gus"; the Hun, Attila IV, is king of Hun Horde No. 17, population 37, not including donkeys.

300   *Ursus of Ultima Thule.* New York, Avon, 1973. 236 p.

Another strong-thewed hero in a primitive culture. Arnten the Bear must conquer the evil being called the Wolf, which he does by turning into a real bear and back again. Much better written than most adventure fantasies.

DAVIES, VALENTINE.

301   *Miracle on 34th Street.* New York, Harcourt, 1947. viii, 117 p.

A novelization of the classic Hollywood movie about how Kris Kringle goes to work at Macy's. One of the extremely small number of readable sentimental fantasies.

302   *It Happens Every Spring.* New York, Farrar, 1949. 224 p.

Another novelization. A chemist who is also a baseball fan happens on a substance that forces baseballs away from wood, which he uses to become a second Babe Ruth. Silly and trite.

DAWSON, CARLEY.

303   *Mr. Wicker's Window.* Illus. by Lynd Ward. Boston, Houghton Mifflin, 1952. 272 p.

Mr. Wicker transports Christopher back through time to post-Revolutionary days and teaches him magic. Christopher then voyages to China to win the fabulous Jewel Tree and defeat the evil pirate Claggett Chew, who is trying to force the young United States into bankruptcy. Very dated, especially in the treatment of blacks, Orientals, and women, though not explicitly racist. Followed by

304   *The Sign of the Seven Seas.* Illus. by Lynd Ward. Boston, Houghton Mifflin, 1954. 287 p.

Chris and Mr. Wicker take ship to Acapulco, where they once again run afoul of Claggett Chew, but defeat him in the end. It's all totally implausible, and while the tale is aggressively strait-laced, there is no check on violence or racist remarks.

DE CAMP, LYON SPRAGUE, 1907– .

305   *Lest Darkness Fall.* New York, Pyramid, 1963 (1941). 174 p.

Martin Padway, a historian visiting Rome, is hit by lightning and transported back to the Rome of the sixth century A.D. He uses his knowledge of Arabic numerals and double-entry bookkeeping to get a little money, borrows a little more, and sets up a still. But he can't keep out of politics however hard he tries and ends up saving Italy from the armies of Belisarius, ruling the country, and starting a printing press so that darkness will not fall on Europe. A thoroughly delightful, amusing, historically accurate, and clever fantasy.

306   *The Glory That Was*. Introduction by Robert Heinlein. New York, Paperback Library, 1971 (1952). 156 p.

A lunatic ruler decides to recreate ancient Greece, so he closes off the country and tampers with the memories of everyone in it. A man whose wife has been shanghaied into this project breaks through the barriers to rescue her. The book has the usual De Camp humor (no pun intended), but it is not up to his normal standard of excellence.

307   *The Tritonian Ring*. New York, Twayne, 1953. 262 p.

The gods of Pusad, an imaginary prehistoric continent, send a man on a quest to find their powerful ring. Competent adventure fantasy.

308   *The Goblin Tower*. New York, Pyramid, 1968. 253 p.

Every king of Xylar, one of the Twelve Cities, is beheaded at the end of his five-year reign, but King Jorian manages to escape his fate with the help of a Mulvanian sorcerer. In return, he must fetch the magical Kist of Avlen so that his benefactor can shine at the next sorcerers' convention. The humorous story is enhanced by clever tales that Jorian tells at need, and humor and action balance each other gracefully. Followed by

309   *The Clocks of Iraz*. New York, Pyramid, 1971. 190 p.

Jorian is now free of the *geas* that forced him to obey the sorcerer, but is no nearer to achieving his own goal of fetching his favorite wife from Xylar. He finds employment in the city of Iraz, only to become involved in a civil war. Not as funny as its predecessor.

310   *The Fallible Fiend*. New York, Signet/NAL, 1973. 143 p.

Short stories set in the world of *The Goblin Tower* and its sequel, which is comprised of: the Twelve Cities, each with a different form of government; the Mulvanian Empire, which combines all the worst features of ancient India and Tammany Hall; and various barbarian and/or piratical nations. De Camp has always been interested in the Hellenistic period in the Mediterranean basin, and this invented world is meant to recall it.

311   *Warlocks and Warriors*. Edited and with an introduction by L. Sprague De Camp. New York, Putnam, 1970. 255 p.

A sword-and-sorcery anthology including stories by Dunsany, H. G. Wells, Robert Howard, Fritz Leiber, C. L. Moore, and others.

DE CAMP, LYON SPRAGUE and PRATT, FLETCHER.

312   *The Incomplete Enchanter*. New York, Holt, 1941. 326 p.

Harold Shea, a psychologist, is sent to the world of heroic Ireland, but ends up in Scandinavian mythology—during Ragnarok—instead. So successful does he become there as an enchanter that he and his colleague, Reed Chalmers, go to the world of the *Faerie Queene* next, to destroy a society of wicked enchanters who are fighting Gloriana. One of the funniest, and most logical, fantasies ever written began as a short-story collaboration between these two writers, who went on to write excellent science fiction, heroic fantasy, adventure fantasy, and historical novels. Followed by

313   *The Castle of Iron*. New York, Gnome Press, 1950. 224 p.

Harold and Reed Chalmers travel to the world of Ariosto's *Orlando Furioso*. Harold's wife, Belphebe, has lost her memory and as-similated herself to Ariosto's character Belphegor, and Harold spends most of the book trying to get her back. This book is not as good as its predecessor, but the scene in which Harold transforms himself and the poet Medoro into the fearsome Jann is hilarious. Followed by

314   *Wall of Serpents*. In *Great Short Novels of Adult Fantasy I*, edited by Lin Carter. New York, Ballantine, 1972.

Harold, Reed, Belphebe, and all the assorted hangers-on who ap-peared in the last book go first to the world of the Kalevala, and then (finally!) to the world of Irish legend. Weakest of the three books, but fans of the first will want to read all of them.

315   *Land of Unreason*. New York, Ballantine, 1973 (1942).

An American visiting England, who mistakenly leaves whiskey in-stead of milk for the Little People, is carried off by them to Fairyland, where no one listens to reason, ever. A marvelous idea, but very badly developed.

316   *The Carnelian Cube*. New York, Gnome Press, 1948. 230 p.

Confusing story about an archaeologist who discovers a strange stone cube which takes him to three different alternate universes—one in which Kentucky is a barony in a society with a rigid caste system, one which is a cross between the antebellum South and a Verdi opera, and one which is a "scholarly" recreation of the time of Sargon of Akkad, complete with blood and gore.

See also Pratt, Fletcher.

DE LA MARE, WALTER, 1873–1956.

317   *The Three Royal Monkeys.* With drawings by Mildred E. Eldridge. New York, Knopf, 1948 (1919). 276 p. (Originally published in England under the title *The Three Mulla-Mulgars*).

A stylized, mystical fairy tale, in which the three sons of a Royal Mulgar, raised in a distant jungle, travel to the land of their father's birth to become princes. On the way they escape a gorilla, a tribe of cannibal monkeys, and a friendly English sailor who keeps the youngest son, Nod, as a pet; and they are helped by the mournful Mountain-Mulgars and a beautiful Water-Midden (or Maiden). Lush and imaginative writing establishes a strange, poetic world of intense natural beauty.

318   *The Magic Jacket.* Illus. by Paul Kennedy. New York, Knopf, 1962 (1923). 277 p.

319   *Broomsticks and Other Tales.* London, Constable, 1925.

320   *A Penny a Day.* Illus. by Paul Kennedy. New York, Knopf, 1960. 209 p.

Three collections of short stories by the most beautifully melancholy fantasist of the twentieth century. "Alice's Godmother" offers Alice eternal life and luxury, at a price. "The Magic Jacket" is the prize possession of an old admiral who gives it to a street-artist boy; but somehow the admiral does not get the satisfaction out of his good deed that he thought he would. "Dick and the Beanstalk" is a funny reversal of the folk tale about Jack, in which Dick can't get the giant to go home. All the stories are informed by the emotions of a poet who knew that we may "wish, even pine" to see fairies, but that they do not pine to see us.

321   Clark, Leonard. *Walter de la Mare.* London, Bodley Head, 1960. 82 p.

Study of de la Mare as a children's writer.

DE REGNIERS, BEATRICE SCHENK, 1914– .

322   *The Enchanted Forest.* From a story by Sophie, Comtesse de Ségur, 1799–1874. Illustrated from old prints by Gustave Doré and others. New York, Atheneum, 1974.

Princess Goldenhair, driven into the forest by her wicked stepmother, is befriended by Bonni-Cat and Gentle-Dog. An evil parrot tells Goldenhair that the cat and dog are not her friends but her captors, and convinces her to escape. The ensuing complications are resolved when Goldenhair learns that the cat and dog are really a queen and a prince, and disenchants them.

DICKENS, CHARLES, 1812–1870.

323 & 324   A *Christmas Carol,* and *The Chimes.* Introduction by Walter Allen. N.Y., Harper, 1965. xviii, 158 p.

A *Christmas Carol* tells how the ghosts of Christmas Past, Present, and Yet to Come cured Ebenezer Scrooge of his miserliness and his irascibility. Perhaps more of a ghost story than a fantasy. Full of joyful vitality.

The Chimes is a powerful though sentimental story about the exploitation of the poor by the rich. The Chimes show an elderly porter the evil results of following the advice of the rich. The atmosphere of the story is excited, even a little hysterical.

See also No. 880 below.

DICKINSON, PETER, 1927– .

325   *The Weathermonger.* London, Gollancz, 1969. 171 p.

Set in an England where everyone has turned against machinery, society has reverted to the Middle Ages, and anyone caught using a machine is killed as a witch. Geoffrey, a weathermonger or weather-maker, and his younger sister Sally are forced to flee when the towns-people catch them using an engine. They eventually travel to Wales in an ancient Rolls-Royce Silver Ghost and discover that Merlin is responsible for the Changes: he has awakened from a centuries-long sleep and changed England to suit his convenience. An excellent fantasy with credible characters, a suspenseful plot, and a well-developed background. Followed by

326   *Heartsease.* London, Gollancz, 1969. 188 p.

A story that takes place while the Changes are still going on. An American spy is sent to England to investigate the Changes, but is caught and stoned for witchcraft. Three children rescue him and set off on an urgent journey to get him out of the country, pursued by their own families intent on killing all four. Dickinson displays warm sensitivity to character relationships in this serious and grim story. Followed by

327   *The Devil's Children*. Boston, Little, Brown, 1970. 188 p.

A story set at the very start of the Changes. An English girl whose mind is in tune with the Changes, but who is not fanatical about them, joins a band of Sikh immigrants who are unaffected and cannot understand why the English are suddenly behaving so strangely. This book is as good as its predecessors.

328   *The Gift*. Boston, Little, Brown, 1974. 188 p.

Davy Price has inherited the gift of clairvoyance, and soon becomes aware that a madman holds a grudge against his father and is trying to destroy his family. The permutations of the relationships among Davy's relatives are beautifully explained, so that the reader understands why Davy's feckless dad is feckless, why his brother Ian has turned to violence, and why his mother keeps leaving and coming back.

DRUON, MAURICE, 1918– .

329   *Tistou of the Green Thumbs*. Translated by Humphrey Hare. Illus. by Jacqueline Duhème. New York, Scribner, 1958 (1957). 178 p.

A nostalgic fairytale about Tistou, the only son of a wealthy arms manufacturer, who can make flowers grow on anything, and who stops a war by making flowers grow out of the mouths of the guns. Delicate, humorous, and unforgettable.

330   *Memoirs of Zeus*. New York, Scribner, 1964. xii, 240 p.

Just what the title says—the rambling memoirs of the king of the Olympians. Very French, satirical and philosophical, but not very fantastical.

DU BOIS, WILLIAM PENE, 1916– .

331   *The Great Geppy*. Illus. by the author. New York, Viking, 1940. 92 p.

A horse becomes a detective in a circus. Fluffy, but with charming illustrations.

332   *The Twenty-One Balloons*. Illus. by the author. New York, Viking, 1947. 180 p.

An eccentric professor flies by balloon to the utopian island of Krakatoa, just before it blows up. Whangdoodleish, funny, and engaging.

333   *The Giant*. Illus. by the author. New York, Viking, 1954. 124 p.

A man touring Europe meets a small boy of Latin-American origin who happens to be a giant, and who, naturally, is the center of a great deal of fuss and bother.

DU MAURIER, GEORGE, 1834–1896.

334   *Peter Ibbetson.* With a preface by Daphne Du Maurier. Illus. by the author. New York, Heritage Press, 1963 (1891). xiii, 344 p.

An old-fashioned, very Victorian, sentimental fantasy. Peter and Mary were friends during their ideally happy Parisian childhood, but now that they have grown up they are separated. Mary has become the Duchess of Towers; Peter has worked for his cruel uncle until he can bear no more and kills him. While he is serving his life sentence for the murder, he begins to meet with Mary again—in his dreams. As a description of a vanished way of life the book is superb.

DUNSANY, EDWARD JOHN MORETON DRAX PLUNKETT, 18TH BARON, 1878–1957.

Dunsany wrote many short stories and sketches between 1905 and 1919, which in their original collections are now mostly out of print and unavailable; but the best of his short pieces have been anthologized and are currently not difficult to get. The original eight collections were:

335a   *The Gods of Pegana.* 1905.
335b   *Time and the Gods.* 1906.
335c   *The Sword of Welleran.* 1908.
335d   *A Dreamer's Tales.* 1910.
335e   *The Book of Wonder.* 1912.
335f   *Fifty-One Tales.* 1915.
335g   *Tales of Wonder.* 1916.
335h   *Tales of Three Hemispheres.* 1919.

Many of these stories were set in the vaguely Oriental, vaguely ancient fantasyland of Pegana, for which Dunsany invented not only a geography and a history, but a cosmology too. Others were set in the modern world, but tinged with horror, the occult, or the exotic. Many were sketches rather than stories. Dunsany's world is not much like the world of the Oriental tale or the Arabian Nights, because it is not experienced, but envisioned. Fantasy, dream, adventure, nostalgia, and horror are far more closely intertwined than in any other author, except, of course, his imitators.

Four anthologies which reprint the best of Dunsany's short pieces are the following:

336   A *Dreamer's Tales and Other Stories*. Introduction by Padraic Colum. New York, Modern Library, 1919. xiv, 212 p.

337   *At the Edge of the World*. Introduction by Lin Carter. New York, Ballantine, 1970.

338   *Beyond the Fields We Know*. Introduction by Lin Carter. New York, Ballantine, 1972.

339   *Gods, Men and Ghosts: the Best Supernatural Fiction of Lord Dunsany*. Selected and with an introduction by E. F. Bleiler. With twenty illustrations by Sidney H. Sime. New York, Dover, 1972. xii, 260 p.

This last includes a number of stories which are more horror than fantasy, and some fantasy pieces about Pegana which are not fiction, but serve to establish the fantasy background. These are written in a pseudo-Biblical prose which is sometimes splendid, but more often turgid. However, among the many excellent stories are "The Exiles' Club," "The Wonderful Window," "The Sword of Welleran," "Bethmoora," and "A Narrow Escape."

340   *The Food of Death: Fifty-one Tales by Lord Dunsany*. Hollywood, Calif., Newcastle, 1974. (Forgotten Fantasy Library series).

A reprint of *Fifty-One Tales*.

341   *Don Rodriguez: Chronicles of Shadow Valley*. New York, Putnam, 1922. v, 318 p.

A dull, episodic romance, rather than a novel. Don Rodriguez goes to seek his fortune across the Spain of the sixteenth century, aided by his servant Morano. The writing is arch and ornate, the story lacks force, and Don Rodriguez has no personality, while Morano is copied from Sancho Panza.

342   *The King of Elfland's Daughter*. Introduction by Lin Carter. New York, Ballantine, 1969 (1924). xiv, 242 p.

Alveric, Prince of Erl, marries the Elf-king's daughter Lirazel. Their son Orion is only three years old when Lirazel returns to Elfland: soon after, Alveric sets out to find her but is prevented by her father's magic for twelve years. Finally, Lirazel convinces her father that Alveric's love should be rewarded, so he uses his greatest rune of power to swallow up Erl in Elfland. The dullness of the plot is more than offset by the power of the writing, which describes mountains "like unchanging dreams" and a palace "that may only be told of in song." The book is a tone poem, a mood piece, not a novel.

343   *The Charwoman's Shadow*. Introduction by Lin Carter. New York, Ballantine, 1973 (1926). 213 p.

Related to *Don Rodriguez* by its setting in chivalric Spain, this novel far outstrips its predecessor. Ramon Alonzo, a poor hidalgo's son, becomes a magician's apprentice. The charwoman is a poor peasant girl from a local village who wanted immortality; the magician gave it to her, but did not give her youth as well, and took her shadow in payment. With Ramon's help she regains not only her shadow but her youth and beauty as well, and they live happily ever after. For once Dunsany's mastery of mood accompanies an excellent plot, rather than making up for the lack of one.

344   *The Blessing of Pan.* Illus. by S. H. Sime. London, Putnam, 1927. vi, 287 pp.

A country vicar becomes aware that a number of disturbing events in his parish are related: the music of Pan-pipes he hears every evening, the strange, wild look in the eyes of the girls and boys that he sees every day, and the sudden disappearance of the last vicar, which no one seems willing to discuss. First his fellow clergymen, then his adult parishioners, then his own wife fail him, and he turns to mad Perkin for help, only to find that Perkin recommends that he too should give in to the tide of paganism.

345   *Patches of Sunlight.* New York, Reynal and Hitchcock, 1938. ix, 309 p.

An autobiography in which Dunsany describes how Coleridge's "Kubla Khan" led him to the idea of Wonder, as opposed to the idea of Reality.

346   Amory, Mark. *Biography of Lord Dunsany.* London, Collins, 1972. 288 p.

347   Carter, Lin. *Journeys to the World's Edge: a Dunsany Bibliography.* New York, Carcosa Press, 1974.

DURRELL, GERALD, 1925– .

348   *The Talking Parcel.* Illus. by Pamela Johnson. Philadelphia, Lippincott, 1975. 189 p.

Simon and Peter, on a vacation in Greece with their cousin Penelope, find the parcel on the beach and open it to find a talking spider and a parrot from the land of Mythologia. The children, the parrot, and the spider (who have comical insult matches) go to Mythologia and join with Ethelred, the renegade Cockney toad; Wensleydale, the Duke of Weaseldom; and others, to defeat the Cockatrice. The Whangdoodlery is mostly inoffensive, and most of the jokes and puns are clever and witty.

EAGER, EDWARD, d. 1964.

349   *Half Magic*. Drawings by N. M. Bodecker. New York, Harcourt, 1954. 170 p.

Jane, Mark, Katharine, and Martha find a magic charm that grants wishes by halves, which not only gives them wonderful magic adventures like going on a quest with Sir Lancelot, but which helps their widowed mother and Mr. Smith find each other. Written with a deadpan humor that never goes stale and with accurate, sympathetic insight into the way children think. Followed by

350   *Knight's Castle*. Illus. by N. M. Bodecker. New York, Harcourt, 1956. 183 p.

Roger and Ann dread going to Baltimore to stay with their cousins Jack and Eliza, but when they arrive things are not so bad, because their Aunt Katharine has bought them a marvelous medieval castle full of toy knights and ladies. They decide to call it Torquilstone, and the knights and ladies become Ivanhoe, Rebecca, Rowena, De Bracy, Bois-Guilbert, and all the other characters from Scott. When the magic begins, their involvement changes everything, and the siege of Torquilstone is lifted by Roger's twentieth-century toy soldiers in a climax that makes all their wishes come true—and Ivanhoe marries Rebecca, a much more satisfactory state of affairs! Anyone who has ever loved (or hated) *Ivanhoe* will be delighted with this parody, and fans of *Half Magic* will recognize Jack and Eliza's mother as the ladylike Katharine, and Roger and Ann's mother as the fiery Martha. Followed by

351   *Magic by the Lake*. Illus. by N. M. Bodecker. New York, Harcourt, 1957. 158 p.

The *Half Magic* children encounter a magic turtle to begin a new series of adventures in which they keep trying to find treasure so that Mr. Smith (now their stepfather) will not have to work so hard. But when Martha breaks all the rules and is captured by cannibals and the other three follow her and get caught too, they are rescued by Roger, Ann, and Eliza, who have been traveling around in time by magical means. This book is not quite as good as the first two. Followed by

352   *The Time Garden*. Illus. N. M. Bodecker. New York, Harcourt, 1958. 188 p.

Roger, Ann, Jack, and Eliza discover that the thyme garden of the old house they are staying at can send them through time. At the climax all four go to England—invisible and immaterial—for the opening of Roger and Ann's father's hit play. This last of the *Half Magic* books is much weaker than the others, although Eager's sense of humor remained intact. Eager had planned to write a final book which would involve all eight children, but he died before he wrote it.

353   *Seven-Day Magic.* Illus. by N. M. Bodecker. New York, Harcourt, 1962. 156 p.

Five children check a book out of the library, which turns out to be magic: when they start reading it, it tells about what they have been doing that morning, and when they wish on it, the adventures start happening. After going to the beginnings of Oz and to the Old West as described by Laura Ingalls Wilder, they turn their thoughts to helping Abigail, Barnaby, and Fredericka's father become a success. In the period between *The Time Garden* and this book, Eager wrote two pseudo-fantasies in which the magic, such as it was, spent all its time getting the characters to be philanthropic, so *Seven-Day Magic* was a welcome return to form although it was not up to the level of the *Half Magic* series.

EDDISON, ERIC RUCKER, 1882–1945.

354   *The Worm Ouroboros.* Illus. by Keith Henderson. Introduction by James Stephens. Introduction to the second edition by Orville Prescott. New York, Ballantine, 1967 (1926). xxii, 520 p.

A magnificent heroic fantasy concerning the war of the noble Demons, led by Lord Juss and Lord Brandoch Daha, with the villainous Witches, led by the necromancer-king Gorice XII. When Juss and Brandoch Daha spend two years trying to rescue Juss's brother Goldry, the Witches take advantage of their absence to invade Demonland and reduce it to slavery. But the Demons return in the nick of time, drive the Witches out, rescue Goldry at last, and finally witness the destruction of the Witches through the overweening pride of Gorice. The story is full of unforgettable scenes; the writing combines seventeenth-century grandeur with a wholly Eddisonian vitality; the invention never flags; and the characters are fascinating, the villains even more than the heroes. The only flaw is the ending, in which the heroes find that they cannot be happy without fighting their noble enemies, so the story begins again (hence the title, an ancient symbol of eternity).

355   *Mistress of Mistresses, a Vision of Zimiamvia.* With decorations by Keith Henderson. New York, Ballantine, 1967 (1935). 405 p.

356   *A Fish Dinner in Memison.* Introduction by James Stephens. New York, Ballantine, 1968 (1941). xxxi, 319 p.

357   *The Mezentian Gate.* Frontispiece and decorations by Keith Henderson. New York, Ballantine, 1969 (1958). xxvii, 275 p.

Zimiamvia was mentioned in *The Worm Ouroboros* as an earthly paradise, inhabited by those who in life were greater than their fellows, and inaccessible to the living. It is a land very like Demonland, which is to say that it is a combination of Renaissance Italy, France, and England; and war, diplomacy, love, and intrigue are its chief concerns. The action of the first book follows the action of the second, which, in turn, is contained within the action of the third; the third book was never completed, but Eddison did compose a plot outline, which makes up the last two-thirds of the book, and which fills in the gaps of the series. *The Mezentian Gate* is a biography of King Mezentius, his wife Rosma, and his mistress Amalie. A *Fish Dinner* divides its time between Zimiamvia and England in the first quarter of this century, and concerns three things primarily: a plot to murder the king; the relationship of Amalie's son by Mezentius, Barganax, and Rosma's daughter by a lover, Fiorinda; and the marriage of Edward and Mary Lessingham, who are avatars of Zeus and Aphrodite, as are all the other important characters. *Mistress of Mistresses* takes place after the death of Mezentius, and concerns the struggle for power going on among his legitimate children, Styllis and Antiope, his bastard son Barganax, and his cousin Horius Parry. All of this complicated history is woven around some abstruse philosophical speculation on the nature of the universe, which Eddison conceives as having been created by Zeus for Aphrodite. The trilogy's faults are greater than those of *The Worm*, but it is trying to achieve something greater: a world with a philosophy.

358   Hamilton, George Rostrevor. "The Prose of E. R. Eddison." In *English Studies, New Series, vol. 2*. London, English Association, 1949. pp. 43–53.

A sympathetic assessment of Eddison's work by his close friend.

EDMONDSON, GARRY COTTON.

359   *The Ship That Sailed the Time Stream.* New York, Ace, 1965. 189 p.

Mediocre science fantasy about a Navy ship, manned by a young lieutenant and a lot of misfits, who are transported back in time to various periods. They are pursued by Roman military vessels who think they are pirates, and Viking pirates who consider them in the light of financial windfalls.

EDWARDS, JULIE ANDREWS, 1935– .

360   *The Last of the Really Great Whangdoodles.* New York, Harper, 1974. 209 p.

The hyperbole of the title alone should warn readers away from this condescendingly cute story about an eccentric but dear old Professor and three children who go to Whangdoodleland. Magic ice cream machines and creatures who look like living stuffed animals finish off what vitality the book had.

ELIOT, ETHEL COOK.

361   *The Wind Boy.* Illus. by Robert Hallock. New York, Viking, 1945. 244 p.

How a refugee family was reunited by the efforts of the mysterious Girl from the Mountains and the Wind Boy from the Crystal Land, which appears to be Heaven and is inhabited by hordes of laughing children.

ENRIGHT, ELIZABETH, 1909–1968.

362   *Tatsinda.* Pictures by Irene Haas. New York, Harcourt, 1963. 80 p.

Tatsinda, the only child with golden hair in her magical home, is accepted by her people after being kidnapped, when the prince she loves rescues her. An average fairy tale.

ERWIN, BETTY K.

363   *Who Is Victoria?* Illus. by Kathleen Anderson. Boston, Little Brown, 1973. 134 p.

Everyone in a tiny, Depression-era Midwestern town is curious about Victoria, who appears one day, dressed in a style fifty years out of date, and proceeds to set the town in an uproar. The Depression setting is faithfully depicted in a sensitive, thoughtful, and often very comical story.

ESTES, ELEANOR, 1906–   .

364   *The Witch Family.* Illus. by Edward Ardizzone. New York, Harcourt, 1960. 186 p.

Two six-year-old girls, Amy and Clarissa, invent a witch family in a game, little realizing that as they invent the characters, they become real. On Halloween, Amy has to be rescued by Malachi, the Spelling Bumblebee, when the little witch girls in school discover that Amy is not a real witch. The development of Amy and Clarissa's game and the development of the live witch family parallel each other in a slightly skewed way which works effectively to establish the Secondary World, and Amy's malapropisms—"banquish," "a haunched house"—are appropriately childlike.

FARJEON, ELEANOR, 1882–1965.

365   *Martin Pippin in the Apple Orchard.* Illus. by Richard Kennedy. Philadelphia, Lippincott, 1949 (1921). 305 p.
366   *Martin Pippin in the Daisy Field.* Illus. by Isobel and John Morton-Sale. Philadelphia, Lippincott, 1937. 294 p.

Two books of short stories centered around Martin Pippin, a sort of cross between a minstrel, a jester, and a nature spirit. *The Apple Orchard* involves a complex singing game in which a girl is held captive and must be rescued by her lover, invented by Farjeon, but with exactly the flavor of real folk games. *The Daisy Field*, written sixteen years later, concerns Martin's efforts to guess the names of the six little daughters of the six original girls. The stories come in between as forfeits. *The Daisy Field* not only has a more accessible frame, but contains the greatest Farjeon story, "Elsie Piddock Skips in Her Sleep" which is the most nearly perfect expression of Farjeon's mature style.
367   *Italian Peepshow.* Illus. by Edward Ardizzone. New York, Walck, 1960 (1926). 96 p.

Stories set in the Italian countryside.

368   *Kaleidoscope.* Illus. by Edward Ardizzone. London, Oxford University Press, 1963 (1929). x, 157 p.

As Anthony grows up he hears all the lovely tales that exist about the flowers, the sun, moon, and stars, and all else in Heaven and Earth.

369   *The Old Nurse's Stocking-Basket.* Illus. by Edward Ardizzone. New York, Walck, 1965 (1931). 102 p.

The Old Nurse's tales are all about the naughty magical children she has been nanny to during her long life, from ancient China to last week.

370   *Jim at the Corner*. Illus. by Edward Ardizzone. New York, Walck, 1958 (1934). 101 p.

An old sailor tells a small boy magical sea stories.

371   *The Silver Curlew*. Illus. by Ernest H. Shepard. New York, Viking, 1954. 192 p.

While pretty, lazy Doll Codling, who has married the King, tries frantically to find out Tom Tit Tot's name, her little sister is trying to help the Man in the Moon, who now lives in a seashore shack, find his Lady. The two threads of the story come together when she realizes that the imp who is tormenting poor Doll is also holding the Lady captive in the form of a silver curlew. The story blends silvery, airy magic with the prosaic (and rather damp) common sense of the Norfolk yeomanry who are its major characters.

372   *The Glass Slipper*. From the play of the same name by Eleanor and Herbert Farjeon. Illus. by Ernest H. Shepard. New York, Viking, 1955. 175 p.

A retelling of "Cinderella," based on a play which Farjeon wrote with her brother Herbert. Ella's enemies are her hypocritical stepmother and her petulant, clumsy stepsisters; her friends are her henpecked father, the Grandfather Clock, and the Prince's zany, who never speaks. The descriptions of the Prince's other possible mates and of the grand feast at the ball are just sumptuous enough to be funny; the scene in which the father and the zany steal sugar-plums to give to Ella is just funny enough not to be heartbreaking. A beautiful balance between melancholy and merriment.

373   *The Little Bookroom, Eleanor Farjeon's Short Stories for Children Chosen by Herself*. Illus. by Edward Ardizzone. New York, Walck, 1956. xii, 302 p.

An anthology of Farjeon's short stories from the Twenties and Thirties (Nos. 365–370), which won the Carnegie Medal in 1956.

374   *Eleanor Farjeon's Book: Stories, Verses, Plays*. Chosen by Eleanor Graham and illus. by Edward Ardizzone. Harmondsworth, Penguin Books, 1960. 208 p.

An anthology which contains religious poetry and plays as well as several fantasy stories, including "Elsie Piddock." At present this is the only paperback collection available in the U.S.

375   *Memoirs*. London, Oxford University Press, 1958.

Primarily a biography of the poet Edward Thomas, who died in World War I, with whom Farjeon was in love.

376   A Book for Eleanor Farjeon: a tribute to her life and work. Illus. by Edward Ardizzone. Introduction by Naomi Lewis. New York, Walck, 1966. 184 p.

A commemorative collection of essays and stories.

377   Blakelock, Denys Martin. Eleanor: Portrait of a Farjeon. London, Gollancz, 1966. 160 p.

A memoir by the actor friend who played King Nollekens in the stage version of The Silver Curlew, and who was instrumental in her conversion to Catholicism.

378   Colwell, Eileen. Eleanor Farjeon. London, Bodley Head, 1961. 94 p.

A short biographical sketch precedes a detailed examination of her work, with emphasis on the stories.

FARMER, PENELOPE, 1939–   .

379   The Magic Stone. Illus. by John Kaufmann. New York, Harcourt, 1964. 223 p.

Memorable characters—working-class Alice and her shrewd grandmother; posh Caroline, her selfish writer father, and her belligerent brother Stephen—interact in this penetrating look at personal and class conflicts, but the magic is disappointing.

380   The Summer Birds. Illus. by James J. Spanfeller. New York, Harcourt, 1962. 155 p.

Emma and Charlotte meet a mysterious, angelic boy who teaches them and the other village children to fly during a quiet, magical summer. Once again, Farmer's tendency to moralize outweighs the meager amount of magic in the story, though the characterizations of Emma and Charlotte are excellent. Followed by

381   Emma in Winter. Illus. by James J. Spanfeller. New York, Harcourt, 1966. 160 p.

While Charlotte is away at boarding school, Emma finds herself meeting one of her schoolfellows—an awkward, unpopular boy—every night in her dreams. At the climax of their adventures, they find they must rely on each other to escape a dangerous situation. Followed by

382   Charlotte Sometimes. Pictures by Charles Connor. New York, Harcourt, 1969. 192 p.

Charlotte's first winter at boarding school is more than difficult because she slips back in time forty years on alternate days, changing places with another girl named Clare. The alternation becomes harder and harder to bear, in spite of the help of Clare's little sister Emily, and one day she is forced to leave school in the past, which makes her fear that she will never get home again. She and Emily manage to get back to school in time, however, and when Charlotte gets back to the present for the last time, she learns that the friendly older girl who has been kind to her is Emily's daughter. This is a first-class fantasy as well as a discerning study of character.

383   *A Castle of Bone.* New York, Atheneum, 1972. 151 p.

An ambiguous, complex, fascinating story of four children who discover that a cupboard bought in a strange secondhand store has the power to return anything put into it to some earlier state of being. This power cannot be predicted or controlled; a pigskin wallet turns into a pig, a plastic one turns into a smelly pool of oily liquid, a woollen sweater turns into a hank of raw wool, and one of the children turns into a baby. The cupboard's power is tied in with a mysterious country where one of the boys repeatedly finds himself. The necessity of dealing with the baby leads all four children to enter the cupboard together, whereupon they find themselves in the other world, which they realize is defined by their own existences. A powerful story that rewards careful and unhasty reading.

384   *William and Mary.* New York, Atheneum, 1974. 160 p.

Two children, forced into each other's company by circumstances, find a magic half-shell that takes them into any picture or poem dealing with the sea. Gradually, William becomes obsessed with finding the other half of the shell, seeing it as the only guarantee of his future happiness, but Mary becomes more and more skeptical. However, in the final crisis, they are enabled to find the shell only because Mary sticks with William in spite of her skepticism.

FENTON, EDWARD, 1917– .

385   *The Nine Questions.* Illus. by C. Walter Hodges. Garden City, N.Y., Doubleday, 1959. 235 p.

Willie Boy's foster-mother gives him the cap, the whistle, and the watch left him by his mother, and he goes out to seek his heritage. In the Weaver's Kingdom, he learns that all the opposition he has met comes from one man, the evil Minister of Light, who is trying to usurp the Weaver's throne. The Minister's hatred for Willie, of course, exists because Willie is the Weaver's rightful heir.

FEYDY, ANNE LINDBERGH.

386   *Osprey Island.* Illus. by Maggie Kaufman Smith. Boston, Houghton Mifflin, 1974. 164 p.

An unconvincingly cute fantasy about three cousins who discover that a mysterious phrase uttered in front of a magic picture can transport them from their homes in Paris and Vermont to the island. The pat ending transports Lizzie's mother to Paris, where the parents figure out everything and promise to take the children to Osprey Island next summer.

FINNEY, CHARLES GRANDISON, 1905– .

387   *The Circus of Dr. Lao.* With drawings by Boris Artzybasheff. New York, Viking, 1935. 154 p.

An ironic fantasy depicting the reactions of the good citizens of Abalone, Arizona to Dr. Lao's magical circus. After the show is over, the Abalonians go home. They are not unwilling, but they are unable to believe in the wonders set so lavishly before them. The book has no plot to speak of; it is a collection of dryly pungent vignettes, which should be read when the reader is in the mood for something different from any other fantasy.

388   *The Ghosts of Manacle.* New York, Pyramid, 1964. 159 p.

A group of miscellaneous short stories and a novella.

FINNEY, JACK.

389   *The Woodrow Wilson Dime.* New York, Simon & Schuster, 1968. 190 p.

Ben finds a dime with Wilson's head on it and discovers that it is the passport into an alternate universe where he is rich, successful, and married to the gorgeous redhead he knew in college. He makes a fortune in his new life by "writing" the songs of Cole Porter, Rodgers and Hammerstein, and Irving Berlin. Funny fluff.

390   *Time and Again.* New York, Simon & Schuster, 1970. 399 p.

Simon Morley, an artist, joins a top-secret government project on time travel and goes back to the New York of 1882 to unravel a mystery concerning his girlfriend's great-grandfather. Back in the twentieth century, however, the military men who run the project announce that they want Simon to change the history of the United States. He does go back, but only to prevent the project from ever happening in the first place, so that no one can tamper with history. This book is a pointed statement of Finney's oft-repeated thesis that the past was preferable to the present, as well as a thrilling suspense story.

391   *Marion's Wall, a novel.* New York, Simon and Schuster, 1973. 187 p.

Marion Marsh, an actress of the 1920s who died before stardom, and her friend Rudolf Valentino possess Nick and Jan and go to Hollywood to resume their careers. At first, everything seems to be going fine: Marion-Jan gets a part dancing the Charleston, and Rudy-Nick does some wing-walking on a biplane. But their dreams crash in ruins when they realize that their parts were in TV commercials. Humorous and sentimental, as Finney's books usually are, but his rueful tone adds dimension to the story.

FLEMING, IAN, 1908–1964.

392   *Chitty Chitty Bang Bang, the Magical Car.* Illus. by John Burningham. New York, Random, 1964. 114 p.

This book possesses many characteristics of Fleming's adult spy novels: a suspenseful plot, lots of gadgetry, plenty of action, and carefully-described but improbable characters. The magical car, which becomes a boat or plane at need, has more personality than any of the humans. But it is saved from mere Whangdoodlery by the air of absolute seriousness which Fleming imparts to it and by his utter lack of condescension.

FOLLETT, BARBARA NEWHALL.

393   *The House Without Windows and Eepersip's Life There.* With a Historical Note by Another Hand, pp. 155–166. New York, Knopf, 1927. 166 p.

A literary curiosity written by a nine-year-old child. Eepersip is a little girl who runs away from home to live on a mountainside and whose family cannot catch her because she becomes the Queen of the Deer. Finally Eepersip goes off to the Snowy Mountains and becomes a nature-spirit. Follett's precocity shows in the formal style and the advanced vocabulary, but most of the plot is about Eepersip's gambols in butterfly-infested meadows.

FORESTER, CECIL SCOTT, 1899–1966.

394   *Poo-Poo and the Dragons.* Illus. by Robert Lawson. Boston, Little, Brown, 1942. viii, 143 p.

A little boy named Harold, or Poo-Poo for short, brings home a dragon, Horatio (get it?), as a pet. Later Horatio acquires a wife and child, Ermyntrude and Maximilian. As if the cutesy names were not enough, the story is full of LOTS and LOTS of capital letters.

FRITZ, JEAN, 1915– .

395   *Magic to Burn*. Illus. by Beth and Joe Krush. New York, Coward-McCann, 1964. 255 p.
While visiting England, Stephen and Ann find Blaze, a tiny boggart or mischief-making fairy. Disgusted with modern progress, Blaze stows away on their ship home, only to find that America is worse than England. Rather dated and sexist, especially in its portrayals of the children's activities.

FRY, ROSALIE, 1911– .

396   *The Mountain Door*. Illus. by the author. New York, Dutton, 1961. 128 p.
An eminently forgettable fantasy about two changelings—that is, the child taken and the child left—who meet when their family leaves for America, and who decide to stay together in Ireland and live with a quaint old couple in a quaint old cottage.

GALLICO, PAUL, 1897–1976.

397   *The Abandoned*. New York, Knopf, 1959. 307 p.
Peter is turned into a cat and learns cat lore from a kind stray, Jennie Baldrin. They ship out as ship's cats to Glasgow, then return to London, where Peter saves Jennie from a cruel tom and becomes a boy again, having learned self-reliance and love from Jennie.
398   *Thomasina, the Cat Who Thought She Was God*. Garden City, N.Y., Doubleday, 1957. 288 p.
Thomasina saves her ill-tempered master from turning into a complete villain with a little love and a lot of coincidences.
399   *Manxmouse*. New York, Coward-McCann, 1968. 188 p.
A charmingly drunken old potter makes a tailless blue mouse that comes to life at the stroke of thirteen and goes out to seek its fortune. When it finally reaches the Isle of Man, the Manxmouse is forced into

a fight with the Manx Cat, but so brave is the Mouse that their fight ends without a blow and they confirm their eternal friendship. These three fantasies are representative of Gallico's work; they suffer from being every bit as mechanical as the Mouse.

GANNETT, RUTH STILES, 1923– .

400   *My Father's Dragon.* Illus. by Ruth C. Gannett. New York, Random, 1948. 86 p.

A family goes to live on a magic island inhabited by dragons. Predictable and slight.

GARD, JOYCE.

401   *Talargain.* New York, Holt, 1964. 251 p.

A grim story, full of feuds and witch-hunts, set in the seventh century. Talargain is a half-Welsh Angle who was cast out by men but accepted by the silkies, or seal-people, who adopt him as one of themselves. He appears to a modern child who is having family problems and tells her his story—perhaps to let her know that her problems are not very serious in comparison with his. Unfortunately, this laudable moral lesson completely overwhelms the story.

GARDNER, JOHN CHAMPLIN, 1933– .

402   *Grendel.* Illus. by Emil Antonucci. Boston, Hall, 1971. 215 p.

The story of Beowulf retold from the monster's point of view. Grendel is a funny, intricate, philosophical sort who is mad with boredom; no one in Hrothgar's hall can talk to him on his intellectual level, and Beowulf is a puritan who refuses to listen to reason. Grendel's acerbic comments and self-conscious *Weltschmerz* make him an outstanding creation.

GARNER, ALAN, 1935– .

403   *The Weirdstone of Brisingamen.* New York, Ace, 1960. 192 p.

Because Susan wears a bracelet with a clear stone that is the key to an enchanted cave full of sleeping knights, guarded by the magician Cadellin, she and Colin are caught up into a nightmarish struggle between Cadellin and his allies, and the terrible Morrigan who commands the goblin-like svarts. Having escaped the svarts, they must get the stone to Cadellin, and flee across country pursued by witches and shrieking trolls. Garner combines elements of Norse mythology, Welsh legend, and English folklore into a fantasy world which is wholly his own and wholly convincing. Followed by

404   *The Moon of Gomrath.* New York, Ace, 1963. 157 p.

The Morrigan has survived her defeat by Cadellin and bends her wrath against Susan, whose new bracelet both protects her and draws her further into the magic. When a vile spirit of evil, the Brollachan, possesses her, Colin must find the magic plant which alone can save her, but in doing so he awakens a spirit of the Old Magic, the Hunter Garanhir who has the horns of a stag. On the night of the Moon of Gomrath, Susan and Colin inadvertently summon up the Wild Hunt, led by Garanhir, which at first seems to be a mistake. But when the Morrigan captures Colin, and Susan and her friends are in dire straits, the Wild Hunt returns and destroys the Morrigan's forces. In these two short children's books Garner creates a Secondary World worthy of comparison with Tolkien's Middle-Earth, and sets it all in a real landscape, his home of Alderley in Cheshire.

405   *Elidor.* New York, Walck, 1965. 158 p.

Four children, exploring some deserted back streets in Manchester, stumble into another world, where the maimed king Malebron entrusts to them the four treasures of Elidor: a cup, a sword, a spear, and a stone. Then invaders from Elidor enter our world in search of the treasures, and the struggle between good and evil in Elidor suddenly becomes urgent in Manchester.

406   *The Owl Service.* New York, Walck, 1967. 202 p.

Alison, her stepbrother Roger, and her housekeeper's son Gwyn, are forced willy-nilly to reenact the ancient Welsh myth of Flowerface when they go to stay in Alison's Welsh country home. Alison finds herself in the role of the woman made of flowers, while the two boys recreate the roles of her murdered husband and her adulterous lover. The situation is exacerbated by their own conflicts, by Alison's mother and stepfather, and by their discovery that Gwyn's mother and Alison's cousin had undergone the same ordeal a generation before. In the final crisis, snobbish Roger, not sensitive Gwyn, saves Alison's life by renouncing his role in the myth. The myth itself, the class and personal conflicts among the characters, and the psychology of each character are inseparably intertwined in this intricate, intense, compelling novel of love and jealousy.

407   *Red Shift.* New York, Macmillan, 1973. 197 p.

The least fantastical and most perplexing and difficult to understand of Garner's books. Three young men—Tom today, Thomas in the seventeenth century, and Macey in Roman Britain—are linked through time by their possession of a prehistoric stone axe. Their interlinked stories center around a crisis in the relationship of each with a woman. Garner skillfully fuses the three stories into one, but he seems to have gone beyond fantasy in the novel, because the three men's lives do not act upon one another, in spite of their resemblances.

408   "A Bit More Practice." *Times Literary Supplement,* June 6, 1968.

GARNETT, DAVID, 1892– .

409   *Lady Into Fox.* Illus. with wood engravings by R. A. Garnett. Introduction by Vincent Starrett. New York, Norton, 1966 (1922). 90 p.

A satirical fantasy in which an English gentleman finds it difficult and, finally, tragic, to deal with his wife's transformation into a vixen. The neighbors, of course, think she ran away with another man, and she does disappear one day, only to return with five cubs. At the end he cannot prevent her from being killed by a hunt. The book's deadpan, bitter humor made it a sensation when it was published in the 1920s; though it would not be considered daring now, it is still a neat little work of ironic art.

410   *Two by Two.* New York, Atheneum, 1964. vii, 143 p.

A retelling of the Noah story, with twin fourteen-year-old orphan girls as heroines. Niss and Fan meet a few good people in their travels —a wolf hunter, a kind cobbler who gives them shelter—but many more evil ones, including Noah himself, who is a drunken, self-righteous old sot getting his revenge on the neighbors who called him names. The twins stow away on the Ark, disguised as woolly monkeys; after the Flood, they and two of Noah's grandsons escape and go to live by the sea. The description of the incredibly brutal lives of the primitive people is first-rate, the characters vary between fascinating creations and humorous parodies, and the whole book is almost excessively well-written. It is more a historical novel with a few fantasy embellishments than true fantasy.

GARRETT, RANDALL.

411   *Too Many Magicians.* Garden City, N.Y., Doubleday, 1966. 260 p.

An eminently satisfactory locked-room mystery set in an alternate universe where the Plantagenets rule England, France, and both continents of the New World, and where the laws of magic are known, but the laws of physics are not. When his chief assistant, Master Sean, is accused of murdering a fellow sorcerer at a convention in London, Lord Darcy, Chief Investigator of the Duchy of Normandy, must solve the case. The characters are wooden, but the fantasy world is so lovingly developed that their shortcomings do not matter. This is the only novel about the Angevin Empire that Garrett has written, but several short stories also exist, including one with the wonderful title, "The Muddle of the Woad."

GASKELL, JANE, 1941– .

412   *The Serpent.* London, Hodder and Stoughton, 1963. 445 p.
413   *Atlan.* London, Hodder and Stoughton, 1965. 286 p.
414   *The City.* London, Hodder and Stoughton, 1966. 190 p.
    The adventures of Cija, princess of a tiny prehistoric South American land, in the great wars for the possession of the mysterious continent, Atlan (Gaskell's version of Atlantis). Cija is intelligent, but her upbringing in a secluded tower does not prepare her for what she encounters as a hostage in the army of Zerd, a half-human, half-lizard general, whom her vengeful lady-in-waiting urges her to murder. Instead, she escapes, and goes to Southern City disguised as a boy, where Zerd hires her to cook for his wife. After a passionate love affair with her cousin Smahil, Cija again escapes, only to be caught by Zerd for the third time and made his wife and the Empress of Atlan. This doesn't last either, and soon she and her children flee again: she becomes a kitchenmaid, a robber queen, a slave, a hostage in the vicious struggle between her mother, the Dictatress, and her father, the High Priest, and finally the mistress of an ape-man in the jungle. To many, the major flaw of the three books is Gaskell's use of anachronisms and slang; but some think it gives the story an immediacy and intimacy which most fantasies lack. Cija herself is a resourceful, funny, and courageous character, and her world is colorful, exciting, and vast.

GILMAN, ROBERT CHAM.

415   *The Rebel of Rhada.* New York, Harcourt, 1968. 192 p.
416   *The Navigator of Rhada.* New York, Harcourt, 1969. 223 p.
    Two science fantasies set in the far future. The Galactic Empire

still possesses space travel, guarded by an elite corps of astronaut-priests, but has otherwise sunk into a quasi-medieval social system of feudal loyalties and internecine wars. The prince of Rhada, a distant planet, leads an insurrection against Earth and its emperor, complicated by the predictable intrigues going on at the imperial court.

GODDEN, RUMER, 1907– .

417   *Impunity Jane.* Illus. by Adrienne Adams. New York, Viking, 1954. 48 p.
    A small boy's doll, Jane, rides on the handlebars of his bicycle with impunity, which is how she gets her name.
418   *The Fairy Doll.* Illus. by Adrienne Adams. New York, Viking, 1956. 67 p.
419   *Miss Happiness and Miss Flower.* Illus. by Jean Primrose. New York, Viking, 1961. 81 p.
    Two Japanese dolls sent to a little girl inspire her to have a Japanese dollhouse made. Followed by
420   *Little Plum.* Drawings by Jean Primrose. New York, Viking, 1962. 91 p.
    A new addition to the Japanese doll family is the object of another child's greed until the dolls bring about a reconciliation.
421   *The Doll's House.* Illus. by Tasha Tudor. New York, Viking, 1962. 136 p.
422   *Home is the Sailor.* Illus. by Jean Primrose. New York, Viking, 1964. 129 p.
    Story of a boy sailor doll. One of the best things about Rumer Godden's doll stories is that she never assumes that any child will, or will not, play with dolls because of his or her sex.

GOLDSMITH-CARTER, GEORGE.

423   *Lord of the Chained.* New York, Lothrop, 1972. 160 p.
    A pretentious, badly written, and pointless time-travel fantasy in which two children help the old Anglo-Saxon gods.

GORDON, JOHN, 1925– .

424   *The Giant Under the Snow, a Story of Suspense.* Illus. by Rocco Negri. New York, Harper, 1968. 200 p.

Jonquil and her friends Bill and Arf join in a battle between Elizabeth Goodenough, a mysterious sorceress, and an evil war-lord who invaded their peaceful English county hundreds of years ago. A skillful blending of past and present, with the awesome thrill of seeing a giant appear out of the earth.

425   *The House on the Brink, a Story of Suspense.* New York, Harper, 1971. 217 p.

An evil woman living in a shabby, decaying house, and a man of frightening strength who is her colleague, nearly manage to capture a boy and girl who have discovered that the couple are trying to recover the lost treasure of King John. A competent horror fantasy, not up to the standard set by Gordon's previous book.

GOUDGE, ELIZABETH, 1900–   .

426   *Smoky House.* Illus. by Richard Floethe. New York, Coward-McCann, 1940. 286 p.

A family of children, whose father and all of whose neighbors and relatives are smugglers, take in the Fiddler, a lonely, embittered man. The Fiddler is a spy sent to betray the smugglers, which he does, but the children, the animals, and the Good People (fairies) save their friends, and finally bring the Fiddler to repent his betrayal and overcome his bitterness.

427   *The Little White Horse.* Illus. by C. Walter Hodges. New York, Coward-McCann, 1946. 280 p.

Maria Merryweather, come to live with her uncle in the West Country, soon learns that there is a secret concerning her family and the robber Sir Wrolf. With the aid of a huge "dog" who is actually a lion, and the enchanted white horse of the Merryweathers, Maria convinces Sir Wrolf to forgive the wrong done to his ancestor and to give up outlawry. A fantasy with a perfect balance between fear, pity, grief, wonderment, and joy.

428   *The Valley of Song.* Illus. by Richard Floethe. New York, Coward-McCann, 1951. 281 p.

How Tabitha and those of her friends who were still children inside entered the Valley, which was the Earthly Paradise, and were given the materials to build the clipper ship *White Swan*. Perhaps a little over-lyrical in its description of the marvels of the Valley, the story emphasizes the beauty of work and of ordinary, daily life.

429   *Linnets and Valerians.* Illus. by Ian Ribbons. New York, Coward-McCann, 1964. 290 p.

The Linnet children become friends with Lady Valerian, whose husband and little son both disappeared many years before, and with a wild man, a mute who lives in a nearby cave. Soon Nan, the eldest child, discovers that the local witch had wanted to marry Sir Hugo Valerian and was responsible for his disappearance. With the help of their uncle's factotum, Ezra, the Linnets lift the curse on the Valerians, which reveals that the Wild Man is the missing son and brings Sir Hugo home from Egypt. A joyous Edwardian story, full of singing, poetry, and sunlight.

430　*The Joy of the Snow.* New York, Coward-McCann, 1974. 319 p. An autobiography.

GRAHAME, KENNETH, 1859–1932.

431　*The Wind in the Willows.* Illus. by Ernest H. Shepard. New York, Scribner, 1961 (1908). 259 p.

A masterpiece of English prose. While the Mole, the Badger, and the Water Rat live their serene lives near the banks of the River, the ebullient Toad gets into one scrape after another. His craze for boats is superseded by a short-lived expedition by horse-drawn caravan, which ends abruptly when a motorcar wrecks the thing, and Toad embarks on the career of a speed-demon, ending up in a dungeon. Meanwhile, the Weasels and Stoats have taken over Toad Hall, and when Toad returns, his faithful friends must help him drive them out. Every aspect of the book is perfect, whether it is the Rat "simply messing about in a boat," the Mole yearning for his lost home, the Badger giving Toad a talking-to, or the Toad's boastful songs and vain swaggering. Shepard's illustrations strike a balance between pastoral lyricism and low humor which perfectly reflects the two poles of the book.

432　*The Reluctant Dragon.* Illus. by Ernest H. Shepard. New York, Holiday House, 1938 (1895). Unpaged.

The charming story of the Dragon who hates fighting, the Boy who tries to heighten his morale, and St. George; first published as a chapter of Grahame's *Dream Days*.

433　Chalmers, Patrick R. *Kenneth Grahame: Life, Letters, and Unpublished Work.* London, Methuen, 1933. xvii, 321 p.

434　Graham, Eleanor. *Kenneth Grahame.* New York, Walck, 1963. 72 p.

GRAY, NICHOLAS STUART, 1922– .

435　*Grimbold's Other World.* Illus. by Charles Keeping. New York, Meredith Press, 1968 (1963). 184 p.

Grimbold the cat's master is Gareth, the son of an enchanter who dislikes his father, and who is consequently always in trouble. Grimbold befriends Muffler, a foundling goatherd, who rescues both Gareth and a lost prince, Jeffrey, whom the enchanter has kept captive. Muffler is also a lost prince, but he decides to stay on the farm, where he is loved, and let Jeffrey take his place. Gray tells the story in language that is poetic, unforced, and ironic all at the same time.

436   *Mainly in Moonlight, Ten Stories of Sorcery and the Supernatural.* Illus. by Charles Keeping. New York, Meredith Press, 1965. 182 p.

Dreamy, melancholy, gently ironic fairy tales. A young lady rescues an enchanted prince, only to realize that the fact that his enchantment lasted a hundred years is going to cause problems; a silly boy who makes a wish is ruthlessly exploited by a succession of magical creatures, but gets his wish after all; a wicked prince learns not to be selfish.

437   *The Apple Stone.* Illus. by Charles Keeping. New York, Meredith Press, 1969. 230 p.

Four children find a magic talking stone inside an apple and have a series of weak Nesbit-ish adventures with it. Disappointing, although their conversation with the Crusader knight whose statue is in their church brings back echoes of a similar conversation in Kipling's *Puck* (q.v.).

GREAVES, MARGARET, 1914– .

438   *The Dagger and the Bird.* Illus. by Laszlo Kubinyi. New York, Harper, 1975 (1971). 133 p.

Luke and Biddy, realizing that their father will never be able to finish the squire's iron gates without the help of their true brother, Simon, go to the fairy world to exchange their changeling Simon for the real one. The fairies are deceitful because they are unable to tell the difference between reality and falsity, but this promising idea is not developed.

GREENWALD, SHEILA, pseudonym of Sheila Ellen Green, 1934– .

439   *The Secret Museum.* Illus. by the author. Philadelphia, Lippincott, 1974. 127 p.

Jennifer finds an abandoned playhouse inhabited by twenty live dolls. The book concentrates on her efforts to clean up the place so that it can be made into a museum, which will help her earn money and allow her parents to stay in the country instead of going back to the city. As such, it is a fine book, but the fantasy of talking, living dolls is totally unnecessary to it; the story of Jennifer's determination would have been just the same without the fantasy.

GRIPE, MARIA, 1923– .

440   *The Glassblower's Children.* With drawings by Harald Gripe. Translated from the Swedish by Sheila La Farge. New York, Dell, 1973 (1964). 170 p.

A didactic fable about love and wishes with a strange, Gothic atmosphere. The Lord of All-Wishes-Town fulfills his Lady's desire for children by kidnaping the glassblower's children, Klas and Klara. At first petted and spoiled, they are soon forgotten except by their ferocious nurse, Nana. Eventually Nana's sister, the good witch Flutter Mildweather, rescues them and returns them to their parents.

441   *The Land Beyond.* Drawings by Harald Gripe. Translated by Sheila La Farge. New York, Delacorte, 1974. 214 p.

This clumsy story concerns the reactions of two kings to an explorer's discovery of a new land: one refuses to believe in it, while the other goes overboard in his acceptance of it. The fantasy is overwhelmed by, indeed is only a vehicle for, the philosophical speculation, and the characters' long, abstruse dialogues are unbelievable and didactic.

GROSSER, MORTON.

442   *The Snake Horn.* Illus. by David K. Stone. New York, Atheneum, 1973. 131 p.

A jazz musician's young son receives an unusual "snake horn" for a present, which, when blown at the proper time, summons its former owner, a musician in Restoration England, to the modern world. Most of the book concerns the boy's efforts to find the proper way to get him home, aided by his many friends of different races. The lightweight but excellent story contains that rare thing in children's books: a portrait of an artist's family life which is realistic without being sensational.

HAGGARD, SIR HENRY RIDER, 1856–1923.

443   *She, a History of Adventure.* New York, Grosset and Dunlap, 1886. 302 p.

A young man, journeying in Africa to learn the answer to a family mystery, discovers a lost civilization in a hidden valley ruled by the beautiful Ayesha—"She-who-must-be-obeyed." Melodramatic, silly, naive, and quite racist by today's standards, *She* is still one of the greatest and most thrilling adventure stories ever written. Followed by a wholly undistinguished sequel,

444   *Ayesha, the Return of She.* New York, Doubleday, Page, 1905. 359 p.

She is reincarnated in Tibet, which was a trendy idea around the turn of the century; but this book has no virtues to redeem that trendiness.

445   *The People of the Mist.* New York, Ballantine, 1973 (1894). xii, 365 p.

A romantic misunderstanding between the Rector's lovely daughter and the noble, impoverished son of a disgraced man sends him to Africa, where he discovers a lost race and makes the fortune which enables him to return to England, only to discover that the girl has died after marrying Another. Mindless melodrama.

446   Cohen, Morton H. *Rider Haggard: His Life and Work.* 2nd ed. London, Hutchinson, 1960. 327 p.

447   Scott, James Edward. *A Bibliography of the Works of Sir Henry Rider Haggard.* Herts., E. Mathews, 1947. 258 p. Illus. (500 copies).

HAGGARD, SIR HENRY RIDER, and LANG, ANDREW.

448   *The World's Desire.* Introduction by Lin Carter. New York, Ballantine, 1972 (1890). xvii, 238 p.

Upon Odysseus's second return to Ithaca, he finds everyone there dead of plague, so he travels to Egypt in search of Helen of Troy. There he is swept up into the intrigues of the court of the sorceress-queen Meriamun, who is protecting Helen, and the struggles of the Apura (Hebrew) minority. This idiosyncratic treatment of the story of Helen in Egypt is even more melodramatic than Haggard's own works and is written in a grossly exaggerated, ornate style. See also Lang, Andrew.

HAIBLUM, ISIDORE, 1935– .

449   *The Tsaddik of the Seven Wonders.* New York, Ballantine, 1971. 185 p.

The Tsaddik is a medieval Polish Jew who has learned to travel in time by magic, which he does accompanied by his friend, the homunculus Greenberg. Naturally, this rips the fabric of the Universe—magic is not allowed in the Milky Way galaxy—so two caseworkers from the cosmic bureaucracy intervene. The three eventually realize that a sharp real estate agent from another galaxy is trying to ensure the Devil's triumph so that the agent can sell the planet after all the aborigines—us—are dead. A unique combination of science fantasy and New York Yiddish humor.

HAMLEY, DENNIS.

450   *Pageants of Despair.* New York, S. G. Phillips, 1974. 175 p.
    A suspenseful time-travel fantasy centered around the medieval play cycle, the Townley Cycle of Wakefield. Peter meets the plays' author on a train and goes back in time with him to try to prevent an evil will from taking over the plays. Well-written and serious without being grim or didactic, though Peter is not especially noteworthy.

HARRIS, ROSEMARY.

451   *The Moon in the Cloud.* New York, Macmillan, 1968. 182 p.
    The first book of a trilogy set in the time of Noah. Noah's lazy, greedy son Ham offers Reuben and Thamar a place on the Ark if Reuben will go to Kemi (Egypt) to get various animals. So Reuben goes, but in Kemi he is imprisoned as a spy. His flute gets him out of prison and into the Pharaoh's palace, where he prevents a plot against the Pharaoh's life from succeeding and wins his eternal friendship. He goes back to Canaan with the animals, rejoins Thamar, and is saved from the Flood (which, fortunately, does not reach Kemi). Satisfying and amusing. Followed by

452   *The Shadow on the Sun.* New York, Macmillan, 1970. 198 p.
    How Reuben rescues the Pharaoh's beloved, Meri-Mekhmet, from the evil men of Punt who have kidnaped her at the instigation of a jealous priest. Much more exciting than *The Moon in the Cloud*, but not less amusing. Followed by

453   *The Bright and Morning Star.* New York, Macmillan, 1972. 254 p.
    Pharaoh's weakling son encourages a wicked counselor, not realizing that he plans to overthrow Pharaoh, kill Meri-Mekhmet and the son himself, and marry Pharaoh's gentle daughter. Reuben and Thamar

are having their own problems with their youngest son, who cannot speak, but they manage to stop the plot, free the royal family, and overcome the child's illness, helped by the sacred cats of Kemi. Though this book is not as humorous as the other two, it has all their virtues: tight and suspenseful plotting, three-dimensional characters, and a thoroughly developed background.

454   *The Seal-Singing.* New York, Macmillan, 1971. 245 p.

Toby, Catriona, and their cousin Miranda are interested in seals and in their ancestress Lucy, a Seal-Singer—a human whom the seals loved and trusted. Miranda becomes obsessed with Lucy, whose treacherous spirit begins to overwhelm Miranda's personality, until finally Miranda is forced to choose between Lucy and the animals. A powerful story of adolescents' conflicts over a bitterly urgent moral question.

HEINLEIN, ROBERT ANSON, 1907– .

455   "Magic, Inc." In *Waldo and Magic, Inc.* New York, Signet/ NAL, 1970 (1942). 192 p.

In a world where all business is run by magical means, what more natural than that a businessman should have to fight a protection racket run by the Devil? When the pressure gets too hot, he and a sweet old lady, who happens to be a top-notch witch, go off to the Other World with an African psychologist, also a witch, a familiar or two, and a G-man investigating the racket. A funny idea developed with relentless logic.

456   *Glory Road.* New York, Putnam, 1963. 288 p.

Oscar Gordon, an opinionated ex-G.I., joins a fabulously beautiful woman named Star on a quest through several alternate universes, trying to find an artifact called the Egg of the Phoenix which is actually a repository of the lives of the rulers of the Twenty Universes. The story is badly plotted.

HILTON, JAMES, 1900–1954.

457   *Lost Horizon.* New York, Morrow, 1933. 277 p.

An ill-assorted group of Europeans and Americans is kidnaped and carried off through the inaccessible Himalayas to the enchanted valley of Shangri-La, which is a bastion of peace, plenty, and civilization hidden from the modern world, ruled by an ancient High Lama, two hundred years old, who came from France in the eighteenth century and made it what it is. The story concerns the Lama's attempt to convince the kidnaped Hugh Conway to become his successor. An immensely, and deservedly, popular fantasy that was made into a memorable Ronald Colman movie.

HOBAN, RUSSELL, 1925– .

458   *The Mouse and His Child.* Pictures by Lillian Hoban. New York, Harper, 1967. 182 p.

A pair of mechanical dancing mice are rescued from a rubbish heap and repaired so they can move, though they can no longer dance. They escape enslavement by the garbage boss, Manny Rat, and after a winter full of adventures and new friendships, they find a home, even converting Manny from a villain to a friend. The story is absolutely unsentimental about animals—many of their friends are eaten by other animals before their eyes—and about friendship and love, but it is optimistic, acute, and sensitive: a superlative fantasy.

HODGSON, WILLIAM HOPE, 1877–1918.

459   *The House on the Borderland and Other Novels.* Bibliography by A. L. Fearles, pp. 638–9. Sauk City, Wis., Arkham House, 1946. xi, 639 p.

Four horror fantasies: "The Boats of the *Glen Carrig*"; "The Ghost Pirates"; "The House on the Borderland"; and "The Night Land," set at the end of the world. What is left of humanity lives in a pyramidal city eternally watched by monsters awaiting its fall. Hodgson masterfully suggests the unguessable terrors of his dismal world.

HOLM, ANNE, 1922– .

460   *Peter.* Translated by L. W. Kingsland. New York, Harcourt, 1968 (1965). 224 p.

Peter travels into the past to ancient Greece and Civil War England for a series of unrelated adventures culminating in the rescue of Charles II from pursuing Roundheads. Too much like a historical travelogue.

HOLMAN, FELICE, 1919– .

461   *The Future of Hooper Toote.* Illus. by Gahan Wilson. New York, Scribner, 1972. 138 p.

Hooper is different from everyone else; he doesn't walk, he "skims," floating a couple of inches above the ground. He gets in trouble with various authorities, is studied by NASA, and is pursued by *paparazzi,* which makes his life more and more difficult, until finally he decides to make his own decisions about life instead of letting himself be pushed around by everyone else. The writing, and the illustrations, are amusing, but the story would have been exactly the same without the fantasy.

HOUSMAN, LAURENCE, 1865–1959.

462   *Cotton-Wooleena.* Illus. by Robert Binks. Garden City, N.Y., Doubleday, 1967, 1974. 58 p.

Cotton-Wooleena, the fairy who lives inside the King's coronation-orb, is the real ruler of the kingdom: she smothers everything in cotton-wool, including the king's affections for his housekeeper and the ideas of the king's counselors. In the end, the king abdicates out of boredom and marries his housekeeper, and Cotton-Wooleena dies, though "in official circles her spirit survives and is immortal." An absurd but acute fairy tale.

463   *The Field of Clover: Five Fairy Tales.* Engravings by Clemence Housman. New York, Dover, 1968 (1898). 148 p.

Five disappointing fairy tales, marred by magic that saves the day too patly and by unorganic, episodic plotting.

464   *The Rat-Catcher's Daughter: a Collection of Stories.* Selected and with an afterword by Ellin Greene. Illus. by Julia Noonan. New York, Atheneum, 1974. 169 p.

A much better group of his stories than No. 463. In the title tale, the greedy Rat-Catcher sells his daughter to the good gnomes, who trick him into thinking she will turn into gold. She does, but the king's son, to whom the Rat-Catcher had wanted to give her, refuses to take her unless she becomes human again. The tales show the influence of Oscar Wilde, but their strange ambience is entirely their own.

HOWARD, JOAN, pseudonym of Patricia Gordon.

465   *The Thirteenth Is Magic.* Illus. by Adrienne Adams. New York, Lothrop, 1950. 169 p.

Ronald and Gillian, who live in a modern apartment building without a thirteenth floor, meet a magical cat one day who takes them to the floor that isn't there. After various adventures with talking wallabies, numismatists who collect fairy gold, the constellations, and the world inside a cuckoo clock, Gillian is stolen by the King of Elfland, and Childe Ronald (!) has to rescue her. Mediocre, forgettable.

HOWARD, ROBERT ERVIN, 1906–1936.

Of all the pulp adventure fantasies published before science fiction went respectable in the 1940s, Robert Howard's have worn better than anyone else's thanks to the intensity and passion with which Howard recorded his visions. His hero, Conan, the model for innumerable heroes with powerful thews, acts with enormous gusto in his barbarian world. Though Howard is endlessly inventive, he creates his effects through simplicity; every story, every character, and every location is reduced to a few all-important essentials to evoke a kind of reader participation in the tale. His stories began to be collected and reprinted fourteen years after his death. Other authors finished stories he had begun, and soon a whole new corps of Conan stories appeared, written by writers who had been fans. A fanzine was also begun by the members of the Hyborian Legion, entitled *Amra*, which contained Howard-like fiction, articles on Howard and other adventure fantasists, and reviews of new adventure fantasies. Gnome Press in the 1950s, and Lancer Books in the 1960s, reprinted or published Howard's work; the Lancer titles include most of the Gnome stories and some others previously unpublished.

From Gnome Press, New York:

466   *Conan the Conqueror: the Hyborian Age.* From the original story "The Hour of the Dragon." 1950.

467   *The Sword of Conan: the Hyborian Age.* 1952.

468   *The Coming of Conan.* 1953.

469   *King Conan.* 1953.

470   *Conan the Barbarian.* 1954.

471   HOWARD and De Camp, L. Sprague. *Tales of Conan.* 1955.

472   HOWARD, De Camp, L. Sprague, and Nyberg, Bjorn. *The Return of Conan.* 1957.

From Lancer Books, New York: 1966–69. *The Complete Conan.*

473   *Conan.*

474   HOWARD and Carter, Lin. *Conan the Freebooter.*

475   *Conan the Adventurer.*

476   HOWARD and De Camp, L. Sprague. *Conan the Warrior.*

477   HOWARD and De Camp, L. Sprague. *Conan the Usurper.*

478   HOWARD and Carter, Lin. *Conan the Conqueror.*

479   *Conan the Avenger.*

480   HOWARD and Carter, Lin. *Conan of the Isles.*

481   HOWARD and Carter, Lin. *Conan of Cimmeria.*

482   HOWARD and Carter, Lin. *Conan the Wanderer.*

All of these stories resemble one another, although Conan's wanderings across the Europe, Asia, and Africa of the prehistoric, post-Atlantean Hyborian Age take him into every possible type of culture, from primitive Norse to primitive Indian. The girls are amazingly beautiful, the gods amazingly callous, the villains amazingly villainous, and Conan amazingly strong, fast, and lucky as he leaves his mark on everyone he encounters—sort of a Lone Ranger with sex appeal and no qualms about survival as his highest priority.

483   De Camp, L. Sprague, ed. *The Conan Reader.* Baltimore, Voyager, 1968.

484   De Camp, L. Sprague, and Scithers, George, eds. *The Conan Swordbook.* Baltimore, Voyager, 1969.

485   De Camp, L. Sprague, and Scithers, George, eds. *The Conan Grimoire.* Baltimore, Voyager, 1972. 261 p.

Selected essays from *Amra.*

486   Miller, P. Schuyler, Clark, John D., and De Camp, L. Sprague. *An Informal Biography of Conan the Cimmerian. Amra,* Vol. 2. No. 4, 1959.

HUDSON, WILLIAM HENRY, 1841–1922.

487   *Green Mansions, a Romance of the Tropical Forest.* Introduction by John Galsworthy. Illus. by E. McKnight Kauffer. New York, Modern Library, 1916 (1904). x, 254 p.

Abel, a young Venezuelan, having fled to the jungles to escape his enemies, meets and falls in love with the mysterious Rima, who seems to be almost a nature-spirit. Though she loves Abel, he cannot comfort her when she realizes that her own people must all be dead; she returns to the jungle alone and is killed by the superstitious, degraded local Indians. The book is grossly melodramatic, turgid and overwritten. It is also racist; Rima's noble bird-people are white, while the Indians, who hate her because she will not allow them to supplement their meager diet by hunting in her forest, are filthy savages without a culture, in the anthropological sense, deceitful, bloodthirsty, and stupid.

488   *A Little Boy Lost.* Illus. by A. D. McCormick. New York, Knopf, 1918. 222 p.

A strange story about Martin, a little boy who lives in the Sierra Nevadas of California, who goes out to live alone in the mountains and becomes a kind of nature-spirit. The Lady of the Hills, the incarnate spirit of the Sierras, adopts him and teaches him how to live. The story is episodic and implausible, and full of gushing emotion about Nature.

HUNTER, MOLLIE, pseudonym of Maureen McIlwraith, 1922–   .

489   *The Smartest Man in Ireland.* Illus. by Charles Keeping. New York, Funk & Wagnall's, 1963. 95 p.

Several related episodes in which Patrick Kentigern Keenan tries to cheat the fairies and is always paid back in his own coin. Amusing and promising, though not first-rate.

490   *The Kelpie's Pearls.* Illus. by Joseph Cellini. New York, Funk & Wagnall's, 1964. 112 p.

Elderly Morag McLeod is a kind soul; she helps a kelpie, or water sprite, with a trapped foot and refuses a reward. She also helps a small boy named Torquil keep his wild pets in spite of his stepmother's prohibition. But Alasdair the Trapper sees the kelpie and the pearls he has given Morag, and begins to plan how to steal them. How Morag, Torquil, Alasdair, and the kelpie all get their just deserts is told by an author with considerable skill in capturing the spirit of Celtic folklore.

491   *Thomas and the Warlock.* Illus. by Joseph Cellini. New York, Funk and Wagnall's, 1967. 128 p.

Thomas catches the evil Warlock in a trap and lames him, but he escapes, bent on revenge, and kidnaps Thomas's wife Janet. Thomas finally defeats the Warlock with his smith's hammer, his skill, and a helpful fairy's rhyme. One of Hunter's best; solid, credible, and exciting.

492   *The Ferlie.* Illus. by Joseph Cellini. New York, Funk and Wagnall's, 1968. 128 p.

Hob Hazeldene is apprenticed to the hot-tempered Archie Armstrong and his virulent wife. Poor Hob finds himself between the Ferlie who wants to capture him and Archie who is exploiting him, but he finally escapes both and gets a better master. Hob's hard life and his wrongs make him Hunter's most sympathetic character in a story that shares all the virtues of its predecessor.

493   *The Walking Stones, a Story of Suspense.* Illus. by Trina Schart Hyman. New York, Harper, 1970. 143 p.

When a new dam is about to drown the magical Standing Stones, Donald must perform an ancient ritual to see the Stones walking before they disappear forever under the lake. His love for the old man who taught him the rite and his admiration for the kind forest ranger who brought the unwelcome news of the dam provided conflict and an impetus for his actions. But the plot seems forced, Donald is passive, and the adult characters are ideally wise rather than credibly real.

494   *The Haunted Mountain, a Story of Suspense.* Illus. by Laszlo Kubinyi. New York, Harper, 1972. 126 p.

McAllister offended the Sidhe, the fairies, by planting the bit of land on his farm which was traditionally theirs, so that he could marry his sweetheart. He cleverly defeats their first attacks; but when they capture him, it is faith, love, and loyalty which save him, not cleverness. The story has some humor, but on the whole it is the most successfully serious of Hunter's novels. Hunter is not a great fantasist, but she is a skillful and entertaining writer whose love for the folklore she works with is apparent in every line.

HYERS, CONRAD, 1933– .

495   *The Chickadees: a Contemporary Fable.* Illus. by Ed Piechocki. New York, Westminster, 1974. 64 p.

A pompous imitation of *Jonathan Livingston Seagull.* A bunch of chickadees "Quest" for "Eaglehood," only to find that true spirituality can be found in their ordinary lives.

HYNE, C. J. CUTLIFFE.

496   *The Lost Continent.* Introduction by Lin Carter. New York, Ballantine, 1972. 274 p.

The Governor of Yucatan, Deucalion, tries to save Atlantis from the wrath of the gods, but is powerless to overcome the curse that the wicked, selfish, bloodthirsty, irresistible Empress, Phorenice, has brought upon it. Only Deucalion and his beloved, Nais, are saved, although Atlantean culture survives in a stunted form in Egypt. There are some interesting fights, but the book is too Victorian in a grandiose, pious way.

INGELOW, JEAN, 1820–1897.

497   *Mopsa the Fairy*. Illus. by Dora Curtis and Diana Stanley. London, Dent, 1964 (1869). xii, 142 p.

Jack finds a nest of fairy babies in a hollow tree and is carried off with them to Fairyland. There he has several adventures of a minor sort. The story is disjointed and episodic; it is one of the last examples of fantasy about gauzy-winged fairies who pop out of bluebells—a literary motif that became popular through Drayton and Shakespeare, but died around the turn of the twentieth century.

INGRAM, TOM, 1924– .

498   *Garranane*. Illus. by Bill Geldart. Scarsdale, N.Y., Bradbury, 1971. 191 p.

The baugrens, evil beings without shadows, who have captured the King and Queen, invade Garranane, and are about to destroy the royal children, Kai and Flor. But Windy the armorer, his wise old Granny, and Tatto, an incompetent but amusing sorcerer, rescue the children, and together they drive their enemies out and save the King and Queen. The book begins slowly, but soon picks up its pace, and the characters are agreeable and credible. The baugrens have plausible motives and means of operation, the destruction they wreak is all too realistic, and the problems of rebuilding are not slighted for the sake of the happy ending.

499   *The Night Rider, a novel*. Jacket and frontispiece by Steve Walker. Scarsdale, N.Y., Bradbury, 1975. 176 p.

Laura finds a gold bracelet which sends her back in time into the mind of Merta, who is under a curse: she will wane with the moon. Laura's possession of the bracelet exposes her to the curse's power also, so she must overcome its debilitating effects twice—as herself and as Merta. The book is less accessible than *Garranane*, but how Laura and Merta resolve their problems makes for a suspenseful, sometimes frightening story.

IPCAR, DAHLOV, 1917– .

500   *The Warlock of Night*. New York, Viking, 1969. 159 p.

A chess story, based on a 1949 championship game: all of the characters are chess pieces, and the story is of a war between the kingdoms of Night and Daylight. The battles are rather grim, but the story is uninteresting except to chess players.

501   *The Queen of Spells*. New York, Viking, 1973. 143 p.

The story is the old Scottish ballad "Tam Lin," updated to the U.S. in the 1870s and 1880s. Tam Lin is a baron's son who was taken to the Green Land, or Elfland, by its Queen in the sixteenth century; but he is also a real farmer's grandson in the America of the 1870s, when Janet meets him for the first time and falls in love. The Queen refuses to let Tam Lin leave the Green Land without a struggle, so she puts Janet through an ordeal in which nothing is as it seems by disguising her fairy train as a traveling circus. The mixture of the old ballad and the American background is masterly and original, and the characterizations of the Queen, of Janet, and of Janet's puritanical mother and kind, rustic father are distinctive.

ISH-KISHOR, SHULAMITH.

502   *The Master of Miracle, a New Novel of the Golem*. Pictures by Arnold Lobel. New York, Harper, 1971. 108 p.

How the Jews of sixteenth-century Prague outwitted their persecutors and restored a young Jewish heiress to her coreligionists with the use of the Golem made by the holy Head Rabbi. The book is full of interesting facts, but short on literary merit.

JANSSON, TOVE, 1914– .

503   *Finn Family Moomintroll*. Translated by Elizabeth Portch. New York, Walck, 1958. 170 p.

First in a series about the charming, roly-poly moomintrolls, who sleep all winter and love good things to eat. Nothing much happens, but Jansson writes with a distinctively dry sense of humor about her jolly little creations, and younger children will enjoy the books unreservedly. Followed by seven sequels:

504   *Moominland Midwinter.* Translated by Thomas Warburton. New York, Walck, 1958. 165 p.

505   *Comet in Moominland.* Translated by Elizabeth Portch. London, Benn, 1959. 192 p.

506   *Moominsummer Madness.* Translated by Thomas Warburton. New York, Walck, 1961. 163 p.

507   *Tales from Moominvalley.* Translated by Thomas Warburton. New York, Walck, 1963. 175 p.

508   *Exploits of Moominpappa.* Translated by Thomas Warburton. New York, Walck, 1966. 156 p.

509   *Moominpappa at Sea.* Translated by Kingsley Hart. New York, Walck, 1966. 192 p.

510   *Moominvalley in November.* Translated by Kingsley Hart. London, Benn, 1971. 175 p.

JARRELL, RANDALL, 1914–1965.

511   *The Bat-Poet.* Pictures by Maurice Sendak. New York, Macmillan, 1963. 43 p.

A fable about poetry with four delightful poems on an owl, a chipmunk, a mockingbird, and a bat. The bat-poet's character is excellent—shy, sensitive, polite, and open-minded, without being the cliché of the rebellious, defiant artist; he behaves just as a bat who became a poet ought to. The self-satisfied, self-pitying mockingbird is also a memorable creation.

512   *The Animal Family.* Decorations by Maurice Sendak. New York, Pantheon, 1965. 180 p.

Another fable, this time about love, family life, and friendship, which is not as successful as the previous one. A hunter who lives alone gradually acquires a family consisting of a mermaid, a bear, a lynx, and a boy. The plot is nonexistent, but the book is written with beautiful, graceful simplicity.

JOHNSTON, THOMAS.

513   *The Fight for Arkenvald.* Illus. by Jane Walworth. Garden City, N.J., Doubleday, 1973. 150 p.

Joseph and Andrew, two schoolboys, stumble through a cave into a savage Inner World where they must kill the witch Ortrad and restore Garth, the rightful king of Arkenvald. The narrative is barbarous and the climax is spoiled by not one but two *deus-ex-machina* intrusions.

JONES, ADRIENNE, 1915– .

514   *The Mural Master*. Illus. by David Omar White. Boston, Houghton Mifflin, 1974. 248 p.

Til Pleeryn, the Mural Master, is a gnome from another world who can paint so well that the pictures come to life. He kidnaps Carrie, Digby, Leo, and Tonio to help him rescue Kreegeth, the human king of the gnomes. The writing is too complex for the story and the digressive plot relies too much on coincidence and ridiculous situations.

JONES, DIANA WYNNE, 1934– .

515   *Witch's Business*. New York, Dutton, 1974. (Originally published in England under the title *Wilkins' Tooth*). 168 p.

Frank and Jess decide to form a "magic" revenge service—a business serving revenge-seekers—but in so doing they are unknowingly competing with Biddy Iremonger, a real witch, who naturally resents their interference. Things get worse and worse until finally they are forced to attack Biddy by magic. Witty and imaginative.

516   *The Ogre Downstairs*. New York, Dutton, 1975. 191 p.

Johnny, Caspar, and Gwinny's mother has married the Ogre, a man with two sons of his own, and none of the five children can get along. When the Ogre unwittingly gives Caspar and his own son magic chemistry sets, a series of near-catastrophes ensues which help the children understand one another better. The two motifs of the book—adjustment to a new family life, and magical toys—are not new ideas, but Jones revitalizes them with verve and originality in this suspenseful and warmhearted story.

JUSTER, NORTON, 1929– .

517   *The Phantom Tollbooth*. Illus. by Jules Feiffer. New York, Random, 1961. 256 p.

How Milo, a bored child who had "nothing to do," went to Dictionopolis and Digitopolis to rescue the Princesses Rhyme and Reason. The book is full of clever, witty word play and has amusing illustrations, but the plot lacks action.

518   *Alberic the Wise and Other Journeys.* Pictures by Domenico Gnoli. New York, Pantheon, 1965. 68 p.

Three inconclusive, overwritten, and dull short stories, in which Alberic, Claude, and two kings learn lessons very different from what they expected.

KENDALL, CAROL, 1917– .

519   *The Gammage Cup.* Illus. by Erik Blegvad. New York, Harcourt, 1959. 221 p.

The Minnipins, who live in the Land Between the Mountains, live lives of dull conformity, ruled by a family descended from the only explorer ever to leave the Land. What few free spirits exist among the Minnipins are forced to leave. It turns out to be a good thing they did, for when an invasion threatens the Minnipins' peaceful lives, the outcasts, especially Muggles, who had wanted to be accepted but wasn't, are the only ones prepared. How Muggles overcomes her fears, the enemies are defeated, and the stuffy rulers of the Minnipins deflated, concludes this excellent miniature-heroic fantasy. Followed by

520   *The Whisper of Glocken.* Illus. by Imero Gobbato. New York, Harcourt, 1965. 256 p.

Five "New Heroes," inspired by Muggles, save the Minnipins from evil foreign invaders, in a story which concentrates on courage and endurance rather than on non-conformity. Not as good as *The Gammage Cup*, but passable.

KINGSLEY, CHARLES, 1819–1875.

521   *The Water-Babies, a Fairy-tale for a Land-baby.* Illus. by Rosalie K. Fry. London, Dent, 1957 (1863).

Tom, a maltreated, much-abused chimney sweep, drowns in a stream and becomes a water-baby, a sort of sprite who learns how to be good so that he may eventually go to Heaven. Ellie, a rich girl, always remembers Tom, and when she later has an accident and dies she too goes to live with the water-babies. Kingsley's evangelical leanings overcame his better judgment in this didactic, moralistic, pompous, and diffuse story.

522   Pope-Hennessey, Una. *Canon Charles Kingsley, a biography*. Millwood, N.Y., Kraus Reprints, 1973 (1948).

KIPLING, RUDYARD, 1865–1936.

523   *The Jungle Book*. Illus. by William Dempster. Chicago, Children's Press, 1968. 217 p.

An anthology containing the two *Jungle Books*, "Rikki-Tikki-Tavi," "The Elephant Boy," and "The Miracle of Purun Bhagat." The stories of Mowgli, brought up in the jungles of India by wise and ferocious animals, are classics, in spite of Kipling's faintly racist and Social-Darwinist ideas.

524   *Just-So Stories*. Garden City, N.Y., Doubleday, 1948 (1897–1902). 249 p.

George Orwell once observed that Kipling is the only modern author who has given as many phrases to the English language as Shakespeare, and no one could forget the Elephant's Child with his " 'satiable curiosity," the Camel who deserved his Humph, or the Rhinoceros whose skin nearly killed him with itching. Somehow Kipling can get away with a condescending tone that in any other author would be unbearable.

525   *Puck of Pook's Hill*. Illus. by Arthur Rackham. New York, Dover, 1968 (1906). 277 p.

Dan and Una, playing at A *Midsummer Night's Dream* at the foot of Pook's Hill in Sussex, attract Puck, who befriends them and calls up the spirits of various people who have lived around the Hill during the history of England: two Roman soldiers; Weland, the Smith of the Gods; Sir Richard Dalyngridge after the battle of Hastings; and many others. The book is steeped in the lore of the Sussex countryside. Followed by

526   *Rewards and Fairies*. Garden City, N.Y., Doubleday & Page, 1910. xix, 344 p.

More of the same, including the wonderful story of stingy Henry VII devising ways to increase thrift in government.

527   Charles, Cecil. *Rudyard Kipling, His Life and Works*. Folcroft, PA., Folcroft Library Editions, 1973.

528   Dobree, Bonamy. *Rudyard Kipling, Realist and Fabulist*. London, Oxford University Press, 1967. x, 244 p.

529   Stewart, John Innes Mackintosh. *Rudyard Kipling*. New York, Dodd, Mead, 1966. vi, 245 p.

530   Sutcliff, Rosemary. *Rudyard Kipling*. New York, Walck, 1961. 61 p.

A study of Kipling's children's books by a prominent historical novelist who considers him her chief inspiration.

KURLAND, MICHAEL.

531   *The Unicorn Girl.* New York, Pyramid, 1969. 159 p.

Sequel to Chester Anderson's *The Butterfly Kid.* Chester and Michael, with two beautiful girls from a magic circus, keep getting BLIPped from world to world because someone in some unknown world dislikes all the others and is trying to destroy them. Their problems are solved by a magician from yet another book, Randall Garrett's *Too Many Magicians* (q.v.), who sends them all back to their own universes.

KURTZ, KATHERINE, 1944– .

532   *Deryni Rising.* Introduction by Lin Carter. New York, Ballantine, 1970. 271 p.

The Deryni, a race with occult powers who once ruled the land of Gwynedd, have been outlawed as witches and sorcerers for two centuries. An evil Deryni sorceress, Charissa, tries to destroy the ruling house of Gwynedd and take over the kingdom. She succeeds in assassinating King Brion, but his teenage son Kelson proves himself a match for her, with the help of his good Deryni cousin Duke Alaric Morgan. Followed by

533   *Deryni Checkmate.* Introduction by Lin Carter. New York, Ballantine, 1972. xiii, 302 p.

The clergy of Gwynedd, determined to destroy Deryni influence, begin a campaign to trump up charges of treason against Alaric Morgan. The mysterious Deryni saint, Camber of Culdi, reappears out of the past to aid him, however. Followed by

534   *High Deryni.* Introduction by Lin Carter. New York, Ballantine, 1973. 369 p.

The conflict between the clergy and the good Deryni of Gwynedd has reached the state of civil war when an evil Deryni king, Wencit of Torenth, invades, forcing the armies of Gwynedd to unite against him.

Kurtz's plots are tight and credible, and the concept of "Deryniness" as a mutation in an otherwise normal human is fascinating and original; but her characters are wooden and her style no better than competent.

KUTTNER, HENRY, 1914–1958.

535   *The Mask of Circe*. Illus. by Alicia Austin. New York, Ace, 1948.
Mediocre adventure fantasy in which a modern man is pulled through time to emerge in barbaric ancient Greece as Jason the Argonaut, the beloved of the witch-priestess Medea.

LA MOTTE FOUQUÉ, FRIEDRICH DE, 1777–1843.

436   *Undine*. Translated by W. L. Courtney. Illus. by Arthur Rackham. London, William Heinemann, 1908 (1811). 136 p.
Undine, a water-sprite, marries a knight, Huldbrand, an action which provides her with a soul and begins her sufferings. When Huldbrand betrays her, Undine is forced by her fairy nature to kill him although she still loves him. This is not a fantasy, but a *Kunstmärchen* with an illogically constructed and motivated plot.

LAMPMAN, EVELYN SIBLEY, 1907– .

537   *The Shy Stegosaurus of Cricket Creek*. Illus. by Robert Buel. Garden City, N.Y., Doubleday, 1955. 220 p.
Joey and Joan, whose widowed mother is having trouble maintaining their Arizona ranch with her meager funds, meet George, a friendly stegosaurus, in the desert. With his help they catch a thief, find an Eohippus fossil for their friend the Professor, and make enough money to live happily ever after. Followed by
538   *The Shy Stegosaurus of Indian Springs*. Illus. by Paul Galdone. Garden City, N.Y., Doubleday, 1962. 232 p.
George, Joey, and Joan help a Klickitat Indian boy and his aged grandfather, a shaman. The friendly dinosaur, unfortunately, seems like an obtrusion on a story with so much genuine love and concern for the maltreated American Indian. The contrast between the rather silly dinosaur fantasy and the Indians' problems is too great.

LANG, ANDREW, 1844–1912.

539   *Prince Prigio and Prince Ricardo*. Illus. with four colour plates and line-drawings in the text by D. J. Watkins-Pitchford. Introduction

by Roger Lancelyn Green. London, Dent, 1961 (1889, 1893). xvii, 171 p.

Prince Prigio, to whom a fairy gave the christening gift of being too intelligent, is disliked by everyone, including his parents, because he can never resist telling everyone everything he knows (and how little they know, and how he would have done things better than they). Of course, he does not believe in magic—too unscientific—until he has sent his brothers to their deaths with his "cleverness," and everyone leaves the palace to get away from him. How Prigio uses his intelligence in the right way at last, kills the Dragon and the Remora, and resurrects his brothers is the subject of this playful fantasy by the great folklorist, subtitled The Chronicles of Pantouflia. *Ricardo* is a sequel.

540　　Green, Roger Lancelyn. *Andrew Lang*. New York, Walck, 1962. 84 p.

See also Haggard, Sir Henry Rider and Lang, Andrew.

LANGTON, JANE, 1922– .

541　　*The Diamond in the Window*. Illus. by Erik Blegvad. New York, Harper, 1962. 242 p.

Eleanor and Eddy follow their long-lost aunt and uncle, Nora and Ned, through a magic treasure hunt which was invented by Prince Krishna, their Aunt Lily's fiancé, who disappeared at the same time as Ned and Nora. Not only do they find all three, breaking the evil power of the Prince's wicked uncle, but they restore their philosopher-uncle Freddy to sanity and prevent the stuffy bank president from foreclosing the mortgage on their house. The fantasy is an extremely vivid and surprisingly believable blending of Indian magic and Transcendentalist philosophy, set in Concord, Massachusetts, and has a strong moral bent, although it is not didactically moralistic. Followed by

542　　*The Swing in the Summerhouse*. Pictures by Erik Blegvad. New York, Harper, 1967. 185 p.

543　　*The Astonishing Stereoscope*. Illus. by Erik Blegvad. New York, Harper, 1971. 240 p.

Two more sets of adventures for Eleanor and Eddy, closely resembling those in *The Diamond in the Window,* in which Prince Krishna arranges for them to experience magic adventures with a moral purpose. Swinging on the summerhouse swing carries them into one set; looking through the old stereoscope enables them to enter the others. Characters, plot, and invention are as good as in the first book, but the moralistic tone is much more pronounced, which detracts from the fantasy.

LANIER, STERLING E.

544   *The War for the Lot, a Tale of Fantasy and Terror.* Illus. by Robert Baumgartner. Chicago, Follett, 1969. 256 p.
The animals of the Lot, a small remnant of forested woodland on the outskirts of a city, enlist the help of a small boy in thwarting an invasion of evil rats from the city dumps. The boy learns to communicate with the forest animals and persuades a bear to join in the struggle.

LAUBENTHAL, SANDERS ANNE.

545   *Excalibur.* Introduction by Lin Carter. New York, Ballantine, 1973. 236 p.
A young archaeologist, who is the secret Pendragon of Britain, comes to Mobile, Alabama, to search for Excalibur in the ruins of Prince Madoc's eleventh-century expedition. This brings him into conflict with Arthur's half-sisters, the priestess Morgan le Fay and the witch Morgause, who seek the sword for their own purposes. Though Laubenthal's borrowings from Tolkien, Lewis, and Williams are often naive and clumsy, the book's plot is complex and coherent, and she combines many disparate fantasy elements into a pleasing, credible whole.

LAWRENCE, ANN.

546   *The Half Brothers.* New York, Walck, 1973. 172 p.
Each of the four princes fifteen-year-old Duchess Ambra meets impresses her, and she occupies herself with all their interests in turn, until she realizes that she has neglected her own real interests trying to please them. Excellent writing and a humorous outlook lend charm and originality to this novel.
547   *Tom Ass or the Second Gift.* Illus. by Mila Lazarevich. New York, Walck, 1973. 133 p.
Tom gets two gifts from an elf-woman: whatever he does at dawn, he will do all day—very handy if he is counting money—and he will be whatever his future wife chooses to make of him. Jennifer subsequently turns him into a donkey by accident, but he becomes a wise man when he realizes her true worth. A delightfully original fairy tale

with a heroine who should be celebrated by anyone who has ever been bored by insipid princesses and tiresome goosegirls.

LAWSON, JOHN.

548   *You Better Come Home With Me.* Illus. by Arnold Spilka. New York, Crowell, 1966. 125 p.

The title of this fantasy is an Appalachian phrase meaning "goodbye." When the Scarecrow says it to the strange Boy who has arrived, the Boy takes it literally and does go home with him. He becomes acquainted with many other local characters: Mr. Fox, a fox in a Norfolk jacket; a witch; the Snowman; and an Old Man living on a moldering farm, who may be the Boy's grandfather. The story is poetically written, with lyrical descriptions of nature, but the plot resolution is confusing and ambiguous.

549   *The Spring Rider.* New York, Crowell, 1968. 147 p.

The Spring Rider is the ghost of Abraham Lincoln who appears every spring to take back the ghosts of Civil War soldiers lingering near an Appalachian battle site. Jacob, a boy living on the farm where the battle was fought, meets the gallant Rebel Colonel Ashby and goes off to ride with him, scouting for Stonewall Jackson, while his sister Gray falls in love with Hannibal, a Union soldier. The past and present mix and blend until the children can hardly tell the difference. Individual and original, with a mood of surrealistic, dreamy, introspective sadness.

LAWSON, ROBERT, 1892–1957.

550   *Ben and Me.* Illus. by the author. Boston, Little, Brown, 1939. 113 p.

The story of Ben Franklin, as told by his faithful mouse Amos, the real brains of the team. Ben is an inept bungler who expends most of his energy flirting with young ladies, who for some unfathomable reason flock around him like ants at a picnic; Amos must not only invent the Franklin stove, the lightning rod, and the Constitution, but must get Ben out of the ridiculous mishaps he gets himself into. The tongue-in-cheek humor of the story is perfectly matched by the clever, absurd illustrations.

551   *I Discover Columbus.* Illus. by the author. Boston, Little, Brown, 1941. xii, 113 p.

Aurelio, a Caribbean parrot, is blown to Spain by a storm, where he meets Columbus, arranges his meeting with grouchy Ferdinand and gracious Isabella, and cozens the hesitant Admiral onto the Santa Maria, where he immediately falls prey to seasickness. The story and the characters are both cliché-ridden; the joke of *Ben and Me* goes stale very quickly. The character of Don Issachar is an inexcusable example of racist stereotyping.

552   *Rabbit Hill.* Illus. by the author. New York, Viking, 1944. 128 p.

A pleasant, slight story for younger children, this is the tale of how the New Folks in the Big House befriended the animals and saved Little Georgie's life when the young rabbit was hit by a car. The illustrations are excellent—clear, graceful, and amusing—and the characters' New England speech scrupulously accurate. Followed by

553   *The Tough Winter.* Illus. by the author. New York, Viking, 1954. 218 p.

The Folks leave Rabbit Hill to go to Kentucky for the winter; with city caretakers in charge and the worst weather in years, the animals have a most difficult time. The best part of the story is Uncle Analdas's trip to Kentucky—he thinks he has reached the paradisal Bluegrass country, when actually he has only gone half a mile and stumbled into a barn full of hay. Again, the story is slight but engaging.

554   *The Fabulous Flight.* Illus. by the author. Boston, Little, Brown, 1949. 152 p.

Peter's "sacro-pitulian-phalangic gland" begins working backwards as the result of a fall, so Peter shrinks as he gets older, until at thirteen he is only four inches high. Peter meets a gull, Gus, on whose back he flies to save the world from a mad scientist. When it is not militaristic and chauvinistic, the story is silly.

555   *Robbut, a Tale of Tails.* Illus. by the author. New York, Viking, 1949. 94 p.

Another story in the vein of *Rabbit Hill*, though not a sequel. Robbut helps an elf escape from a trap, and in return the little man gives him the new tail he wanted. He first tries a cat's tail, but it gets all wet and covered with burrs; then a garter snake's, but even his mother thinks he must be part rat; then a fox's, which gets him chased by a pack of hounds. Finally he realizes he is better off with his own tail after all. Short and sweet.

556   *Mr. Revere and I.* Illus. by the author. Boston, Little, Brown, 1953. 152 p.

Another tongue-in-cheek look at American history, this one told by Paul Revere's horse, an ex-British trooper named Scheherazade. Perhaps because the story deals with the Revolution, where *Ben and Me* concentrated on Ben's inventions, it is rather didactic and lacks the earlier book's sly humor.

557   *Captain Kidd's Cat*. Illus. by the author. Boston, Little, Brown, 1956. 152 p.

By far the weakest of Lawson's American-history parodies, this book tells the story of a pirate who didn't want to be one but was henpecked into it.

558   *Robert Lawson, Illustrator: a selection of his characteristic illustrations*. With an introduction and comment by Helen L. Jones. Boston, Little, Brown, 1972. 120 p.

Includes a biographical sketch (pp. 109–113) and a bibliography of books Lawson illustrated.

LEE, TANITH, 1947– .

559   *The Dragon Hoard*. Illus. by Graham Oakley. New York, Farrar, 1971. 162 p.

King Minus forgets to ask his cousin, the enchantress Maligna, to the birthday feast for Prince Jasleth and Princess Goodness. As a result, Jasleth must spend an hour every day in the form of a raven, while Goodness becomes just as silly as she is good, which is very silly indeed. A very funny fairy tale for both adults and children.

560   *The Birthgrave*. New York, DAW Books, 1975. 408 p.

A nameless woman, cursed with demonic ugliness, is the only survivor of a superhuman race that used its powers to exploit and murder. Since she is more than human, she can neither die nor be killed. Unable to escape the curse of her hideousness, she becomes the concubine of a bandit, then the unwilling goddess-wife of a sorcerer, and starts a furious and bloody war among the Cities of an imitative human culture. In spite of an unfortunate ending that is anti-climactic enough to be funny, *The Birthgrave* is a superb achievement of adventure fantasy, so good that it escapes the limitations of the form and reaches heroic stature.

LE GUIN, URSULA KROEBER, 1929– .

561   *A Wizard of Earthsea*. Drawings by Ruth Robbins. Berkeley, Parnassus, 1968. 205 p.

Sparrowhawk, whose true name is Ged, a boy of immense natural powers of magic, goes to the school for wizards on the Isle of Roke. There, his hot temper and his conflict with another boy cause him to upset the Balance of Nature out of bravado, so that he is attacked by a hideous, nameless thing from the shadows of death. Through numerous subsequent adventures he flees from the Shadow-thing, yet cannot escape it and find peace. Finally he realizes that the only way to escape it is to pursue it, find it, and accept it as the shadow of himself. The book is based on American Indian and Far Eastern religious ideas, but, while deeply philosophical, is tightly plotted with exciting action, and set in a lovingly fashioned world. Followed by

562   *The Tombs of Atuan*. Illus. by Gail Garraty. New York, Atheneum, 1971. 163 p.

Ged, searching for the Ring of Erreth-Akbe in the forbidden Tombs of Atuan, is discovered by the high priestess Arha, "The Eaten One," a young girl, who for reasons of her own does not reveal her discovery to her fellow priestesses. With Ged's help, she rejects the service of her evil gods and learns her own true name for the first time. The book concentrates on Arha's journey from hatred and suspicion to freedom and is a delicate portrait of a young woman's developing personality. Followed by

563   *The Farthest Shore*. Illus. by Gail Garraty. New York, Atheneum, 1972. 223 p.

Ged, now Archmage of all Earthsea, and Arren, a young prince, journey together to seek the source of a mysterious force which is draining magical ability from men's minds. In the land of the dead, Ged heals the breach in the Balance which an evil mage has opened by his refusal to accept death, and Arren proves himself worthy to restore the kingship of Earthsea, to which he is heir. This final volume of the Earthsea trilogy is the most serious, moving, and intense of the three books. The episodes of the Dyer of Lorbanery, the Children of the Open Sea, and the journey through the world of the dead are especially memorable.

564   *The Lathe of Heaven*. New York, Scribner, 1971. 184 p.

A science fantasy set in the near future. George Orr is sent to a psychologist, Dr. Haber, who is skeptical when George tells him that his dreams can change reality, but begins to manipulate the dreams when George proves his claim is true. Haber tries to improve the world, which is grossly overpopulated and engaged in vicious wars, but every change he forces on George backfires, because Haber is essentially power-hungry and out of touch with reality. Based on studies of sleep and dreaming, the book is a wry, profound essay on the need for balance and wholeness and is original, well-developed, and fascinating.

LEIBER, FRITZ, 1910– .

565   *Conjure Wife.* New York, Award Books, 1968 (1953). 188 p.
    Though they keep it a dark secret from men, women still practice real witchcraft. A man interrupts the serene course of his college career and renders himself and his wife helpless against their enemies when he forces her to give witchery up. Well-written, but lightweight.
566   *Swords and Deviltry.* New York, Ace, 1970.
567   *Swords Against Death.* New York, Ace, 1970.
568   *Swords in the Mist.* New York, Ace, 1968.
569   *Swords Against Wizardry.* New York, Ace, 1968.
570   *The Swords of Lankhmar.* New York, Ace, 1968. 224 p.
    Collected short stories and one novel (No. 570) about the adventures of two mercenary soldiers in Lankhmar, a country in the barbaric world of Nehwon ("No-when"). Fahfrd is a gigantic blond berserker from some cold northern clime; his partner, the Grey Mouser, is a quiet little fellow even quicker with a stiletto than with a broadsword. These adventure fantasies are distinguished by a sophisticated style and an excellent sense of humor. The internal chronology is in the order given.

LEITCII, PATRICIA.

571   *The Black Loch.* Illus. by Janet Duchesne. New York, Funk and Wagnall's, 1968. 160 p.
    Kay, one of six cousins visiting the family home in Scotland, learns that she has inherited the guardianship of a magical Water Horse, a gigantic creature living at the bottom of the Black Loch. When one of the cousins sells the secret of the Horse to an animal-catcher, Kay and the rest of the family must prevent him from getting to it. The plot is confusing and focuses more on the suspenseful chase than on the fantasy.

L'ENGLE, MADELEINE, 1918– .

572   *A Wrinkle in Time.* New York, Farrar, 1962. 211 p.
    Meg Murry's father, a government scientist, has been missing for a long time, captured by a frightful, evil being called IT. Meg, her favorite brother Charles Wallace, and their friend Calvin embark on a fantastic journey through space to rescue Dr. Murry, aided by the

angels Mrs. Who, Mrs. Which, and Mrs. Whatsit. When all else fails, Meg must invoke the power of love to set Dr. Murry free. The science-fiction trappings of travel to alien planets, scientific experiments, and a fourth-dimension time warp fit in well with the fantasy. Followed by

573   A *Wind in the Door.* New York, Farrar, 1973. 211 p.

Meg, aided by the cherub Proginoskes, must find a way to save Charles Wallace from dying of a strange disease caused by a pervasive evil in both the miniature universe of his body and the greater universe without. To do this she undergoes a series of moral tests, but since every one of these tests is rigged—with other characters shouting advice and moral support at Meg, and everything labeled GOOD or EVIL so she will know which to choose—it is impossible to care whether Meg makes the right choice or not. Since there is no real risk that things will go wrong, there is no story.

LEVIN, BETTY.

574   *The Sword of Culann.* New York, Macmillan, 1973. 280 p.

Claudia and Evan stumble into the world of Bronze Age Ireland and the story of Cuchulain, where they become servants in the camp of Queen Maeve. They are primarily spectators of the action, although Claudia helps Cuchulain's master, Fergus, and is saved from becoming a human sacrifice. The description of the physical discomforts of the primitive Irish culture is excellent. Followed by

575   A *Griffon's Nest.* New York, Macmillan, 1975.

Claudia and Evan become the servants of an unpleasant, elderly Irish princess in tenth-century Orkney and see the great battle between Brian Boru and the Vikings. The story is confusing, and the children's presence is both unmotivated and unnecessary.

LEVITIN, SONIA.

576   *Jason and the Money Tree.* Illus. by Pat Grant Porter. New York, Harcourt, 1974. 121 p.

Jason is worried about money because his father is going to law school at night, so when his grandfather wills him a tree that grows ten-dollar bills he is delighted. But he soon finds that the money is more trouble than it is worth, what with the tax laws, fearing that he will be accused of robbery, and watering the tree in secret. A mild little story, with some amusing new twists on an old idea.

LEWIS, CLIVE STAPLES, 1898–1963.

577   *Out of the Silent Planet.* New York, Macmillan, 1938. 174 p.

The first book of Lewis's "space" or "Perelandra" trilogy. The philologist Ransom is kidnapped by the scientist Weston and the wealthy dilettante Devine and carried off by them to Mars, where (they think) he will be sacrificed to some native god. On Mars, or Malacandra, Ransom escapes and goes to live with the gentle *hrossa*, one of three races on the planet, and gradually realizes that Weston and Devine had misled him. Then Oyarsa, the tutelary angel ruling the planet, sends for him, and in a climactic scene he must interpret a conversation between Oyarsa and Weston, whose crazy, grandiose, "scientific" dreams of expansion and conquest receive a rude setback. Ransom himself realizes that Maleldil, the deity whom Oyarsa serves, is the God of Christianity. The theology that forms the story's base is not obtrusive, and Lewis's powers of imagination were never better expressed. Followed by

578   *Perelandra.* New York, Macmillan, 1944. 222 p.

Ransom is sent by God to Venus, or Perelandra, to prevent Weston, who has been possessed by Satan, from tempting the Eve of that planet, the Green Lady. Once there, he finds that mere argument is not enough and finally fights Weston to the death. The theology is only too obtrusive in this book, since all the action depends on Ransom's and Weston's arguments; but the background of the story is lovely: the warm, sweet-scented seas, the floating islands, the golden sky, and the mysterious caves of Perelandra. Followed by

579   *That Hideous Strength.* New York, Macmillan, 1946. 382 p.

A young couple, Jane and Mark Studdock, find themselves at the center of a struggle between the forces of good, represented by Ransom and his few friends, and the forces of evil, represented by a scientific institute with the ironic initials N.I.C.E. Jane's discovery that she is clairvoyant sets in motion a plot which is resolved by the reappearance of Merlin the enchanter and the eventual destruction of the city and university of Edgestow. This book was Lewis's only attempt to write a novel in the style of Charles Williams, and, while the Arthurian, Perelandrian, and Christian strands of fantasy in it are fully integrated, the novel is not a success, in spite of Lewis's gratifying, fluent style. His patronizing attitude toward women in general and Jane in particular is especially offensive.

580   *The Lion, the Witch, and the Wardrobe.* Illus. by Pauline

Baynes. New York, Macmillan, 1950. 154 p.

Peter, Susan, Edmund, and Lucy get into Narnia through a magic wardrobe and are immediately caught up in the struggle between the evil White Witch and the good Aslan the Lion. Aslan dies and is resurrected to save Edmund, and the children become kings and queens of Narnia. After many long and happy years, the children return to England to find that no time has passed since they left. Followed by

581   *Prince Caspian, the Return to Narnia.* Illus. by Pauline Baynes. New York, Macmillan, 1951. 186 p.

The children return to Narnia a year later. Hundreds of years have passed there, and they join with Aslan in restoring the rightful king, Caspian the Tenth, who wants to restore the rights of the non-human creatures of Narnia—Talking Animals, dryads, fauns, unicorns, centaurs, giants, and dwarfs. To do so, they must overcome both treachery in Caspian's own ranks and his wicked, usurping uncle Miraz. Followed by

582   *The Voyage of the "Dawn Treader."* Illus. by Pauline Baynes. New York, Macmillan, 1952. 210 p.

Edmund, Lucy, and their disagreeable cousin Eustace return to Narnia and join Caspian on a voyage to the Eastern End of the world. At first, Eustace is an unmitigated nuisance, but after a spell of being turned into a dragon he begins to reform. Caspian locates all of the seven noble lords he is seeking, finds a wife in the Star Ramandu's daughter, and returns home, while the three children go through the end of the world back to England. Followed by

583   *The Silver Chair.* Illus. by Pauline Baynes. New York, Macmillan, 1953. 208 p.

Eustace and his friend Jill, escaping from bullies at their badly run experimental school, go through a door in the wall to Narnia, where Aslan sends them on a quest for Caspian's son Rilian. Many years have gone by in Narnia during the few weeks Eustace has been at home, and Rilian has been missing for a decade. After a narrow escape from man-eating giants, the children and Puddleglum, a Marsh-wiggle, find Rilian in Underland, where an evil witch is holding him captive. Together they defeat the witch, thwart her planned invasion of Narnia, and rescue the Prince. Followed by

584   *The Horse and His Boy.* Illus. by Pauline Baynes. New York, Macmillan, 1954. 191 p.

Set during the reign of Peter, Susan, Edmund, and Lucy, in the great southern empire of Calormen. Shasta, who has always thought himself the son of a poor Calormene fisherman, learns that he is actually a foundling and determines to escape to the North with a Narnian Talking Horse, Bree. On the way, they meet a Calormene aristocrat, Aravis, and her Talking Mare Hwin, and join forces. While they are passing through the capital city, Tashbaan, they learn of a plot by the hot-tempered Prince Rabadash to invade Narnia, carry off Queen Susan, and conquer Narnia's southern neighbor, Archenland. But after a race across the great desert, they manage to warn the Archenlanders in time, and Shasta learns that he is the lost prince of Archenland. Followed by

585   *The Magician's Nephew.* Illus. by Pauline Baynes. New York, Macmillan, 1955. 167 p.

The beginning of Narnia. The magician is Digory's Uncle Andrew, who sends Digory and Polly via magic ring to another world. They soon realize that this place is not a "world" at all, but a sort of ante-chamber to the worlds, and they begin to explore. But in a dying world they encounter a fearsome witch who forces them to take her back to London, where she causes so much trouble that they must get rid of her. Unfortunately, they not only pick the wrong world to return her to, but they also drag along Uncle Andrew. The new world is Narnia, just being created, and since Digory has brought an evil into it, Aslan sends him on a quest to protect it. Followed by

586   *The Last Battle.* Illus. by Pauline Baynes. New York, Macmillan, 1956. 184 p.

Tirian, the last king of Narnia, is faced with an invasion of Calormenes, who are aided by a wicked Talking Ape who has disguised a Donkey as Aslan. Eustace and Jill return to help him, but their task is heartbreakingly difficult, as the false Aslan has an iron grip on the good Narnians. During a fearful battle, Tirian and the children enter a darkened stable, which they find is the gateway to a beautiful country. There they meet Digory, Polly, Peter, Edmund, and Lucy, who have been magically transported there from England, and many other friends whom they thought were dead. Finally, they realize that they *are* dead, and are now in Heaven, and Aslan comes and conducts the Last Judgment of Narnia.

Although every story in this series is a reworking in Narnian terms of some aspect of Christian theology, the seven Chronicles of Narnia are among the freshest and most enchanting of fantasies, because they are an utterly satisfying expression of Lewis's imagination. Narnia itself, with its cool green glades, its castles and galleons, its magical blending of English and Mediterranean mythology, its grumpy Marsh-wiggles, gallant Talking Mice, graceful dryads, busy dwarfs, and child Kings and Queens, comes alive despite any flaws in the stories, because Lewis makes it a real place.

587   Gibb, Jocelyn. *Light on C. S. Lewis.* New York, Harcourt, 1966. 160 p.

588   Gilbert, Douglas, and Kilby, Clyde S. *C. S. Lewis: Images of His World*. Grand Rapids, Mich., Eerdmans, 1970. 192 p.

589   Green, Roger Lancelyn. *Tellers of Tales*. Leicester, Edmund Ward, 1946. 288 p.

590   Green, Roger Lancelyn, and Hooper, Walter. *C. S. Lewis, a Biography*. New York, Harcourt, 1974. 320 p.

A standard biography by two of Lewis's closest friends, which is an excellent introduction to Lewis for those with little previous acquaintance with his work. It does not, however, provide any new perspective on him; those who have already read a great deal about him will find it disappointing.

591   Keefe, Carolyn, ed. *C. S. Lewis: Speaker and Teacher*. Foreword by Thomas Howard. Grand Rapids, Mich., Zondervan, 1971. 144 p.

592   Kreeft, Peter. *C. S. Lewis, a Critical Essay*. Grand Rapids, Mich., Eerdmans, 1969. 48 p.

593   *Letters of C. S. Lewis*. Ed. by W. H. Lewis. New York, Harcourt, 1966. 308 p.

594   *Surprised by Joy: the Shape of My Early Life*. New York, Harcourt, 1955. ix, 238 p.

His spiritual autobiography.

595   White, William Luther. *The Image of Man in C. S. Lewis*. Nashville, Abingdon, 1969. 239 p.

596   Fowler, Helen. "C. S. Lewis: Sputnik or Dinosaur?" *Approach*, No. 32 (Summer 1959), pp. 8–14.

597   Reddy, Albert F. "The Else Unspeakable: an Introduction to the Fiction of C. S. Lewis." *Dissertation Abstracts Index*, Vol. 33 No. 6 (December 1972), p. 2949A.

598   Spacks, Patricia Meyer. "The Myth-Maker's Dilemma: Three Novels by C. S. Lewis." *Discourse*, Vol. 2 No. 4 (October 1959), pp. 234–243.

599   Fuller, Edmund. *Books With Men Behind Them*. New York, Random, 1962. 241 p.

Essays: "The Christian Spaceman: C. S. Lewis," pp. 143–168; "The Lord of the Hobbits: J. R. R. Tolkien," pp. 169–196; "Many Dimensions: The Images of Charles Williams," pp. 197–234.

600   Hillegas, Mark R., ed. *Shadows of Imagination: the fantasies of C. S. Lewis, J. R. R. Tolkien, and Charles Williams*. Carbondale, Ill., Southern Illinois University Press, 1969. xix, 170 p.

601   Moorman, Charles. *Arthurian Triptych: Mythic Materials in Charles Williams, C. S. Lewis, and T. S. Eliot*. Berkeley, University of California Press, 1960. xii, 163 p.

601.1   Purtill, Richard. *Lord of the Elves and Eldils: Fantasy and*

Philosophy in C. S. Lewis and J. R. R. Tolkien. Grand Rapids, Mich., Zondervan, 1974. 216 p.

602   Reilly, Robert J. *Romantic Religion: a Study of Barfield, Lewis, Williams, and Tolkien.* Athens, Ga., University of Georgia Press, 1971. x, 249 p.

603   Irwin, W. R. "There and Back Again: the Romances of Williams, Lewis, and Tolkien." *Sewanee Review,* Vol. 69 No. 4 (Autumn 1961), pp. 566–578.

604   Sale, Roger. "England's Parnassus: C. S. Lewis, Charles Williams, and J. R. R. Tolkien." *Hudson Review,* Vol. 17 No. 2 (Summer 1964), pp. 203–225.

See also No. 260 above.

LEWIS, HILDA, 1896–1974.

605   *The Ship That Flew.* Illus. by Nora Lavrin. New York, Criterion, 1958 (1939). 246 p.

Four English children buy a magic toy ship with all the money they have "and a bit over." It is Skidbladnir, the flying ship of the Norse god Frey, which can be folded up and put into a pocket, upon which they travel through time and space. Their happiest adventure brings the Norman child Matilda home with them for a week's visit. But finally the ship must go back to the odd little shop where they first bought it, where they not only get back all their money, but also receive their hearts' desire. Light, pleasant, enjoyable.

LINDSAY, DAVID, 1876–1945.

606   *A Voyage to Arcturus.* Introduction by Loren Eiseley. New York, Ballantine, 1968 (1920). 287 p.

A man named Maskull meets two strange persons, Krag and Nightspore, who persuade him to go with them to the distant planet Tormance which revolves around the double star Arcturus. There, he embarks on a spiritual voyage through an incomprehensible, chimerical landscape in which nothing is certain and everything is possible. In the end Maskull dies and is reborn—as Nightspore. Meaning in Lindsay's weird odyssey is ambiguous and elusive, but its alien beauty and passionate intensity make it unforgettable.

607   Pick, John Barclay, *et al. The Strange Genius of David Lindsay.* London, John Baker, 1970. viii, 183 p.

LITTLE, JANE.

608   *Sneaker Hill.* Drawings by Nancy Grossman. New York, Atheneum, 1967. 183 p.

When Susan goes to visit her Aunt Miranda, she finds that her aunt's latest craze is witchcraft, and Susan and her cousin Matthew have to help Miranda out when she must suddenly take her "witch tests" unprepared.

609   *The Philosopher's Stone.* Illus. by Robin Hall. New York, Atheneum, 1971. 123 p.

The wizard Nyvrem's liege lord, Sir Egbert Sauvepeut, is in financial difficulties, so Nyvrem travels from the twelfth century to the twentieth in search of the Stone. But his signals cross, and the Stone's unwitting owner, Stephen, is inadvertently transported back to the wizard's time.

LIVELY, PENELOPE, 1933– .

610   *Astercote.* New York, Dutton, 1970. 153 p.

Two children living in an English country town decide to try to help a half-mad man they meet in the ruins of a nearby medieval village, which was depopulated in the Black Plague. A religious relic has disappeared, and as the effects of its loss begin to be felt in the modern town, the children become more and more determined to get it back. The story is obscure in places, but the characters are strong, and the book shows considerable promise.

611   *The Wild Hunt of the Ghost Hounds.* New York, Dutton, 1971. 141 p. (Originally published in England under the title *The Wild Hunt of Hagworthy*).

A young girl visiting a West Country village befriends a lonely, unpopular, timid boy. The local vicar is trying to revive an ancient pagan hunting dance as "local color" which he hopes will attract tourists to the village fair. Instead, the dance unlooses vicious passions in the participants, who subconsciously choose the boy as the Hunt's victim, and in a horrifying climax the girl must save the boy from being torn to pieces by the ghost hounds the dancers have summoned. Well-motivated, terrifying, and effective.

612   *The Driftway.* New York, Dutton, 1972. 140 p.

Resentment of his new stepmother makes Paul run away with his little sister. Together they hitch a ride with an old man in a horse cart on an ancient road called the Driftway, where history comes alive in different places. As Paul travels, he hears the stories of many different people and begins to realize that his own opinions and beliefs are not necessarily always right. The author does not overemphasize Paul's lesson, while the various historical characters are vivid and engaging, and the plot develops logically.

613   *The Ghost of Thomas Kempe.* New York, Dutton, 1973. 186 p.

The ghost of an Elizabethan wizard who once lived in his house makes James's life miserable with ill-tempered orders to do his bidding. As Thomas Kempe does not understand modern life at all, he gets James in a lot of trouble. Finally, having burned down a neighbor's house, Thomas Kempe begins to realize that he cannot succeed in a world he does not understand and consents to return to his grave. Both Thomas Kempe's rash behavior and James's resentment are sensitively drawn in a well-plotted, humorous story.

614   *The House in Norham Gardens.* New York, Dutton, 1974. 154 p.

Clare, who lives with her octogenarian aunts in an old house, has strange dreams caused by the presence of a carved shield from New Guinea in the attic. Each dream shows her another step in the making and using of the shield by a primitive tribe who considered it sacred. When she finally reaches the tribe in her last dream, bent on returning the shield to them, they have experienced deculturation because of Western influence, and no longer even understand, let alone desire, the shield. In this beautifully written story of a young girl coming to understand both herself and another culture, Lively has created a small masterpiece of sensitivity.

LOFTING, HUGH, 1886–1947.

615   *The Story of Doctor Dolittle.* Illus. by the author. New York, Stokes, 1920. xvi, 172 p.

The first book of a classic series about the little doctor who learned to speak animal languages and became the best animal doctor in the world. In this story he goes to Africa in order to save the monkeys from a great plague. Unfortunately, this otherwise charming story contains many slighting and derogatory references to black people. Followed by

616   *The Voyages of Doctor Dolittle.* Illus. by the author. New York, Stokes, 1922. 364 p.

The Doctor, accompanied by Tommy Stubbins, his ten-year-old

assistant, voyages to South America to find the missing Long Arrow, the world's greatest (though unsung) naturalist. Followed by

617   *Doctor Dolittle's Post Office.* Illus. by the author. New York, Stokes, 1923. 359 p.

The story of the Post Office run by birds that the Doctor set up in the African kingdom of Jolliginki. Again, a pleasant story is badly marred by racist remarks. Followed by

618   *Doctor Dolittle's Caravan.* Illus. by the author. New York, Stokes, 1924. ix, 342 p.

How the Doctor and his family of animals joined a circus, with the help of the two-headed Pushmi-Pullyu, and how the Doctor rescued Sophie the seal from her cruel trainer. Followed by

619   *Doctor Dolittle's Circus.* Illus. by the author. New York, Stokes, 1924. 307 p.

How the Doctor took over the circus when its owner ran away with all the money and made it into a huge success with his unique Puddleby Pantomime. Followed by

620   *Doctor Dolittle and the Green Canary.* Illus. by the author. Philadelphia, Lippincott, 1950. xi, 276 p.

The expanded story of Pippinella, the mezzo-soprano canary, whom the Doctor first found languishing in a pet shop in *Doctor Dolittle's Circus.* In return for all her help with the Canary Opera, the hit of the London season, the Doctor helps her find her old master, who was unjustly accused of a crime. Followed by

621   *Doctor Dolittle's Zoo.* Illus. by the author. Philadelphia, Lippincott, 1925. 338 p.

622   *Doctor Dolittle's Garden.* Illus. by the author. Philadelphia, Lippincott, 1927. 252 p.

623   *Doctor Dolittle's Puddleby Adventures.* Illus. by the author. Philadelphia, Lippincott, 1952. 241 p.

Three sequels to the *Voyages,* featuring Tommy Stubbins, telling of the Doctor's doings at home in Puddleby-on-the-Marsh. Followed by

624   *Doctor Dolittle in the Moon.* Illus. by the author. Philadelphia, Lippincott, 1928. 186 p.

The Doctor and Tommy fly to the Moon via giant Moon Moth, where they meet the prehistoric man Otho Bludge, who has grown gigantic over the ages. Otho, having heard of the Doctor's fame even on the Moon, has sent for him hoping for a cure for his gout. Tommy is shanghaied home again, but the Doctor stays. Followed by

625   *Doctor Dolittle's Return.* Illus. by the author. Philadelphia, Lippincott, 1933. 183 p.

When the Doctor finally returns, he has also grown enormous from eating Moon food and must spend weeks reducing. The Moon

Cat, Itty, whom he has brought back with him, causes quite an upset in the Dolittle household. Followed by

626　*Doctor Dolittle and the Secret Lake.* Illus. by the author. Philadelphia, Lippincott, 1948. xii, 366 p.

The Doctor, despondent because he has been unable to grow the Moon seeds he brought home, is perked up again by the prospect of a voyage to Africa. There, he revisits Mudface the Turtle, the last survivor of Noah's Ark, who tells him, Tommy, and the animals the true story of the Flood.

627　*Gub-Gub's Book: An Encyclopedia of Food.* Illus. by the author. Philadelphia, Lippincott, 1932. 185 p.

Some of the stories about food, feasts, and food fairies that Gub-Gub, the Doctor's pet pig, was always threatening to write down in the other books.

Perhaps the best thing about the Doctor is his wonderful kindness, common sense, and straightforwardness; there is something so reassuring and irresistible about the plump little man with the strong, sure hands who never fails to speak the truth to wrongdoers and who always knows the sensible thing to do. The unfortunate attitudes towards blacks which disfigure some of Lofting's books are generally peripheral and should be removed; such attitudes were commonplace fifty years ago, and Lofting probably used them without thinking about them, like many other writers (John Buchan comes to mind), unaware that they would offend anyone.

628　*The Twilight of Magic.* Illus. by Lois Lenski. Philadelphia, Lippincott, 1930. xii, 303 p.

Lofting's only non-Dolittle book, this is a fairy tale set in medieval times. Giles saves the king's life with a magic shell given him by Agnes the Applewoman, whose enemies call her a witch. Later, however, Giles realizes that he cannot rely on magic to help him best serve the king, but must use his own wits and good faith. Smoothly written, though the plot is incoherent and relies too much on coincidence. The illustrations resemble the Dolittle pictures, but are not as good.

629　Blishen, Edward. *Hugh Lofting.* Bound with *Geoffrey Trease* by Margaret Meek and *J. M. Barrie* by Roger Lancelyn Green. London, Bodley Head, 1968. 188 p.

LONGMAN, HAROLD S., 1919– .

630　*Andron and the Magician.* Illus. by Richard Cuffari. New York, Seabury, 1971. 143 p.

A boy quests for magic, meets a lot of unscrupulous criminals, finds a "magician" whose magic consists of teaching him how to use his brain, helps the true sheriff defeat the criminals, and returns home, wiser and richer. Dull and didactic, with an extremely muddy plot.

LOVE, EDMUND G., 1912– .

631   *An End to Bugling.* Illus. by Bob Bugg. New York, Harper, 1963. 150 p.

A not-quite-successful ghost fantasy. The Archangel Michael orders the Army of Northern Virginia to reenact the Battle of Gettysburg as a training exercise for Armageddon. The Army comes to Gettysburg in 1963, coincident with the Civil War Centennial, unaware that any time has passed since the real battle. Their attempts to behave like a real wartime army quite naturally create havoc as they steal horses, commandeer supplies, and try to use gasoline credit cards without any idea of what they are. The blend of past and present, ghosts and living, never quite succeeds in convincing the reader.

LOVECRAFT, HOWARD PHILLIPS, 1890–1937.

632   *The Dream-Quest of Unknown Kadath.* Edited and with an introduction by Lin Carter. New York, Ballantine, 1970 (1926). 242 p.

The title-novella and five short stories, including "Celephais" and "The White Ship." The *Dream-Quest* is a derivative, but well-done, Dunsanyesque blend of horror and adventure in an Oriental wonderland.

633   De Camp, L. Sprague. *Lovecraft: A Biography.* Garden City, N.Y., Doubleday, 1975. 510 p.

634   Derleth, August. *H.P.L., a memoir.* New York, Ben Abramson, 1945. 122 p.

635   Derleth, August, and Wandrei, Donald, eds. *Selected Letters by H. P. Lovecraft.* Sauk City, Wis., Arkham House, 1965. 3 vols.

LYNCH, PATRICIA, 1900–1972.

636   *Brogeen Follows the Magic Tune.* Illus. by Ralph Pinto. New York, Macmillan, 1968 (1952). ix, 165 p.

Brogeen, a leprechaun shoemaker, lives in the Fairy Fort of Sheen with the other sidhe (fairies). One night he lets a quarrelsome human fiddler into the fort out of pity, but the fellow steals the Magic Tune of the sidhe—the music a true fiddler hears in his dreams—and Brogeen has to go after him. An episodic plot and a little too much brogue weaken an otherwise entertaining story. Followed by

637   *Brogeen and the Bronze Lizard.* Illus. by H. B. Vestal. New York, Macmillan, 1970 (1954). 181 p.

A monster is in Ireland, and the Queen of the Sidhe talks Brogeen into going to meet it. Eventually he brings it back after joining Brid, Garry, Madame Rose, and Prof. Cornelius Mulrooney in a circus. Lightweight, silly, happy.

MacDONALD, GEORGE, 1824–1905.

638   *Phantastes.* Introduction by Lin Carter. New York, Ballantine, 1970 (1858). 212 p.

Anodos wanders in Fairy-Land, where his spiritual adventures are crowned by death and resurrection; death is a cool green land of dreamy bliss, while life—our life—is like stepping into a shadow. This first of MacDonald's romances owes a great deal to the German Romantic mystic, Novalis, and strongly resembles his *Kunstmärchen* with its diffuse, dreamlike plot.

639   *At the Back of the North Wind.* With 75 illustrations by Arthur Hughes; frontispiece and cover-design by Laurence Housman. London, Blackie and Son, 1908 (1871). vi, 378 p.

The story of Diamond, the cabman's son, whose dearest friend is the beautiful North Wind. Although she carries him over all the world on her back, he is not satisfied, and longs to go with her to her own country, the land "at the back of the north wind," where once she took him when he was very ill. At last he dies, which is the only way to return to that wonderful country. Diamond is perhaps a little too good and kind, like those other Victorian children, Little Eva and Little Nell, but his death is neither unnecessary nor maudlin, and his adventures with North Wind are original—even startling.

640   *The Princess and the Goblin.* With the original illustrations by Arthur Hughes. Baltimore, Penguin, 1964 (1872). 207 p.

How Curdie the miner's son saved little Princess Irene from the goblins who planned to kidnap her, with the help of Irene's great-great-grandmother, the princess who lived in the tower. Full of memorable scenes. Followed by

641   *The Princess and Curdie.* Illus. by Helen Stratton. Baltimore, Penguin, 1966 (1882). 221 p.

In which Irene's grandmother sends Curdie to the capital city, Gwyntystorm, to save the King and Irene from the Chancellor's wicked plot. Not only does he defeat the plot, but he punishes the greedy servants and the selfish burghers of Gwyntystorm and makes them reform. This sequel is rather better than its predecessor, because Curdie and Irene are more mature, and therefore more sophisticated and interesting, and because the threat to Irene and the King is more serious.

642   *Lilith.* Introduction by Lin Carter. New York, Ballantine, 1969 (1895). xii, 274 p.

Mr. Vane, much like Anodos, gets into a strange, Faerielike world, helped by Mr. Raven, a bird who was his father's librarian and is also Adam; but Vane distrusts him and refuses his aid. Instead, he begins to travel through this lovely new world, and soon is caught up in a conflict which centers around two women: the tyrannous, exotic Queen Lilith, who repeatedly betrays him, and the beautiful child Lona, motherly eldest of a brood of wild, happy children. He eventually returns to our world, aware at last of the real meaning of life. This reworking of the theme of *Phantastes*, written nearly forty years later, is far more successful and effective.

643   *The Golden Key.* Pictures by Maurice Sendak. Afterword by W. H. Auden. New York, Farrar, 1967. 85 p.

The story of Mossy and Tangle's journey to the country "whence the shadows fall" is an allegorical fairytale, and very lovely, though a little diffuse.

644   *The Light Princess.* Pictures by Maurice Sendak. New York, Farrar, 1969. 110 p.

Another allegorical tale, which begins humorously when the princess loses her gravity, but ends seriously, with the princess's recovery of both her gravity and her suitor. The illustrations are typically Sendak's—grave, dark, and evocative.

645   *Evenor.* Edited with introduction and notes by Lin Carter. New York, Ballantine, 1972. xiv, 210 p.

Three stories: "The Wise Woman," about a princess who learns not to be spoiled; "The Carasoyn," about a boy who rescues a girl from the fairies, because the Fairy Queen wanted a bottle of magical wine; and "The Golden Key."

646   MacDonald, Greville. *George MacDonald and His Wife.* Introduction by G. K. Chesterton. London, Allen and Unwin, 1924. 575 p.

A biography by MacDonald's son.

647   Wolff, Robert Lee. *The Golden Key: a Study of the Fiction of*

George MacDonald. New Haven, Conn., Yale University Press, 1961. xi, 425 p.

648   Hein, Rolland. "Faith and Fiction." *Dissertation Abstracts Index*, Vol. 32 No. 2 (Aug. 1971), pp. 919A–920A.

649   Hines, Joyce R. "Getting Home: a Study of Fantasy and the Spiritual Journey in the Christian Supernatural Novels of Charles Williams and George MacDonald." *Dissertation Abstracts Index*, Vol. 33 No. 2 (Aug. 1972), p. 755A.

MacDONALD, GREVILLE, 1856–1944.

650   *Billy Barnicoat, a Fairy Romance for Young and Old.* Illus. by Francis D. Bedford. With an introduction by Anne Carroll Moore. New York, Dutton, 1925. xi, 246 p.

Set in Cornwall in 1815, this is the story of a foundling saved from a shipwreck. Mermaids and other Cornish fairies help him find his true heritage, but in the end he decides to stay in Cornwall with his foster parents. This confusing, repetitive story shows that Greville MacDonald was not the writer his father was.

McGOWEN, TOM, 1927– .

651   *Sir Machinery.* Illus. by Trina Schart Hyman. Chicago, Follett, 1970. 155 p.

The brownies and their allies, a wizard and a good witch, need a champion against the evil trolls. Having sneaked into the house of an American scientist nearby, they discover a crate marked MACHINERY which contains a talking, walking robot, which they mistake for a knight in armor with the good Scots name of MacHinery. They enlist the robot and his scientist master too, and with their help invade and destroy the trolls' kingdom. Clever and funny.

McHARGUE, GEORGESS.

652   *Stoneflight.* Illus. by Arvis Stewart. New York, Viking, 1975. 222 p.

Janie, tired of her parents' marital problems, escapes by spending all her time with a stone griffin who comes to life. Griff takes her on magical flights over New York City, which she loves all the more as the contrast with her miserable home life becomes more and more acute. But when the queen of all the Stonefolk, lion-headed Sekhmet, tries to get Janie to turn into stone too, she refuses and goes back home to work on her real problems. The characters are depicted with sensitivity, but the book is strongly didactic in condemning Janie's escapist behavior.

MACHEN, ARTHUR, 1863–1947.

653   *Tales of Horror and the Supernatural*. Edited and with an introduction by Philip Van Doren Stern. With a note on Machen by Robert Hillyer. New York, Knopf, 1948. xxiii, 427 p.

Includes the horror fantasy "The Novel of the Black Seal" from Machen's horror story *The Three Impostors*, and the lovely story of the Grail's return, "The Great Return," set in a tiny Welsh village. However, most of the stories included are pure horror story, full of reasonless, inexorable evils and characters without choices.

654   Cassazza, Alice C. "Arthur Machen's Treatment of the Occult and a Consideration of Its Reception in England and America." *Dissertation Abstracts Index*, Vol. 32 No. 5 (Nov. 1971), pp. 2633A–2634A.

MacKELLAR, WILLIAM, 1914– .

655   *Alfie and Me and the Ghost of Peter Stuyvesant*. Illus. by David K. Stone. New York, Dodd, Mead, 1974.

Peter Stuyvesant is haunting the Staten Island ferry because New York hasn't named a bridge after him, but no one notices him except Billy and Alfie, to whom he gives a treasure map. Since the treasure is buried in the middle of Times Square, Billy and Alfie have to disguise themselves as Con Ed workmen to dig it up. This causes all sorts of havoc for the Mayor, the newspapers, and the boys, but in the end everything works out and Peter gets a ferry named in his honor. The tale is told by Billy in a snide adolescent tone, and the events are totally implausible.

McKENZIE, ELLEN KINDT.

656   *Taash and the Jesters*. New York, Holt, 1968. 233 p.

Taash, a foundling, goes to live with a good witch and the Queen's

Jester and soon is caught in a struggle between a band of evil witches who have kidnapped the baby Prince, and the Jester and his twin, the King's Jester. The plot is complicated but not difficult or incoherent, the characters are credible, and the background is imaginatively designed.

657   *Drujienna's Harp.* New York, Dutton, 1971.

Tha and Duncan are magically transported into a country inside a curious, antique bottle. It is ruled by the wicked Jadido, who, though forbidden to shed blood by an ancient wizard's curse, sends those who displease him to die of hunger and overwork in the mines. Tha and her friends eventually fulfill the ancient prophecies of destruction by asking Drujienna, the wizard's daughter, to play her harp. Many incongruities indicate that the Jadido's world is not an organic conception, the plot is confusing, episodic, and tedious, and the writing is dull.

McKILLIP, PATRICIA A., 1948– .

658   *The House on Parchment Street.* Drawings by Charles Robinson. New York, Atheneum, 1973. 190 p.

An American girl visiting English relatives finds a secret in their basement: the ghosts of a man and woman from the Civil War period. She and her boy cousin finally discover the reason for the ghosts' presence and help put them to rest. This well-written story wavers back and forth between fantasy and ghost story.

659   *The Throme of the Erril of Sherill.* Illus. by Julie Noonan. New York, Atheneum, 1973. 63 p.

Cnite Caerles searches for the nonexistent Throme, a literary work, so that he may marry the King's Damsen, but finally has to write it himself. The writing and the illustrations are delicate and graceful, but on the whole this is a perfect example of how a good writer can get misdirected. The invented names ("norange" and "noak" trees, for example) are both clumsy and cutesy.

660   *The Forgotten Beasts of Eld.* New York, Atheneum, 1974. 217 p.

Sybel, a wizardess with power over many strange and fantastic beasts, brings up Tamlorn, the only son of King Drede, at the request of Coren, Tamlorn's uncle and Drede's enemy. Thus she becomes involved in the human world of love, war, and revenge, almost destroying herself and those she loves in the process. Her beasts—the Black Swan of Tirlith, the Cat Moriah, the Boar Cyrin, Gyld the dragon, the Falcon Ter, and the Lyon Gules—prevent her from carrying out her revenge, so that she realizes what she has almost done. Magnificent, many-colored prose, elaborate without being either "forsoothly" or pretentious, tells this amazing story of human and Faerie love.

McNEILL, JANET, 1907– .

661   *Tom's Tower.* Illus. by Mary Russon. Boston, Little, Brown, 1967 (1965). 182 p.

Tom becomes the Guardian of the Castle Treasure in a magic world he enters, with the help of the Hermit and Cassandra Peach, a witch. However, it turns out that the treasure is not supposed to be guarded, but to be released to the people. McNeill doesn't say, but the treasure appears to be Hope. Then, back in our world, Tom's father comes home at last. The ending is maudlin, but the story is otherwise enjoyable.

MANNING, ROSEMARY, 1911– .

662   *Dragon in Danger.* Illus. by Constance Marshall. Garden City, N.Y., Doubleday, 1960. 169 p.

Susan's friend, R. Dragon of Cornwall, decides to come home with her to London after her holidays end. Since the dragon refuses to part with even one of his precious possessions, which of course are really junk, he has to go in a moving van, driven by William and Fred, two rather servile Cockneys. Strictly pedestrian.

MASEFIELD, JOHN, 1878–1967.

663   *The Midnight Folk.* Illus. by Rowland Hilder. Harmondsworth, Penguin, 1963 (1927). 233 p.

With the help of the Midnight Folk—the cats Nibbins and Greymalkin, the fox Rollicum Bitem, and all the toys his governess, Sylvia Daisy, had banished—Kay Harker beats the witches to the Harker treasure, exposes Sylvia Daisy as a witch, and returns the treasure to its rightful owner, the Cathedral of Santa Barbara of the West Indies. This classic story combines everything desirable in a fantasy: pirates, mermaids, talking animals and toys, English lore and legends, witches on broomsticks, a treasure hunt, and the incredible Miss Susan Pricker, ninety years old, who sings songs about flirting with all the men and drinks a quart of rum every day. Followed by

664   *The Box of Delights, or When the Wolves Were Running.* London, Heinemann, 1935. 418 p.

Kay, home for the Christmas holidays, meets a mysterious peddler who gives him the wonderful Box of Delights, a sort of magic miniature theatre. Soon Kay realizes that the peddler is opposed to Sylvia Daisy and her friends, who have returned and are attacking Kay and his friends. How Kay uses the box to save his mother's friend, dear Caroline Louisa, and defeat the witches once again is the subject of this excellent sequel.

665   Fisher, Margery T. *John Masefield.* New York, Walck, 1963. 67 p.

A study of Masefield's writing for children.

MASON, ARTHUR, 1876– ?

666   *The Wee Men of Ballywooden.* With illus. by Robert Lawson. Garden City, N.Y., Doubleday, 1930. 266 p.

Two separate stories about the Wee Men. In "The Night of the Big Wind" they are blown away and must make their way back; in "Coggelty-Curry" they sail after the Jackdaw who has stolen their bagpipes. The Wee Men are an unattractive lot, each named for his duty —Cradle-Rocker, Weaver, Pilot, Stirrer-of-Gruel—who spend most of their time being stupid and quarrelsome.

MATHESON, RICHARD.

667   *Bid Time Return.* New York, Viking, 1975. 278 p.

A writer dying of a brain tumor falls in love with the photograph of a beautiful actress, taken in 1896. He travels back through time and meets her during the only week of her life which is not accounted for in her biography, and they share a brief love. Sentimental, unbelievable, and banal.

MAYNE, WILLIAM, 1928– .

668   *Earthfasts.* New York, Dutton, 1967 (1966). 154 p.

Two hundred years before the start of this story, a drummer boy went into an underground passage to search for King Arthur's treasure and never came out. Keith and David hear a strange sound coming from under the ground one summer night, which turns out to be the drummer, who emerges carrying a candle he found inside and is unaware that more than a few hours had passed. Some startling and unpleasant experiences make him return to the tunnel, but he leaves the candle behind. This action begins a series of strange events. Finally, Keith discovers that all the enchantments in the countryside have stopped because the candle is not in its proper place in King Arthur's cave. The magical blending of times and spells in the story is made more effective by Mayne's matter-of-fact attitude. His tight, intricate plotting, skillful prose, and distinctive, individual characters, especially the drummer boy and gentle, passive Keith, combine with the immense profundity of his invention to make this one of the best of all fantasies, a classic of speculative literature.

669   *The Hill Road.* New York, Dutton, 1969. (Originally published in England under the title *Over the Hills and Far Away*). 144 p.

Magra, a Celtic girl in the Dark Ages, thought to be a witch because of her red hair, finds a magic stone that has the power to make the past or the future come real. When sent to the king—Mayne hints that it may be as a sacrifice—Magra uses the stone to escape pursuit by enemies: she changes times until another red-headed girl comes along, then changes places with her. The other girl, Sara, and her sister and brother live in the past for two days, pursued by Magra's enemies, until Magra chooses to return and exchange places again. The book is excellent on Dark Age living conditions and beliefs, but has no real plot; since the modern children escape the pursuers, just as Magra would have, there is no point to her exchange.

MEREDITH, GEORGE, 1828–1909.

670   *The Shaving of Shagpat, an Arabian Entertainment.* New York, Scribner, 1909 (1855). 298 p.

The adventures of Shibli Bagarag in the city of Shagpat, the villainous clothier, who is hated by the Vizier because of his monumental beard. Full of exotic pseudo-Arabic splendiferousness, people whose conversation consists of saying "Wullahy!" and tearing their hair, names of unique ugliness, and invented quotations from nonexistent, sententious poets. Overdone.

671   McKechnie, James. *Meredith's Allegory: The Shaving of Shagpat Interpreted.* Havertown, Pa., R. West, 1973 (1910). 247 p.

Argues that *Shagpat* is an allegory of remarkable opaqueness. The argument itself is also remarkably opaque.

MERRITT, ABRAHAM, 1882–1943.

672   *The Moon Pool.* New York, Liveright, 1919. 432 p.

The "Dweller" in the Moon Pool is a being of supernatural power and unearthly beauty, deriving from the lost continent of Mu, who may only emerge when the moon is shining and who possesses evil, forbidden knowledge. A scientist describes to a friend how the Dweller took his wife from him, then mysteriously disappears at moonrise. The friend determines to search for him, and the rest of the book concerns his adventures, beset by gorgeous priestesses, savage guardians, and the usual trappings of pulp adventure fiction.

673   *The Ship of Ishtar.* Illus. by Virgil Finlay. Los Angeles, Borden, 1924. 309 p.

John Kenton receives a block of stone from ancient Babylon, out of which comes a magic ship which transports him back in time six thousand years with the beautiful Sharane, priestess of Ishtar.

674 & 675   *Dwellers in the Mirage and The Face in the Abyss.* Complete and unabridged. With an introduction by Donald A. Wollheim. New York, Liveright, 1953 (1932, 1931). 295, 343 p.

Dwellers in the Mirage. The Ayjir, an ancient race, live in a hidden valley in Alaska. Leif Langdon, the hero, is their Redeemer, reincarnated from the far past, and has the power to summon an evil being, Khalkh'ru, the Dissolver, whom the Ayjir worship by offering scantily clad maidens as a sacrifice.

The Face in the Abyss. The scene is another hidden valley, this time in the Andes, inhabited by the remnant of Atlantis, their Indian serfs and the good serpent-woman, Adana. Nick Graydon leads the struggle of Adana and her few adherents against the evil forces of Nimir.

These are probably Merritt's best works. They are nothing more than a good, fast read, but they are first-class examples of it.

676   *Burn, Witch, Burn!* New York, Liveright, 1933. 301 p.

"I say to you—to hell with your science! . . . beyond the curtain of the material at which your vision halts, there are forces and energies that hate us. . . ."

677   *The Fox Woman*, by A. Merritt; continued as *The Blue Pagoda* by Hannes Bok. Illus. by Hannes Bok. New York, New Collector's Group, 1946. 109 p.

An American woman's husband is murdered by bandits in China, so, dying in childbirth, she asks the fox woman, a Chinese nature-spirit, for revenge. The story is seductively readable, although full of the usual inscrutable Orientals and a villain named Lascelles—villains in pulp fiction are *always* named Lascelles.

MIAN, MARY.

678   *Take Three Witches.* Illus. by Eric von Schmidt. Boston, Houghton Mifflin, 1971. 279 p.

Two teenage girls, Lynn and Sammy, join with three witches—an Anglo, a Mexican, and an Indian—in their little New Mexico town, to defeat and reform the greedy mayor who is trying to drive all the poor people out of their homes. Some funny episodes balance some serious ones. Not a great book, but better written than average, with an original, multi-ethnic premise.

MILNE, ALAN ALEXANDER, 1882–1956.

679   *Once On a Time.* New York, Avon, 1962 (1917). vii, 242 p.

When King Merriwig of Euralia goes off to war, his daughter Hyacinth is left in charge, but the devastating, scheming, utterly charming Countess Belvane tries to run everything. Lightweight and amusing: Belvane, who loves to fling largesse and writes the funniest epic poetry imaginable, is a marvelous character, and the love story of Hyacinth and Coronel strikes all the requisite chords.

680   *Winnie-the-Pooh.* With decorations by Ernest H. Shepard. New York, Dutton, 1961 (1926). xi, 161 p.

The adventures of Christopher Robin and his toys in the Hundred-Aker Wood. A book which even very small children can understand, while adults enjoy the deadpan humor. Followed by

681   *The House at Pooh Corner.* With decorations by Ernest H. Shepard. New York, Dutton, 1961 (1928). xi, 180 p.

More adventures of Pooh, Piglet, Owl, Kanga, Roo, and Eeyore, and introducing a new character in fierce Tigger. At the end, Christopher Robin says goodbye to Pooh and goes away to school.

682   *Winnie-Ille-Pu.* Translated into Latin by Alexander Lenard. Illus. by Ernest H. Shepard. New York, Dutton, 1960. 121 p.

A translation of Milne's classic into idiomatic classical Latin, which started a minor vogue for similar works, notably a version of *Through the Looking Glass.*

683   *Prince Rabbit and The Princess Who Could Not Laugh.* Illus. by Mary Shepard. New York, Dutton, 1966. 72 p.

Two tongue-in-cheek fairy tales. Rabbit enters a footrace for competitors for the position of Prince, which he wins, which forces the King to think of various cheating ways to get out of having a rabbit for an heir. Extremely funny.

684   Milne, Christopher. *The Enchanted Places.* Illus. with photographs and drawings. New York, Dutton, 1975.

A memoir by the real Christopher Robin, who recalls both the happy times he spent with his father in the English countryside and the more difficult times when he was unmercifully teased by other children.

MIRRLEES, HOPE.

685   *Lud-in-the-Mist.* Introduction by Lin Carter. New York, Ballantine, 1970 (1926). xiii, 273 p.

When Master Nathaniel Chanticleer, the Mayor of Lud-in-the-Mist, learns that his son Ranulph has been eating the forbidden fairy fruit, he calls in the services of Lud's chief doctor, Endymion Leer, a foreigner. His call for help starts a chain of events which sends both his children to Fairyland, loses him his position and standing, solves a long-ago murder, and finally requires him to go into Fairyland himself. There, he not only rescues his children and many others, but mets Duke Aubrey of Fairyland and convinces the citizens of Lud that the rejection of all things Faerie has been a mistake.

No synopsis can begin to convey the atmosphere of this magnificent fantasy: its Englishness; its evocative, lovely names—Swan-on-the-Dapple, Moongrass, Dreamsweet, Moonlove Honeysuckle, Dame Ivy Peppercorn, the fields of Grammary; its smooth modern prose which calls up faint echoes of Sir Thomas Browne and seventeenth-century herbals; its melancholy air of secret amusement; its dreamy, yet piercingly sweet, enchantment.

MOLESWORTH, MARY LOUISA STEWART, 1839–1921.

686   *The Cuckoo Clock.* Illus. with line drawings and color plates by Ernest H. Shepard. London, Dent, 1954 (1877). x, 165 p.

Griselda, who has come to live with her great-aunts, is befriended by the cuckoo from the clock, who takes her on several adventures. Eventually she grows good and patient enough not to need the cuckoo any more in order to make friends and enjoy life. A charmingly Victorian story.

MOON, SHEILA, 1910– .

687   *Knee-Deep in Thunder.* Illus. by Peter Parnall. New York, Atheneum, 1967. 307 p.

Maris enters a magic land based on Navajo mythology, which is inhabited by giant, friendly, talking insects and animals. She and the insects must destroy the kingdom of the savage Beasts in order to save the Great Land from the Beasts, and the Beasts from themselves. Followed by

688   *Hunt Down the Prize.* Illus. by Laurel Schindelman. New York, Atheneum, 1971. 244 p.

Some of the Beasts who are not yet cured of their evil ways escape from the wise Old Ones and set out to destroy the Great Land. Maris and her friend Jetty return, and, with some old and some new friends, recapture the bad Beasts and save the Land. Both these books are moralistic and pompous, especially when the mysterious Old Ones interfere with the plot.

MOORCOCK, MICHAEL, 1939– .

689   *Stormbringer.* London, Mayflower, 1968 (1965).

The first novel of a long and complicated series of Howard-like adventure fantasies, featuring a number of heroes who are all avatars of one another. In this particular book, Elric of Melniboné is the last ruler of the dying, ten-thousand-year-old empire of Melniboné. As the world ends in a final battle between Law and Chaos, Elric blows the divine Horn that begins life in the newly formed universe of humanity. In later books he is a wanderer through this new, chaotic world of many small kingdoms. Followed by

690   *The Stealer of Souls and Other Stories.* London, Mayflower, 1968 (1963).

691   *Elric of Melniboné.* London, Mayflower, 1969. (Published in the U.S. under the title *The Sleeping Sorceress*).

692   *The Singing Citadel: Four Tales of Heroic Fantasy.* London, Mayflower, 1970.

These are the only books about Elric. Another avatar, Dorian Hawkmoon, stars in the following books:

693   *The Jewel in the Skull: the History of the Runestaff.* New York, Lancer, 1967.

Granbretan is the chief nation of Europe, a Dark Empire ruled by the sorcerer King Huon, whose power is spreading all over the Continent. Followed by

694   *The Mad God's Amulet.* London, Mayflower, 1969.

695   *The Sword of the Dawn.* London, Mayflower, 1969.

696   *Runestaff.* London, Mayflower, 1969.

Dorian Hawkmoon is also Erekosë, the Eternal Champion, who appears in the following:

697   *The Eternal Champion.* London, Mayflower, 1970.

698   *The Silver Warriors.* New York, Dell, 1973. (Originally published in England under the title *Phoenix in Obsidian*).

699   *The Champion of Garathorm: The Chronicles of Castle Brass, being a sequel to the High History of the Runestaff.* London, Mayflower, 1973.

Here Erekosë and Hawkmoon merge, more or less. A fourth avatar, Corum, appears in six novels, in the last three of which he is reincarnated in a different setting from that of the first three. They are:

700   *The Knight of the Swords.* New York, Berkley, 1971.

701   *The Queen of the Swords.* New York, Berkley, 1971.

702   *The King of the Swords.* New York, Berkley, 1971.

703   *The Bull and the Spear.* New York, Berkley, 1973.

704   *The Oak and the Ram.* New York, Berkley, 1973.

705   *The Sword and the Stallion.* New York, Berkley, 1974.

Corum is the last prince of the Vadhagh, who have been destroyed on order of the Gods by the Mabden, ordinary humankind. Corum eventually destroys the Gods and marries Rhalina, a Mabden, with whom he reigns over a Renaissance of culture and intelligence. But she dies, and Corum wanders off again to escape the attentions of ignorant men who think him a god. Moorcock's adventure stories are distinguished chiefly by their pessimism, their competent style, their eclectic use of mythology and history, and their pretentiousness.

MORRIS, WILLIAM, 1834–1896.

706   *The Hollow Land.* In *Great Short Novels of Adult Fantasy, Vol. I.* Edited by Lin Carter. New York, Ballantine, 1972 (1856). Pp. 231–276.

A strange, incoherent story, written thirty years before his other fantasies, in which a young knight, defeated by his brother's enemy, enters the Hollow Land. The style is completely different from the quasi-medieval prose of his later work, and the story is chiefly interesting only as an example of Morris's early thought.

707   *The Story of the Glittering Plain, which has been also called the Land of Living Men, or the Acre of the Undying.* Frontispiece by Howard Pyle. Hollywood, Calif., Newcastle, 1973. xvii, 174 p.

The first and weakest of Morris's prose-romance fantasies. Hallblithe, a young man of a chieftain's family, pursues the men of the Isle of Ransom who have kidnapped his betrothed, the Hostage. He meets the Puny Fox, who deceives him and sends him to the Glittering Plain to seek her.

708   *The Wood Beyond the World.* New York, Dover, 1972 (1894). 261 p.

This paperback edition is a facsimile of Morris's original Kelmscott Press edition, with the decorations and black-letter type Morris designed. Walter sees two lovely women in what proves to be a vision, and follows them. One woman is a beautiful, desirable, wicked Queen; the other, her slave, is a beautiful, desirable, chaste Maid. Walter and the Maid arrange matters so that the Queen kills her old lover, thinking he is Walter, and then kills herself. The Maid and Walter subsequently become the King and Queen of a neighboring country.

709   *The Water of the Wondrous Isles.* Introduction by Lin Carter. New York, Ballantine, 1971 (1895). xv, 366 p.

A witch kidnaps the child Birdalone, who grows up into a blithe and lovely woman and, with the help of the wood-spirit Habundia, escapes her cruel mistress. She meets three ladies captured by the witch's equally cruel sister and helps them by summoning the three knights who are their lovers. One knight, Arthur, discovers that he loves Birdalone better than his plighted lady, so Birdalone goes away in sorrow, but after many adventures is reunited with Arthur and her other friends. Intriguing and readable, although Birdalone is perhaps a little too good to be true.

710   *The Well at the World's End.* Introduction by Lin Carter. New York, Ballantine, 1970 (1896). 2 vols.

The best of Morris's romances. Ralph, the youngest son of the king of Upmeads, sets out against his father's will to seek adventure, and decides to search for the fabulous Well whose water cures all evils and hurts. Two women whom he meets change his life: the maiden Ursula (sometimes called Dorothy), who kisses him at an inn; and the Lady of the Wildwood, whom he rescues from a knight, and with whom he has a love affair. But the knight returns and kills the Lady, and Ursula is carried off by a band of robbers. Ralph revenges the

Lady, rescues Ursula, finds the Well, and returns in triumph to Up-meads, where he and Ursula live to a great and happy old age. The world of Ralph's adventures is complete and vivid, and the characters strong, attractive, and credible.

711   *The Sundering Flood.* Introduction by Lin Carter. New York, Ballantine, 1973 (1896). xv, 238 p.

How Osberne, a young hero befriended by the mysterious Steel-head (who repeatedly pops up to help him), and Elfhild, a lovely girl, meet on opposite sides of an unbridgeable river and fall in love. The weak story is badly organized (Morris died just after completing the first draft, which he did not have time to revise), and the Flood's un-bridgeability is not convincing.

712   Clutton-Brock, Arthur. *William Morris: His Work and In-fluence.* London, Williams, 1914. 256 p.

713   Drinkwater, John. *William Morris, a critical study.* New York, M. Kennerley, 1912. 201 p.

714   Faulkner, Peter, ed. *William Morris: The Critical Heritage.* London, Routledge & Kegan Paul, 1973. xiii, 465 p.

An annotated collection of contemporary reviews of Morris's major works from *The Defence of Guinevere* (1858) to *The Sundering Flood.* Background information on each critic is given, and Morris's other activities are discussed in the introduction.

715   Henderson, Philip. *William Morris: His Life, Work, and Friends.* Foreword by Allan Temko. With 82 black-and-white illustra-tions and eight color plates. New York, McGraw-Hill, 1967. 388 p.

716   Mackail, J. W. *The Life of William Morris.* London, Long-mans, Green, 1901 (1899). 2 vols.

A standard work undertaken at the request of Morris's friend, the painter Sir Edward Burne-Jones.

717   Albrecht, Wilbur T. "William Morris' *The Well at the World's End.*" *Dissertation Abstracts Index,* Vol. 31, No. 8 (Feb. 1971), p. 5347A.

MUNN, H. WARNER, 1903– .

718   *Merlin's Ring.* New York, Ballantine, 1974.

Semi-heroic adventure fantasy in a conglomeration of barbaric and medieval cultures. Merlin, who is also Quetzalcoatl, gives his ring to his godson Gwalchmai, whose great love is the Atlantean sorceress Corenice. Their story spans millenia between 9564 B.C. and A.D. 1492, during which they meet Bronze Age Irishmen, Normans, Atlanteans, Faery Folk, and Joan of Arc, among others.

MYERS, JOHN MYERS, 1906– .

719   *Silverlock*. New York, Dutton, 1949. 349 p.

A shipwrecked American businessman is saved by a mysterious minstrel, Taliesin, and the two set off on a picaresque journey across the realm of Literature, meeting all the great heroes and heroines— Don Quixote, Robin Hood, Odysseus, the Queen of Sheba, and more. The American's college degree in business is given as the justification for his never having heard of *any* of these characters, an unlikely proposition. However, the story is funny and well-planned.

NATHAN, ROBERT, 1894– .

720   *Portrait of Jennie*. New York, Knopf, 1939. 125 p.

A young artist, starving in a garret, meets a sweet little girl who inspires him to paint a great portrait. Over the next few months, she seems to grow older by years instead of weeks. Finally, as he is about to meet her as an adult for the first time, she drowns, but her ghost saves him from drowning too. Soppy, contrived, and trite.

721   *The Devil With Love*. New York, Knopf, 1963. 208 p.

Lucifer sends a demon to buy, not the soul, but the heart of a boy who loves the beauteous Homecoming Queen, Gladys Millhouser.

722   *The Fair*. New York, Knopf, 1964. 208 p.

An Arthurian story, stuffed with anachronisms. The heroine, Penrhyd, marries her cousin Godwin, who is supposed to be a Briton in spite of his Saxon name, and all the knights and ladies of Malory appear.

723   *Mia*. New York, Knopf, 1970. 179 p.

A failed writer meets a young girl through a warp in time; she is the child who grew up into the woman he loves in the present. Just as he is about to declare his love, the girl, who resents the woman's failures, kills the woman—that is, her older self.

724   *The Summer Meadows*. New York, Delacorte, 1973. 117 p.

A middle-aged couple have just heard the news of an old friend's death when he appears, and together they go on a fantastic journey which reaffirms the meaning of life and love. The hokey situation is not redeemed by any vestige of originality.

NESBIT, E., pseudonym of Edith Nesbit Bland, 1858–1924.

725   *The Complete Book of Dragons.* Illus. by Erik Blegvad. New York, Macmillan, 1972 (1899). 198 p.

Amusing fairy tales; a typical one is "The Book of Beasts," in which Lionel (aged six) becomes king and opens a magic book, out of which flies a dragon who carries off the football team and the Parliament.

726   *Five Children and It.* With illus. by H. R. Millar. Introduction by Roger Lancelyn Green. Baltimore, Penguin, 1959 (1902). 215 p.

Five children at the seashore discover a Psammead, or Sand-Fairy, an odd-looking, grumpy creature, who grants their wishes. But the wishes don't come out as well as they should. They become as beautiful as the day, but they can't get anything to eat; they have wealth beyond the dreams of avarice and are accused of theft; they wish for wings, but lose them at the top of a tower. But finally everything works out, their Mother comes home, and the Psammead promises to return some day. Followed by

727   *The Phoenix and the Carpet.* With illus. by H. R. Millar. Baltimore, Penguin, 1959 (1904). 281 p.

The children, having set fire to their nursery carpet in practicing for Guy Fawkes' Day, get a new carpet which is not only a flying one, but which contains the egg of the phoenix. The phoenix hatches, and the children learn that the carpet is magic, thus beginning a new series of thrilling adventures. Followed by

728   *The Story of the Amulet.* With illus. by H. R. Millar. Baltimore, Penguin, 1959 (1906). 281 p.

The children find the Psammead once again in a pet shop cage, and in gratitude for its rescue it tells them where to find half of a wonderful magic amulet. They buy it and use it to go through time and space looking for the other half, for then it will give them their hearts' desire: Mother well and home again, and Father safely returned from a dreadful foreign war. The adventures, though frequently still as complicated and difficult for the children and funny to the reader, are more serious; many of Nesbit's humanitarian concerns and hopes are shown.

729   *The Enchanted Castle.* Illus. by Cecil Leslie. London, Dent, 1964 (1907). 231 p.

Four children find a ring in a great old house which they believe is an enchanted castle. They pretend that the ring is a magic ring of invisibility and are astonished to find that it is exactly that. Then the ring changes unexpectedly into a wishing ring, which is even more disconcerting. Meanwhile, they gradually become aware that their kind governess, Mademoiselle, is unhappy because she is parted from her lover, and the magic obligingly helps them reunite the pair. This is the longest, best-developed, and most imaginative of Nesbit's fantasies; the magic ring's unexpected change is a brilliant idea.

730   *The House of Arden*. Illus. with four colour plates and line drawings in the text by Clarke Hutton. New York, Dutton, 1968 (1908). 244 p.

731   *Harding's Luck*. Illus. by Desmond E. Walduck. New York, Coward, 1960 (1910). 348 p.

Two interrelated time-travel fantasies. In the first, Edred and Elfrida inherit Arden Castle and discover the Mouldiwarp of Arden, whose magic takes them back in time to Tudor, Stuart, and Napoleonic days to search for the Arden treasure, which they must find before Edred's birthday. In the second book, Edred and Elfrida's cousin Richard Arden, or Harding, comes to the fore. Richard is a lame beggar-boy, who travels back to Tudor times, when he is not lame, and is the heir of Arden. But he is suddenly brought back to the present and declared the true heir of the modern Ardens, thus supplanting Edred and Elfrida's father. The magic eventually straightens this tangle out and everyone gets what he wants. The stories can be quite confusing unless they are read together, since their plots depend on one another. Nesbit tried to deal with subjects that are much more serious than in her other books, and so stifled her normally acute sense of humor.

732   *The Magic City*. Illus. by H. R. Millar. London, Benn, 1958 (1910). 333 p.

Philip is left alone as punishment for behaving badly to Lucy, his new brother-in-law's daughter. Out of boredom he builds a toy city from books and dominoes and bottles; then, one night, when Lucy has come home without his knowing, the magic starts and both get into the city. Philip must perform seven knightly deeds before they can get out again; in the process he learns to like Lucy and reconciles himself to his sister. The plot rambles, but the children's quarrels are accurately and humorously detailed.

733   *Wet Magic*. Illus. by H. R. Millar. London, Benn, 1958 (1910). 274 p.

Four children visiting the seaside rescue a mermaid from a carnival, visit her undersea home, reconcile two groups of warring merpeople, and reunite a friend with his parents. One of Nesbit's weakest:

there is not enough contrast between the magic adventures and the children's everyday lives.

734   *The Wonderful Garden*. Illus. by H. R. Millar. London, Benn, 1959 (1911). 402 p.

Three children think· they are having magic adventures, but every episode has a natural explanation, so the book is not a fantasy.

735   *Oswald Bastable and Others*. Illus. by Charles E. Brock and H. R. Millar. London, Benn, 1960. 369 p.

Four non-fantasy Bastable stories and eleven fairy tales which are among the worst Nesbit ever wrote, full of magic pussycats and seas of emotional treacle.

736   Bell, Anthea. *E. Nesbit*. New York, Walck, 1960. 84 p.

A thorough and comprehensive study of Nesbit's work.

737   Moore, Doris Langley. *E. Nesbit, a Biography*. Rev. ed., with new material. London, Benn, 1967 (1933). 335 p.

A definitive biography.

738   *Long Ago When I Was Young*. Illus, by Edward Ardizzone. Introduction by Noel Streatfeild. New York, Watts, 1966. 127 p.

Reminiscences of Nesbit's "unsettled" and stormy childhood.

739   Streatfeild, Noel. *Magic and the Magician: E. Nesbit and Her Children's Books*. London, Benn, 1958. 160 p.

A rambling essay on Nesbit's work which seems to consist largely of quotations.

NETHERCLIFT, BERYL.

740   *The Snowstorm*. Illus. by Joseph Schindelman. New York, Knopf, 1967. 182 p.

Three children, visiting their Aunt Amethyst at her great country house, soon realize that she is very poor and determine to help her. They discover that the glass paperweight in the drawing room suspends time whenever it is shaken to produce a toy snowstorm, which allows them to travel into the past in search of the lost treasure that will save the house. Suspenseful, detailed, historically accurate, and engaging.

NEWMAN, ROBERT, 1909– .

741   *Merlin's Mistake*. Illus. by Richard Lebenson. New York, Atheneum, 1970. 237 p.

Merlin endows a medieval boy, Tertius, with all *future* knowledge, so he knows all about computers and quasars, but nothing practical about witchcraft and sorcery. But Tertius's brains and seemingly useless knowledge save him and his friend and enable the other boy to break the enchantment on his long-lost father. A competent treatment of an amusing premise. Followed by

742   *The Testing of Tertius.* Illus. by Richard Cuffari. New York, Atheneum, 1973. 186 p.

Attila the Hun is about to conquer all Europe, so the forces of good, headed by Arthur, Merlin, and Merlin's new apprentice—Tertius —sail to France to battle the Huns. The forces of Attila keep winning until at last Tertius combines his two kinds of knowledge, science and sorcery. This book is inferior to its predecessor.

NICHOLS, RUTH.

743   *A Walk Out of the World.* Illus. by Trina Schart Hyman. New York, Harcourt, 1969. 192 p.

Tobit and Judith stumble into a world of brilliantly colored stars, enormous pine forests, and simple, noble people, who welcome them as the promised deliverers from an evil usurper. At first they think only of going home, but at the end discover that they do not wish to leave. A beautifully written, sad story, set in a world of enchanted loveliness.

744   *The Marrow of the World.* Illus. by Trina Schart Hyman. New York, Atheneum, 1972. 168 p.

Philip and his adopted cousin Linda discover a magic lake, inside which is another world. There, Linda is a witch-queen's daughter, whose evil sister has sent for her to fetch the Marrow of the World, a magic soil created at the beginning of time. Much weaker than Nichols's other book.

NIVEN, LARRY, 1938– .

745   *The Flight of the Horse.* New York, Ballantine, 1975. 209 p.

Time-travel stories set in the far future. Svetz's master, an exigent autocrat, sends him on trips into the past to retrieve extinct animals for his zoo. Sent for a dog, Svetz finds a lady werewolf; sent for a horse, Svetz doesn't know what to do about the sharp horn on its forehead. Slyly funny.

NORTH, JOAN, 1920– .

746   *The Cloud Forest.* New York, Farrar, 1965. 180 p.

Andrew and a girl who is his only friend must struggle against both his adoptive mother and an evil uncle who is trying to capture him. The "mother" and the uncle have already delivered Andrew's father to an evil being possessing him. An eerie horror fantasy which builds inexorably to a terrifying climax.

747   *The Whirling Shapes.* New York, Farrar, 1967. 183 p.

The whirling gray funnels seen and painted by Liz's cousin James come out of the unknown and lay a spell of paralysis on her family. In the land beyond a magic door, Liz must rescue everyone, because the indecision which has plagued her means that she alone is free of the spell. The story is didactic, but the characters are lively and intelligent.

748   *The Light Maze.* New York, Farrar, 1971. 186 p.

When Kit comes to visit her godparents, Tom and Sally, she finds that Tom has left a clue to his sudden disappearance: the mysterious Lightstone. Kit and her friends follow Tom into the Maze with the Stone, find their true selves in the Light, and return, wiser and happier. The plot is confused and undramatic, and the theology is overemphasized and pretentious.

NORTON, ANDRE, pseudonym of Alice M. Norton.

749   *Star Gate.* New York, Harcourt, 1958. 192 p.

The Terrans, Starlords of Gorth, are leaving the planet to allow it to develop free from outside influence. Because they love Gorth, they are not going into space, but into an alternate Gorth where, they hope, its native race never evolved. But the new Gorth is so similar to their own that alternate versions of themselves are vicious tyrants. A realistic, well-developed Secondary World and a fascinating premise make this one of Norton's best.

750   *Witch World.* New York, Ace, 1963. 222 p.

Simon Tregarth, a hunted spy, escapes from pursuit into another world, where he saves a witch-woman from her enemies and joins her people as a soldier. After countless battles, sieges, and journeys, he destroys the soulless enemies of the witch-folk—monstrous villains from another universe who murder and maim for fun—and marries the witch Jaelithe. This is the first book of a long series which is afflicted with wooden characters, overwritten prose, and disjointed plotting. Followed by seven sequels:

751   *Three Against the Witch World.* New York, Ace, 1965.

752   *Year of the Unicorn.* New York, Ace, 1965.

753   *Warlock of the Witch World.* New York, Ace, 1967.

754   *Sorceress of the Witch World.* New York, Ace, 1968.

755   *Spell of the Witch World.* New York, DAW Books, 1972.

756   *The Crystal Gryphon.* New York, Atheneum, 1972. 234 p.

A Witch World story. Kerovan, a mutant hated by his mother, Tephana, is married to Joisan by proxy. He and Joisan have never met when bloodthirsty invaders conquer the Dales, and Joisan has to flee. Meanwhile, Kerovan too must flee his mother's evil spells. Husband and wife meet in the wilderness, but Kerovan keeps his true identity a secret until his mother has Joisan kidnaped to serve as a sacrifice. The story is not unified, because the brutal invasion is merely a red herring, and the narrative is stiff and unconvincing.

757   *The Jargoon Pard.* New York, Atheneum, 1974. 194 p.

Very similar to No. 756. Kethan's mother is a witch who wishes to use him as an avenue to power. The panther-shaped gem called the "jargoon pard" gives him some power to oppose her, but he must be helped by a witch-couple who turn out to be his real parents. Except for the mutant appearance, Kethan recreates Kerovan of *The Crystal Gryphon* down to his speech patterns and adolescent hangups.

758   *Steel Magic.* Illus. by Robin Jacques. Cleveland, World, 1965. 155 p.

A book for children (rather than adolescents). Three children go through a magic door into Avalon, where they meet Huon, Merlin, and Arthur and learn that Avalon is at war with dark but undefined powers. The children quest for the lost treasures of Avalon—a sword, a horn, and a ring—and find that the quest requires each of them to overcome his worst faults or fears. Pompous and uninspired.

759   *Octagon Magic.* Illus. by Mac Conner. Cleveland, World, 1967. 189 p.

Laurie meets elderly Miss Ashemeade of Octagon House and goes back in time to the Civil War, where she helps young Miss Ashemeade save several fugitives. The plot goes on forever, the conclusion is a little too obvious, and Miss Ashemeade's pressure on Laurie to be ladylike is outdated.

760   *Fur Magic.* Illus. by John Kaufmann. Cleveland, World, 1968. 174 p.

Cory, on a visit to the West, is magically transported back to the days of Indian legend, where, in the shape of a beaver, he goes on a mission to prevent the powerful Changer from abusing his powers. Cory proves himself by this ordeal, overcoming his former timidity. The story's moral didacticism and *machismo* cannot spoil the Indian material, which is excellent.

761   *High Sorcery.* New York, Ace, 1970. 156 p.

Five short stories in Norton's usual vein.

762   *Ice Crown.* New York, Viking, 1970. 256 p.

Roane, a member of an archaeological expedition to the closed planet Clio, helps the Princess Ludorica regain the fabulous Ice Crown. But the Crown is really a machine controlling Ludorica's people, so Roane finds that she must now destroy it. A complex plot and characters less wooden than usual make this one of Norton's better novels, although Roane's home civilization is too cold and sterile to be believable.

763   *Dragon Magic.* Illus. by Robin Jacques. New York, Crowell, 1972. 213 p.

Four American boys break into a deserted house, where they find a magic box that transports each into his ancestral past: Sig to the time of Fafnir and Siegfried; Ras to ancient Babylon; Kim to the China of emperors and warlords; and Artie to the death of King Arthur. The result of the magic is that the four boys overcome their prejudices against one another.

764   *Forerunner Foray.* New York, Viking, 1973. 216 p.

Ziantha, an ESP sensitive, finds a strange stone, an artifact of a vanished civilization. When she "reads" it psychically, she is thrown into the past. A young archaeologist is also flung into the past by the stone, and after he and Ziantha save each other's lives there, they return and defeat Ziantha's evil employer. The story relies too heavily on lovely villainesses, loyal subalterns, and scheming servants.

765   *Here Abide Monsters.* New York, Atheneum, 1973. 205 p.

Nick and Linda, riding down a mysterious road, find themselves in an alternate universe, called Avalon, which is inhabited by ordinary humans like themselves, two sets of flying saucer people, and the Fairy Folk. All of these peoples are in constant conflict, and Nick and Linda must try to reconcile them, although the flying saucers prove intractable. The plot is, at best, incoherent.

766   *Lavender-Green Magic.* Illus. by Judith Gwyn Brown. New York, Crowell, 1974. 241 p.

The three black Wade children, who have come to live with their grandparents, discover that the maze in the old garden can take them back in time to Puritan New England. There they must choose between helping Tamar, the healer, or her sister Hagar, a witch. The Puritans are shown as the usual frowning clichés, but the children's personalities, conflicts, and difficulties are unusually well-developed. This book shows evidence of painstaking attention and serious effort.

767   *The Many Worlds of Andre Norton.* Ed. by Roger Elwood. Introduction by Donald A. Wollheim. Radnor, Pa., Chilton, 1974. x, 208 p.

Seven stories of fantasy and science fiction, and an essay entitled "On Writing Fantasy," constitute Norton's contribution to this collection. Also included is an essay by Rick Brooks entitled "Andre Norton: Loss of Faith." A complete bibliography of Norton's work through 1973 is given on pp. 201–208.

768   *Merlin's Mirror.* New York, DAW Books, 1975. 205 p.

Retells the story of Merlin on the assumption that both he and Arthur are extra-terrestrial in origin, guided by miraculous machines which sense (somehow) everything happening in Britain. Earth is an outpost in a terrific galactic war between Merlin's father and his cohorts on the side of Good and another group of aliens who are Evil, headed by the witch Nimue. Unfortunately, the story is distorted to fit the premise.

Norton has written many other books which blend some elements of fantasy with an essentially science-fiction treatment, and which are therefore not included here.

NORTON, MARY, 1913– .

769   *Bedknob and Broomstick.* Illus. by Erik Blegvad. A combined edition of "The Magic Broomstick" and "Bonfires and Broomsticks." New York, Harcourt, 1957 (1943). 189 p.

Three children learn that eccentric Miss Price's ankle was sprained when she fell off her broomstick, so they persuade her to put a spell on their bedknob which will take them wherever they wish to go. After several E. Nesbit-like adventures, they and Miss Price rescue a Restoration-era sorcerer. A charming, amusing fantasy.

770   *The Borrowers.* Illus. by Beth and Joe Krush. New York, Harcourt, 1952. 180 p.

The Borrowers are miniature people, even smaller than Lilliputians, who live in our houses by "Borrowing"—taking all the little things like pins and scraps and thimbles which are never where we want them. This story tells how Arrietty, a young girl Borrower, went Borrowing with her father, Pod, and was "Seen by the Boy." This starts a complicated series of events which put Arrietty and her family in danger of being captured and shown at fairs, and end in their having to leave the house where they have always lived. It is not a sad story, however, but exciting, fast-moving, and optimistic. Followed by

771   *The Borrowers Afield.* Illus. by Beth and Joe Krush. New York, Harcourt, 1955. 215 p.

772   *The Borrowers Afloat.* Illus. by Beth and Joe Krush. New York, Harcourt, 1959. 191 p.

773   *The Borrowers Aloft.* Illus. by Beth and Joe Krush. New York, Harcourt, 1961. 193 p.

The adventures of Pod, his wife Homily, and Arrietty out in the big world. Arrietty loves the danger and the freedom of being outside, and they are helped by another Borrower, a wild boy, whom Homily rather looks down on, but whom Arrietty begins, gradually, to love. The problems of miniature people in a world too large for them have rarely been better depicted, and Arrietty, with her curiosity and delight in life, is one of the best fantasy characters ever created.

774   *Poor Stainless, a new story about the Borrowers.* Illus. by Beth and Joe Krush. New York, Harcourt, 1971 (1966). 32 p.

A short story about Arrietty's cousin Stainless.

O'BRIEN, ROBERT C., pseudonym of Robert L. Conly, 1918–1973.

775   *The Silver Crown.* Illus. by Dale Payson. New York, Atheneum, 1968. 174 p.

A girl wakes up on her birthday and finds a beautiful silver crown, which she interprets as long-overdue recognition for her superior qualities from her hitherto unappreciative parents. She goes out for a quiet walk before the rest of the family wakes up, but when she returns, the house is in flames and a bystander tells her the family are all dead. Later, she learns that the crown was sent by the evil leader of an army of children who, controlled by the crowns, plan to conquer the world. The premise is too elaborate and farfetched to be plausible.

776   *Mrs. Frisby and the Rats of NIMH.* Illus. by Zena Bernstein. New York, Atheneum, 1972. 233 p.

Mrs. Frisby, a mouse, goes to the Rats for help when her youngest child gets sick. The Rats help her, and in the process she learns that they are super-rats, escapees from NIMH, a scientific institute, where they were the subjects of an experiment which increased their intelligence to human level. When the Rats must relocate their brilliant civilization, Mrs. Frisby and the children join them. A science fantasy with memorable characters and a serious, but not didactic, purpose.

ORMONDROYD, EDWARD.

777   *David and the Phoenix.* Illus. by Joan Raysor. Chicago, Follett, 1957. 173 p.

David helps the Phoenix avoid being trapped by the over-zealous Scientist; in reward, the Phoenix takes David to meet his many magical friends. For younger children, although the story contains much literary humor accessible to—perhaps intended for—adults.

778   *Time at the Top.* Illus. by Peggie Bach. Berkeley, Parnassus, 1963. 176 p.

Susan is given three magical rides on the elevator in her apartment building. On the first she steps into a house that occupied the building's site in the 1880s and makes friends with the boy and girl who live there with their widowed mother. She uses her second ride to help the children prevent a crooked con man from marrying their mother, and the third to convince her father to return to the past with her. A satisfying story, with realistic and engaging characters.

779   *Castaways on Long Ago.* Illus. by Ruth Robbins. Berkeley, Parnassus, 1973. 182 p.

Three children vacationing on a farm visit a nearby lake in spite of warnings to stay away and become dangerously involved with the ghost of a drowned child. The muggy, stifling summer atmosphere of the farm provides a convincing background for the suspenseful plot.

PARKER, RICHARD.

780   *The Old Powder Line.* New York, Nelson, 1971. 143 p.

Brian and Wendy discover a new railway platform and line in their tiny, familiar home station, which takes them back in time. When Brian's crippled friend Mr. Mincing tries to follow them, the time warp traps him in the modern railway tunnel, and Brian and Wendy must try to rescue him at great risk to themselves. An excellent analysis of the nature of time and the fascination of the past.

781   *A Time to Choose, a Story of Suspense.* New York, Harper, 1973. 151 p.

Stephen and his intelligent but acid-tongued schoolmate, Mary, become friends when they discover that they can enter the future.

Severe family problems for both finally impel them to take their chances in the new world. Though the plot is sometimes difficult to follow, the characters are attractive and intelligent.

PEAKE, MERVYN, 1911–1968.

782   *Titus Groan.* With an introduction by Anthony Burgess. London, Eyre and Spottiswoode, 1968 (1946).
783   *Gormenghast.* New York, Ballantine, 1968 (1950).
784   *Titus Alone.* New York, Ballantine, 1968 (1959).
A passionately overwritten trilogy of novels about the life of Titus, heir of Gormenghast, a gigantic castle—almost a city—which is all the world there is to its inhabitants. The novels are not, strictly speaking, tales of horror, but they are horrific; their atmosphere is deliberately the same as that of nineteenth-century Gothic novels—gloomy, grim, terrifying, secretive, and mysterious. Titus grows up surrounded by characters out of a Dickensian nightmare: Mr. Flay, Mr. Rottcodd, Nannie Slagg, the sly, rebellious Steerpike; his earliest emotions are of foreboding and dread. His struggle to master, or, alternatively, to escape Gormenghast is told in ornate, artificial language.

The Gormenghast trilogy is the effusion of an almost distracted mind, the only fantasy world without a constructive moral framework to sustain it. As an exercise in the weird, the eccentric, and the remote, Gormenghast is unique, a fantasy which is whole, solid, and complete, but has no relation to Primary reality: not a metaphor for the real world, but a frozen distortion of the popular image of Victorian life, full of poverty, oppression, Philistinism, and heartlessness.

PEARCE, ANN PHILIPPA, 1920– .

785   *Tom's Midnight Garden.* Illus by Susan Einzig. London, Oxford University Press, 1958. 154 p.
One night, when the clock strikes thirteen, Tom makes his way into the garden that once existed around the old house he is staying in. There he meets Hatty, a little girl of the 1880s, and makes friends; but soon, on his later visits, he sees that she is growing up into a young lady. When the garden disappears entirely one night, Tom screams in panic for Hatty, waking the elderly landlady—Hatty herself, grown old. A delicate, nostalgic story with excellent characters, especially resentful Tom, his kind but pompous uncle, and Hatty's cold, unfeeling aunt; a joyous, soul-satisfying ending; and a magical blend of times.

PEARSON, EDWARD.

786   *Chamiel*. New York, Pocket Books, 1973. 143 p.
    War in Heaven, narrated by an angel on special courier duty
between God, Earth, and Satan. Undistinguished.

PEEPLES, EDWIN A., JR., 1915– .

787   *A Hole in the Hill*. Illus. by George Wiggins. Camden, N.J.,
Nelson, 1969. 189 p.
    Colin and Geoffrey and their friends, Ian and Deirdre, find a lost
cave which was once part of the Underground Railroad, and inside it
meet the ghost of an escaped slave. Ian and Deirdre's parents tell a
newsman about the cave, against the wishes of Colin and Geoffrey's
parents. How the children cope with an influx of sightseers, the ghost,
the terrible drought that follows, and their warring elders, makes up
the rest of this better-than-average ghost fantasy.

PHIPSON, JOAN, pseudonym of Joan M. Fitzhardinge, 1912– .

788   *The Way Home*. New York, Atheneum, 1973. 184 p.
    Three Australian children, stranded alone in the outback, are
transported back to prehistoric times, full of volcanoes, carnivorous
dinosaurs, floods, and similar disasters, through which they are guided
by a mysterious Voice. The novel is a competent wilderness-survival
story, but the use of "fantasy" to give it a "moral" framework is pointless and condescending.

PICARD, BARBARA LEONIE, 1917– .

789   *The Mermaid and the Simpleton*. Illus. by Philip Gough. London, Oxford University Press, 1949. 253 p.
790   *The Faun and the Woodcutter's Daughter*. Illus. by Charles
Stewart. New York, Criterion, 1964 (1951). 255 p.
791   *The Lady of the Linden Tree*. Illus. by Charles Stewart. New
York, Criterion, 1962 (1954). x, 214 p.
792   *The Goldfinch Garden*. Illus. by Anne Linton. New York,
Criterion, 1965 (1963). 121 p.

Four collections of fairy tales written in a tender, nostalgic style by this excellent historical novelist. Typical is the charming, wry "The Goldfinch Garden," which tells how an inept gardener won the king's gardening prize with the help of a flock of goldfinches, which opportunely settled on the only plants he had been able to grow—thistles.

PLATT, KIN, 1911– .

793   *Mystery of the Witch Who Wouldn't.* Philadelphia, Chilton, 1969. 265 p.

Sequel to another mystery, *Sinbad and Me*, not a fantasy, about a boy and his intelligent dog. In this one Sinbad and the boy solve a mystery about a witch who refuses to cast spells.

POOLE, JOSEPHINE, 1933– .

794   *Moon Eyes.* Illus. by Trina Schart Hyman. Boston, Little, Brown, 1967. 151 p.

A young girl, living with her aunt, sees a huge, frightening dog with glowing, saucer-shaped eyes near the house and gradually becomes aware that the beast is a witch's familiar and is trying to possess her. But is it her aunt's familiar? She must fight against it, unable to find out who has sent it until the climax of this spooky horror fantasy.

795   *The Visitor, a Story of Suspense.* New York, Harper, 1972. 148 p.

A boy convalescing from a wasting disease begins to realize that his tutor has some grudge against his family and intends to revenge himself. After an attempt to burn the house down is frustrated by the boy's sister's husband, the tutor reveals himself as a pagan deity whose worship—old ceremonial rituals—includes human sacrifice. An exciting, terrifying story with well-observed characters, in which the fantasy elements are gradually, quietly, and effectively introduced until their cumulative power is overwhelming.

POPE, ELIZABETH MARIE, 1917– .

796   *The Sherwood Ring.* Illus. by Evaline Ness. Boston, Houghton Mifflin, 1958. 266 p.

A young girl living in an eighteenth-century farmhouse in New York State meets an Englishman who seems to be interested in her family. Thanks to the ghosts of her ancestors, she learns that he is a distant cousin, descended from a British captain of irregulars who fell in love with her great-great-grandfather's sister. The love stories of both past and present are delightful and exciting.

POST, J.B., comp.

797   *An Atlas of Fantasy.* Baltimore, Mirage, 1973.
Imaginary maps of all dates and kinds, including many non-fantasy ones like those of Baskerville Hall and Barsetshire. Some of the maps are badly drawn and/or photocopied, but most are clear and well reproduced. Annotations are provided for most of the maps.

POTTER, BEATRIX, 1866–1943.

798   *The Fairy Caravan.* New York, Warne, 1929. 225 p.
When Tuppenny, a guinea pig, is rubbed all over with hair-growing oil and his life made a misery, he runs away and joins the animals' circus—the Fairy Caravan—with Pony Billy, Sandy the terrier, Jenny Ferret, Paddy Pig, Xarifa Dormouse, and Iky Shepster the starling. The Caravan travels up and down the North-of-England countryside and has various encounters with sheep, cats, and foxes, but only one with humans, when Pony Billy forgets the fernseed that makes him invisible. An ideal story to read aloud to small children.
799   *The Journal of Beatrix Potter from 1891 to 1897.* Transcribed by Leslie Linder from her original coded diaries. With an appreciation by H. L. Cox. London, Warne, 1966. xxix, 448 p.
800   Godden, Rumer. *The Tale of the "Tales": the Beatrix Potter Ballet.* Including illustrations by Beatrix Potter, designs by Christine Edzard, and photographs from the E.M.I. film production *Tales of Beatrix Potter.* London, Warne, 1971. 208 p.
801   Lane, Margaret. *The Tale of Beatrix Potter.* London, Warne, 1946. 176 p.
The standard biography.
802   Linder, Leslie. *A History of the Writings of Beatrix Potter.* Includes unpublished work. 150 plates. London, Warne, 1971. xxvi, 446 p.
803   Linder, Leslie, and Herring, W. A., comps. *The Art of Beatrix*

Potter. Text by Enid and Leslie Linder. Appreciation by Anne Carroll Moore. New and enlarged ed. London, Warne, 1975 (1955). 336 p.

Contains 205 color illustrations, 125 black-and-white, in two sections: "Her Work as an Artist"; "Her Art in Relation to Her Books."

PRATT, FLETCHER, 1897–1956.

804   *The Well of the Unicorn.* New York, William Sloane, 1948.

This story tells the rise of Airar of Dalarna, a young man taxed out of his home by the oppressive Vulks, who joins a revolt and becomes its leader. He is aided by a band of fisher-folk, a guild of merchants, a magician, and four warrior captains, including the savage Amazon Evadne, who loves him. Most of the plot is a narrative of battles, sieges, and forced marches; only the unpleasant Evadne has any personality, while Airar seems an unlikely leader. An unsuccessful heroic fantasy, rather than a successful adventure story.

805   *The Blue Star.* Introduction by Lin Carter. New York, Ballantine, 1969 (1952). 242 p.

An idealistic young clerk, Rodvard, joins a revolutionary society, which orders him to seduce the witch-girl, Lalette. This will enable him to gain her magic power, which is symbolized by and centered in the witch-jewel, the Blue Star. The act catapults the two into a maelstrom of conflicting loyalties, treachery, assassination, exile, religious persecution, and a revolution which quickly becomes a reign of terror. The bond of the Blue Star helps them mature from dislike and suspicion to love. The ambiguities of their situation are beautifully developed in this important and engrossing fantasy.

See also De Camp, Lyon Sprague, and Pratt, Fletcher, Nos. 312–316.

PYLE, HOWARD, 1853–1911.

806   *Pepper and Salt, or Seasoning for Young Folk.* Illus. by the author. New York, Harper, 1885. xiii, 109 p.

807   *The Wonder Clock, or Four-and-Twenty Marvelous Tales.* Illus. by the author. Embellished with verses by Katharine Pyle. New York, Harper, 1887. xiv, 319 p.

808   *The Twilight Land.* Illus. by the author. New York, Harper, 1894. 438 p.

Fairy tales told in Pyle's unique quasi-medieval style, which has great emotional resonance despite its inauthenticity. Illustrated with his superb black-and-white drawings.

809   Nesbitt, Elizabeth. *Howard Pyle*. New York, Walck, 1968. 72 p.

810   Pitz, Henry Clarence. *A Plethora of Talent: the Creative Life of Howard Pyle*. Illustrated. New York, Potter, 1975. 320 p.

Not so much a biography as an analysis of Pyle's work.

QUILLER-COUCH, SIR ARTHUR, 1863–1944, and DU MAURIER, DAPHNE, 1907– .

811   *Castle Dor*. Garden City, N.Y., Doubleday, 1962.

Romantic nonsense about two nineteenth-century peasants in Cornwall who re-enact the story of Tristan and Isolde, influenced by some miasmal mental force.

RASKIN, ELLEN, 1928– .

812   *Figgs and Phantoms*. Illus. by the author. New York, Dutton, 1974. vi, 152 p.

Though the jacket notes call it fantasy, this is a fanciful, whimsical dream-story with a touch of fabulation and a whole lot of confusion. Mona Lisa Newton hates belonging to her mother's family, the Fabulous Figgs of vaudeville, although her uncle Florence Italy Figg is her dearest companion. When Uncle Florence dies and goes (as all good Figgs do) to Capri, Mona tries to follow him, which helps her realize that being from an unusual family is not so bad after all.

RAYNER, WILLIAM.

813   *Stag Boy*. New York, Harcourt. 1973. 160 p.

Jim, a timid, weak teenager, finds an ancient stag-horned helmet; wearing it, he meets Herne the Hunter, who gives him the power to enter the mind of a great black stag. Unaware that his own death is at stake, Jim loves being the animal and finds that he can win his childhood friend Mary away from a rich boy because she loves to ride on the stag. As the stag, Jim eludes the hunters all summer long, but when he is caught Mary desperately offers herself to Herne as the sacrifice in his place. The perception of Herne as both a Stone Age hunter and shaman and as a godlike being of numinous power gives the fantasy great depth.

REIT, SEYMOUR.

814   *Benvenuto.* Illus. by Will Winslow. New York, Addisonian Press, 1974. 126 p.

Paolo brings a baby dragon home from camp to his parents in Greenwich Village. The SPCA and the Health Department try to make the family give Benvenuto up, but a smart black lawyer gets the case dismissed. The light little story is not too heavily laden with brotherly love.

RIOS, TERE, pseudonym of Maria Teresa Rios Versace, 1917–   .

815   *The Fifteenth Pelican.* Illus. by Arthur King. Garden City, N.Y., Doubleday, 1965. 118 p.

Sister Bertrille's small size and huge cornice-shaped hat give her the ability to fly (or glide) and get her into various kinds of hot water with the Mother Superior and the CIA, until they weight down her habit with fishing weights.

ROBERTSON, KEITH.

816   *Tales of Myrtle the Turtle.* Illus. by Peter Parnall. New York, Viking, 1974.

Myrtle tells tall tales about her deceased husband, Herman, to her niece and nephew, Gloria and Witherspoon. Some of the jokes are funny.

RUSKIN, JOHN, 1819–1900.

817   *The King of the Golden River.* Illus. by Fritz Kredel. Introduction by May Lamberton Becker. Cleveland, World, 1946 (1841). 113 p.

The immortal fairy tale of a boy, mistreated by his rowdy, selfish older brothers, who is rewarded for his kindness by the gnomish King. The freeing of the little King from his enchanted shape as a soup mug, the destruction of the brothers' house by South-West Wind, Esquire, and the transformation of the wicked brothers into twin black stones are the most vivid episodes of this old favorite.

ST.-EXUPERY, ANTOINE DE, 1900–1944.

818   *The Little Prince*. Illus. by the author. Translated by Katherine Woods. New York, Harcourt, 1943. 93 p.
A gravely childlike, philosophical fable about a little boy, a prince from a distant planetoid, searching the world to find out the meaning of love and happiness.

SARBAN, pseudonym of John W. Wall.

819   *Ringstones*. New York, Ballantine, 1961 (1951). 139 p.
Daphne Hazel, a young governess, goes to an old mansion as companion and teacher to a foreign boy, Nuaman, and his two girl cousins. He turns out to be the Syrian god Tammuz, trying to enslave her and lead her into another world where he rules. A competent horror fantasy.

SAXTON, MARK. See WRIGHT, AUSTIN TAPPAN.

SCHMITZ, JAMES H.

820   *The Witches of Karres*. New York, Ace, 1966. 286 p.
A humorous science fantasy set in the far future. Captain Pausert, a young misfit, rescues three unusual girl-children from slavery on a foreign planet, an act of generosity which forces him to embark on a life of adventure. The girls are from the forbidden planet Karres, a mysterious place which seems to move from place to place in the galaxy at will and whose inhabitants are all "witches," who deal with an extra-universal energy called "klatha." A well-plotted, tongue-in-cheek story with an original premise.

SELDEN, GEORGE, pseudonym of George Selden Thompson, 1929– .

821   *Oscar Lobster's Fair Exchange*. Pictures by Peter Lippman. New York, Harper, 1957. 172 p.

An episodic story for younger children centered around a typical Long Island beach summer. Oscar, Peter Starfish, James Fish, and Hector Crab decide to build an undersea garden on the same basis as the local humans' rock gardens—by taking anything they can find on the beach. Thin, but entertaining.

822   *The Cricket in Times Square.* Drawings by Garth Williams. New York, Farrar, 1960. 151 p.

Mario, whose parents run a newsstand in Grand Central Station, discovers Chester Cricket visiting from Connecticut and puts him in a Chinese good-luck cage. Chester soon grows to love Mario and his parents, and he and his friends Tucker Mouse and Harry Cat try to help their newsstand business, which is doing poorly. But when Chester becomes a famous concert artist, all ends happily. A whimsical, winning story. Followed by

823   *Tucker's Countryside.* Drawings by Garth Williams. New York, Farrar, 1969. 167 p.

Tucker and Harry go to Connecticut to visit Chester, where Tucker is immediately disgusted by the accommodations (an old stump, which is flooded), the food (seeds and shoots), and the little girl who pets and overfeeds Harry. But Tucker gets over his problems and leads the animals' fight to save the meadow from bulldozers, which they do by faking a historic monument, an inspired idea which mere humans might do well to imitate in similar situations. Has all the virtues and none of the faults of its predecessor. Followed by

824   *Harry Cat's Pet Puppy.* Illus. by Garth Williams. New York, Farrar, 1974. 167 p.

Back in New York, Tucker and Harry find an abandoned puppy in a sleazy neighborhood and adopt it, but Huppy quickly grows too large and rambunctious for their drainpipe home. With the help of Lulu Pigeon, they keep Huppy from joining a band of dog thieves and get him adopted by the mild-mannered Mr. Smedley and his haughty Siamese cat. The story is much weaker than either of the two previous books.

825   *The Genie of Sutton Place.* New York, Farrar, 1973. 175 p.

After Tim's father dies, Tim goes to live with Aunt Lucy, but she is allergic to his beloved dog, Sam. Tim finds a genie in a museum, Abdullah (Dooley for short), who saves Sam from the pound by turning him into a man—who promptly falls in love with Aunt Lucy. Everything is going fine until Dooley falls in love too, which cancels all the spells, and Tim has to straighten out the mess. Well-contrived, bright, and enjoyable.

SEVERN, DAVID, pseudonym of David Storr Unwin, 1918–　.

826　*The Girl in the Grove, a Story of Suspense.* New York, Harper, 1974.
Jonquil's friend Paul has a problem: his relationship with a ghost, Laura, a little girl who died in 1901 and is spoiled and bad-tempered. Jonquil finally realizes that only she can help both of them, and when she does so, she overcomes her own feelings of shame and hurt due to her father's conviction for embezzling. The resolution of the children's conflict is neatly done.

SHARP, MARGERY, 1905–　.

827　*The Rescuers.* Illus. by Garth Williams. Boston, Little, Brown, 1959. 149 p.
Miss Bianca, an aristocratic white mouse, decides to accompany a Norwegian sailor mouse and Bernard, the pantry mouse, on a mission of mercy for the Mouse Prisoners' Aid Society. Together the three enter the Black Castle, deceive the jailer and the Castle Cat, rescue the prisoner, and return to civilization. The first and best book of a series in which Miss Bianca and the trusty Bernard extend the M.P.A.S.'s mission to include not only comforting prisoners, but rescuing them. Followed by
828　*Miss Bianca.* Illus. by Garth Williams. Boston, Little, Brown, 1962. 152 p.
829　*The Turret.* Illus. by Garth Williams. Boston, Little, Brown, 1963. 138 p.
In which Miss Bianca becomes ever more ladylike and refined, but rescues a prisoner alone, without the help of the M.P.A.S. and its new chairwoman, who is bent on turning it into a gymnasium. Followed by
830　*Miss Bianca in the Salt Mines.* Illus. by Garth Williams. Boston, Little, Brown, 1966. 148 p.
831　*Miss Bianca in the Orient.* Illus. by Erik Blegvad. Boston, Little, Brown, 1970. 144 p.
832　*Miss Bianca in the Antarctic.* Illus. by Erik Blegvad. Boston, Little, Brown, 1971. 134 p.
833　*Miss Bianca and the Bridesmaid.* Illus. by Erik Blegvad. Boston, Little, Brown, 1972. 123 p.

None of these sequels, especially the last, is as good as the first three books, but Miss Bianca is indomitable, and the tales are far better written than most.

SHERBURNE, ZOA, 1912– .

834   *Why Have the Birds Stopped Singing?* New York, Morrow, 1974. 189 p.

Katie, an epileptic teenager, goes back in time to help her epileptic great-grandmother, Kathryn, escape from her heartless and ignorant relatives, who think she is insane. A realistic treatment would have been more in keeping with the spirit of the novel, which centers on the problems faced by epileptics, and uses the fantasy merely as a vehicle.

SHURA, MARY FRANCIS, 1923– .

835   *The Nearsighted Knight.* Illus. by Adrienne Adams. New York, Knopf, 1964. 111 p.

A very minor children's book about ten-year-old Prince Todd, whose sister marries the eponymous hero, also known as the Knight Before Glasses.

SIMAK, CLIFFORD D., 1904– .

836   *Enchanted Pilgrimage.* New York, Berkley-Putnam, 1975. 230 p.

In an alternate universe, a scholar and a tavern "wench" undertake a quest to the Misty Mountains to search for the mysterious Old Ones, accompanied by gnomes, ogres, witches, harpies, wolves, flying saucers, and an American anthropologist. Shoddy writing, rather than lack of imagination, appears to be the cause of both the setting's lack of coherence and the characters' incongruous twentieth-century flippancy.

SLEIGH, BARBARA, 1906– .

837   *Carbonel, the King of the Cats.* Illus. by V. H. Drummond. Indianapolis, Bobbs-Merrill, 1955. 253 p.

Rosemary inadvertently buys both a witch's broom and her cat, Carbonel, who talks her into trying to break the witch's evil spell which prevents him from taking his rightful position as the King of the Cats. Followed by

838   *The Kingdom of Carbonel*. Illus. by D. M. Leonard. Indianapolis, Bobbs-Merrill, 1960. 287 p.

Rosemary and her friend John are to care for the royal kittens while Carbonel is away, unaware that a wicked cousin, the old witch from the previous book, and a scheming cat-queen from the next street are threatening the kittens' lives. Both these stories are full of clichés, and the fantasy is fatally weakened by Rosemary's belief that she dreamed it all.

839   *Jessamy*. Indianapolis, Bobbs-Merrill, 1967. 246 p.

While staying at Posset Place, Jessamy goes back in time to 1914, where the children of the house think she is the cook's niece, and she becomes fast friends with the middle boy, Kit. Back in her own time, she finds a valuable missing book, and returns it to Posset Place's elderly owner—Kit. A few loose ends do not detract from this pleasant, readable time fantasy.

840   *Stirabout Stories*. Illus. by Victor G. Ambrus. Indianapolis, Bobbs-Merrill, 1971. 143 p. (Originally published in England under the title *West of Widdershins*).

Fairy tales about crabby elves, eccentric teachers whose wishes come true, which wreaks havoc on the students, and princesses named Peridot, in the style of Joan Aiken.

SMITH, DODIE.

841   *The Hundred and One Dalmatians*. Illus. by Janet and Anne Grahame-Johnstone. New York, Viking, 1956. 199 p.

How the dalmatians escaped from Cruella de Vil, who was planning to make them into fur coats. Maintains a nice balance between humor and suspense. Followed by

842   *The Starlight Barking*. Illus. by Janet and Anne Grahame-Johnstone. New York, Simon and Schuster, 1967. 156 p.

A grossly inferior sequel in which all the humans go into a magic sleep brought on by Sirius, the god of the Dog Star, who wants all the dogs on earth to leave their masters and live with him. The dalmatians become the dogs' leaders, and eventually decide to stay home with their masters, who would be incapable of getting anything done without them.

SMITH, THORNE, 1893–1934.

843   *Topper, an improbable adventure.* New York, McBride, 1926. 292 p.

Topper is the story of a stuffy, middle-aged banker whose life is abruptly altered—for the better, on the whole—by his adventures with a pair of gin-swigging Bright Young Things, George and Marion Kirby (and their dog), who happen to have recently become ghosts. Poor Topper's difficulties in coping with careless, shingled, ultra-modern Marion and jealous, quick-tempered George, not to mention the unfortunate Mrs. Topper, who rightly fears that Topper may be losing his mind, are artfully and hilariously detailed. Followed by

844   *Topper Takes a Trip.* Garden City, N.Y., Doubleday, 1932. 325 p.

In which Marion drags Topper off to the Riviera (with the dog), where both contemplate sin, gin, and winning at cards. A pleasant rerun of the first book.

845   *Turnabout.* Garden City, N.Y., Doubleday, 1931. 312 p.

A young married couple wake up one morning in each other's bodies. The wife starts smoking cigars and telling unmentionable stories, while the husband puts on unmentionables and begins flirting with other men.

846   *Skin and Bones.* Garden City, N.Y., Doubleday, 1934. viii, 306 p.

Quintus Bland, a jealous photographer with a sexy wife, sniffs too much of the fumes of a fluoroscopic solution and turns into a skeleton, *à la* the Invisible Man, only not so much.

847   *The Glorious Pool.* Illus. by Herbert Roese. Garden City, N.Y., Doubleday, 1934. 292 p.

A female Greek statue—called Baggage—comes to life via the miraculous swimming pool, after which an old roué and his old mistress regain their youth, after which his wife and her French maid, Fifi. . . . Eventually all are restored to their original condition, happier and wiser. Pure bedroom farce.

848   *The Night Life of the Gods.* Garden City, N.Y., Doubleday, 1934. 311 p.

Hunter Hawk, a scientist, discovers a ray which turns people to statues and back again, and acquires a girlfriend, Megaera, daughter of a drunken leprechaun, who can turn statues into people and back again. The two go off to New York, where they proceed to bring to life the gods who loved to drink, climb in bedroom windows, carouse, and generally enjoy life. And they do enjoy it—all over Prohibition-era New York City.

849   *The Passionate Witch.* Completed by Norman Matson. Illus. by Herbert Roese. Garden City, N.Y., Doubleday, 1941. vi, 267 p.

A middle-aged millionaire marries a witch, over the loud protests of his fifteen-year-old daughter and his sexy secretary, and the fur begins to fly. Unfortunately, the break between Smith's work and Matson's is so abrupt that one can practically hear it happen.

SNYDER, ZILPHA KEATLEY, 1927–   .

850   *Black and Blue Magic.* Drawings by Gene Holtan. New York, Atheneum, 1972. 186 p.

Clumsy Harry Houdini Marco's mother has to run a boarding house because his magician father is dead. One day Harry helps a little man who left his briefcase on the bus, and in return the man, Mr. Mazzeeck, gives Harry the gift of wings. Over the summer, as Harry learns to use the wings, he is enabled to help several other people, as well as learn to be better coordinated, and finally his efforts result in his mother's marrying their nicest boarder. The author shows a good sense of humor, understands Harry's problems without over-emphasizing them, and makes her fantasy delightful, credible, and ingenious.

851   *Season of Ponies.* Drawings by Alton Raible. New York, Atheneum, 1974. 133 p.

Pam meets the elusive, mysterious Ponyboy, who hates questions, and who leads a troop of pastel-colored magic ponies which he teaches her to ride. At the end, the knowledge of how she and Ponyboy defeated the evil Pig Woman helps Pam defeat her aunt's well-meant but stifling plans, to find out about her dead mother, and to go off with her father. The plot is not quite coherent and the resolution is a little too pat, but these are small faults in a shimmering, ethereal, gentle story.

852   *The Truth About Stone Hollow.* Illus. by Alton Raible. New York, Atheneum, 1974. 211 p.

Amy, who lives in a small, conservative California town in the 1930s, is curious about "haunted" Stone Hollow, but has never had the nerve to go there until Jason comes to town. Together they explore the Hollow, learning that the Stone is an ancient Indian power center which allows them to see the "truth" about several deaths that had occurred there. Later, the Stone helps Amy understand some events that concern her own family, and she realizes that truth has many faces. The interplay of feeling in Amy's family and the way peer pressure operates on her to force her to conform are especially notable. A thoughtful, touching story about sincerity, truth, and their contradictions.

853   *Below the Root.* Illus. by Alton Raible. New York, Atheneum, 1975. 231 p.

Raamo, aged thirteen, is a new member of the ruling elite, the Ol-zhaan, on the planet of Green-Sky, who learns that the Ol-zhaan have lied to the people in order to retain their power and tries to do something about it. This is a fine book, if perhaps a little didactic, but it is not a fantasy, in spite of the jacket description and the Library of Congress classification. Another planet, not another universe, is the location; the powers of the Ol-zhaan are specifically described as ESP, developed by scientific effort, not as supernatural in origin; and there is nothing in the society or geography of Green-Sky, unusual and utopian though it may be, which is inherently impossible according to the physical laws of our universe. The book is science fiction and is included here only to dispel the incorrect notion that it is fantasy.

STAHL, BEN, 1910– .

854   *Blackbeard's Ghost.* Illus. by the author. Boston, Houghton Mifflin, 1965. 184 p.

855   *The Secret of Red Skull.* Illus. by Ben F. Stahl. Boston, Houghton Mifflin, 1971. 243 p.

Two sloppily plotted, inept fantasies. In the first, Hank and J. D., two teenage boys, accidentally call up the ghost of Blackbeard, who proceeds to make life unlivable for them until they manage to save his (former) home from being replaced by a gas station. In the second, Blackbeard, his cook Scousy, his house witch, Lady Aldetha, and the boys foil a James Bond-ish plot by the evil Red Skull and his henchmen, the Secret Ten, who plan to take over the world.

STEIG, WILLIAM, 1907– .

856   *Dominic.* Illus. by the author. New York, Farrar, 1972. 146 p.

A rambling and inconclusive fantasy about a dog who goes out to see the world. There are some amusing characters, and the book is graced with Steig's cartoon-style illustrations, but essentially this is just an attenuated picture book with too much text.

STEPHENS, JAMES, 1882–1950.

857   *The Crock of Gold.* London, Macmillan, 1912. 311 p.
    A story about a Philosopher, his two children, a wise woman, some leprechauns, and the hidden pot of gold which every leprechaun keeps as his darkest secret. The fantasy is nearly swallowed up by the philosophical ramblings of the Philosopher and the author, the poetic diction, the characters' brogue, and the Irish folklore which was Stephens's main interest.
858   Pyle, Henry. *James Stephens: His Work and an Account of His Life.* London, Routledge and Kegan Paul, 1965. xi, 196 p.
    A study of his literary influences and achievements.

STEWART, MARY, 1916– .

859   *The Crystal Cave.* New York, Morrow, 1970. xviii, 521 p.
860   *The Hollow Hills.* New York, Morrow, 1973. 512 p.
    The story of Arthur, as told by Merlin the enchanter. In the first book, Merlin comes into his power, which is a sort of strange ESP, controlled by a mysterious crystal cave, manifesting itself in precognition, clairvoyance, and the power to cloud men's minds. In the sequel, Merlin narrates the story of Arthur's birth, as plotted by himself; his escape with the babe to Brittany; his return with the child to Ector, who brings him up with his own son, Kay; and his coming to power in a time of war along the northern border of Britain. Merlin is an interesting character, full of self-doubt, cynicism, and frustrated love for his father and his cousin, but no one else in the books is notable. Stewart notes in *The Hollow Hills* that the Arthurian legend combines fact, imagination, and allegory, but her own combination of these elements does not quite come off.
861   *The Little Broomstick.* New York, Morrow, 1972. 192 p.
    Child defeats witch yet again. Derivative and uninteresting.
862   *Ludo and the Star Horse.* Illus. by Gino d'Achille. New York, Morrow, 1975.
    Ludo and his old horse, Renti, learn that they must travel all around the Zodiac in order to claim Renti's destiny as a Star Horse

who will pull the Sun Chariot. So they go off through the Star Land, which is a real country with rocks and trees, meeting each sign of the Zodiac along the way. A little didactic, but otherwise a good story with an interesting premise. The portrait of the Gemini as a pair of athletic thugs is excellent.

STOCKTON, FRANK R., 1834–1902.

863   *The Griffin and the Minor Canon.* Illus. by Maurice Sendak. New York, Holt, 1963. 56 p.

When the Griffin came to see his likeness on the church door, only the humble Minor Canon would speak to him. But the ungrateful townspeople sent the Canon away, because they said he was the only thing keeping the beast in the town. How the Griffin finally punished the offending burghers and brought the Minor Canon home is the rest of this warm, slyly funny story with its perfectly realized modern illustrations.

864   *The Bee-Man of Orn.* Illus. by Maurice Sendak. New York, Holt, 1964. 46 p.

The Bee-Man is convinced that he has been transformed into his present state from something else; not wanting to be what he ought not to be, he goes out to seek his original form. In a sulphurous cave, inhabited by gnomes, imps, and dragons, he rescues a baby who is about to be eaten, and so pleased is he that he realizes he must have been transformed from a baby. A helpful wizard, naturally, changes him back—for all the good that does. A rollicking, lively story with comically absurd illustrations.

865   *The Storyteller's Pack, a Frank R. Stockton Reader.* Illus. by Bernarda Bryson. New York, Scribner, 1968. xv, 358 p.

A collection of Stockton's best stories, not all of which are fantasy, but all of which are well worth reading.

866   Griffin, Frank R. *Frank R. Stockton, a critical biography.* Philadelphia, University of Pennsylvania Press, 1939.

STONE, ANN.

867   *The Balloon People.* Illus. by Philip Gough. New York, McGraw-Hill, 1974. 179 p.

Ben, Miranda, and Pushkin the cat help the good Balloon People against their enemies. Lacks coherence.

SWANN, THOMAS BURNETT, 1928– .

868   *Day of the Minotaur*. New York, Ace, 1966. 159 p.

Thea and Icarus must flee to the country of the Beasts, a hidden valley of peace inhabited by six fantastic peoples: dryads, centaurs, the fat female Bears of Artemis, the sly male Panisci or Fauns, the insect-like Telchin artisans, and the Thriae or Bee-People. One other fantastic creature lives there: Eunostos, the last Minotaur, a literary fellow who falls in love with Thea. A jealous Bee-Queen betrays the secret of the valley to Achaeans searching for the children, but the Beasts defeat the invaders. An excellent mixture of authentic and invented myth-elements, with an exciting plot. Followed by

869   *The Forest of Forever*. New York, Ace, 1971. 158 p.

A "prequel" to *Minotaur* which tells how Thea and Icarus's father and mother fell in love, while Eunostos, a hairy adolescent, tagged along with both. Without its sequel, the story is a little confusing, and very sad, but together they make an interesting if repetitive story.

870   *The Weirwoods*. New York, Ace, 1967. 125 p.

An Etruscan teenager runs away to live in the enchanted forest with the fauns. A very weak retracing of *Day of the Minotaur*.

871   *The Dolphin and the Deep*. New York, Ace, 1968. 160 p.

Three stories, of which the only one worth mentioning is the brilliant "The Manor of Roses," Swann's most successful tale. Three medieval English children, delicate John, sturdy Stephen, and passionate, intense Ruth, run away to join the Children's Crusade. Lost in the forest, they are captured by the man-eating Mandrakes, who, though inhuman, are Christians of a sort, and so release the children when Ruth convinces them that she is an angel. They take refuge in the Manor of a beautiful lady, who tries to persuade John to stay with her. Only after they leave does the lady learn that she, too, is a Mandrake, which means that her motives for wanting to keep John were not as altruistic as she thought. As penance, she opens her doors to the other Mandrakes. A beautifully balanced story.

872   *Moondust*. New York, Ace, 1968. 158 p.

The story of Rahab of Jericho. Sent to Jericho to get pregnant and produce more slaves for the evil fennecs, she is befriended by a Cretan exile, Bard, and his friend Zeb. When Bard's baby brother is stolen by the fennecs, Bard and Zeb rescue him and Rahab-Moondust, incidentally helping the Hebrew Joshua. The scenes in the fennecs' land, the underground Honey Heart, are just barely plausible in a weird,

Freudian way, and the story's premise is most original.

873   *Where Is the Bird of Fire?* New York, Ace, 1970. 155 p.

Three stories: the title story, told by a Faun, is on the founding of Rome by Romulus and Remus; "Vashti" tells what became of Persia's queen after her banishment by Ahasuerus and her return to Petra; and "Bear" tells how a Druidess cheats an innocent Bearon, a half-bear, half-human boy, and then repents her mistreatment of him. None of the tales is particularly well done.

874   *The Goat Without Horns.* New York, Ballantine, 1971. 175 p.

A dolphin tells the story of his dearest friend, a young Victorian tutor, who gets involved with voodoo on a Caribbean isle. Disorganized.

875   *How Are the Mighty Fallen.* Illus. by George Barr. New York, DAW Books, 1974. 160 p.

Ahinoam and Jonathan are Cretan refugees—Bee-People—who are trying to escape Goliath the Cyclops. Ahinoam marries King Saul, who adopts Jonathan. Most of the story concerns the homosexual love of David and Jonathan and is remarkably bad, but the love scenes are not explicit.

876   *The Not-World.* New York, DAW Books, 1975. 160 p.

Deirdre, an invalid, eighteenth-century Gothic novelist, and Dylan, a sailor, are lost together in the Not-World, a dismal enchanted forest outside Bristol. There they meet the poet Thomas Chatterton, who guides them. After a good deal of complicated maneuvering, the witch Arachne captures Dylan, forcing Deirdre to overcome her weaknesses and rescue him, and Chatterton is revealed as the spirit of the forest. The writing is awkward, the plot is incoherent, and the characters are simply unbelievable, as when Deirdre asks Dylan if she can become his "moll" because she thinks it would be "gutsy." A waste of originality.

SYKES, PAMELA.

877   *Mirror of Danger.* New York, Nelson, 1974. (Originally published in England under the title *Come Back, Lucy*).

Lucy must go to live with a hitherto-unknown family of cousins, whose lifestyle distresses her: she has to share a room, the boys are noisy, no one mentions the death of her beloved, elderly aunt, and everyone likes rock music. Out of resentment, she becomes involved with a girl from the past and must choose between her and the acceptance of her new family. A thrilling, suspenseful story with intelligent, distinctive characters, sensitivity, and strength.

TARN, SIR WILLIAM WOODTHORPE, 1869–1957.

878   *The Treasure of the Isle of Mist*. New York, Putnam, 1920. 192 p.
   Two children, searching for treasure on a Scottish island, stumble upon a cave which leads them into Fairyland, and, with the fairies, foil a stupid, greedy Professor who tries to follow them. An old-fashioned, thin, but pleasant little story imbued with the author's great love of Scottish folklore.

TERROT, C.

879   *The Angel Who Pawned Her Harp*. New York, Dutton, 1954. 254 p.
   When an Angel on holiday comes in to pawn her harp, the shop owner thinks she is a gang member planning a robbery. Only the shop assistant, gawky, spotty Len, believes her story and is rewarded by her help in winning his Jenny. A sentimental, predictable, and snobbish story.

THACKERAY, WILLIAM MAKEPEACE, 1811–1863.

880   *The Rose and the Ring*. With "The Magic Fishbone" by Charles Dickens. Illus. with color plates and drawings in the text by Thackeray, John Gilbert, and Paul Hogarth. New York, Dutton, 1959 (1855, 1868). 179 p.
   A riotous, farcical fairy tale about Prince Giglio, Princess Angelica, the serving-maid Betsinda/Rosalba, and Prince Bulbo of Crim Tartary, enlivened by the presence of the hideous Countess Gruffanuff, the wise Fairy Blackstick, and a Pride of Lions. Thackeray's comic illustrations are priceless. The Dickens fairy tale centers around the Princess Alicia, who had to take care of the seventeen other princes and princesses because her King-Papa would have no money until quarter-day, and is also a delight.
   See also Dickens, Charles, Nos. 323–324.

THURBER, JAMES, 1894–1961.

881   *Many Moons.* Illus. by Louis Slobodkin. New York, Harcourt, 1943. Unp.

A classic fairy tale, as good as Andersen. When the Princess falls ill because she wants the Moon, the King asks all his wisest men to help, but none of their wisdom avails him. Only the Jester knows what the Princess really wants—because only he asks *her*.

882   *The Great Quillow.* Illus. by Doris Lee. New York, Harcourt, 1944. 54 p.

How Quillow the Toymaker convinced the marauding giant Hunder to leave the town alone by making him think he was insane. Not quite first-rate Thurber, which means it is still better than almost anyone else.

883   *The White Deer.* Illus. by the author and Don Freeman. New York, Harcourt, 1945. 115 p.

How King Clode and his three sons—Thag, Gallow, and Jorn—found the Princess, enchanted into a white deer; how the King thought her a deer in truth; and how Jorn's unfailing love broke her enchantment. Very sweet, in spite of the preponderance of punning wordplay.

884   *The Thirteen Clocks.* Illus. by Mark Simont. New York, Simon and Schuster, 1950. 124 p.

The story of a wicked Duke and his beautiful niece in the castle where none of the clocks run, until a hero comes to deliver her. Thurber's most literary story, full of allusions, puns, plays on words, private jokes, and wisecracks, but ultimately rather melancholy.

885   *The Wonderful O.* In *The Thirteen Clocks and The Wonderful O.* Illus. by Ronald Searle. Harmondsworth, Penguin, 1972 (1957). 158 p.

A pirate, who hates the letter "O" because his mother was pushed out of a porthole, conquers an island and forbids all use of the letter, which naturally disrupts everything. But the islanders revolt, throw the pirates out, and restore love, humor, and—most important—freedom. The mood of the story is, of course, optimistic, and the pirate is suitably odious.

886   Bernstein, Burton. *Thurber: A Biography.* Illus. with drawings by James Thurber and photographs. New York, Dodd, Mead, 1975. 532 p.

An "authorized" biography.

887   Holmes, Charles S. *The Clocks of Columbus: a Literary Portrait of James Thurber.* New York, Atheneum, 1972. xiv, 360 p.

TOLKIEN, JOHN RONALD REUEL, 1892–1973.

888a   *The Hobbit, or There and Back Again.* Illus. by the author. Boston, Houghton Mifflin, 1937. 317 p.

888b   *The Hobbit, or There and Back Again.* 2nd rev. ed. Illus. by the author. Boston, Houghton Mifflin, 1965. 315 p.

This was Tolkien's first published fantasy, although he had been working on the languages and histories of his Middle-Earth since World War I. The hobbit, Bilbo Baggins, joins with Gandalf the wizard and thirteen dwarves—Thorin Oakenshield and his companions—on a journey to the Lonely Mountain, there to recapture the dwarves' treasure from the dragon, Smaug. Along the way, Bilbo finds a magic ring of invisibility, which helps him out of many tight spots. During Smaug's attack on nearby Lake-Town, Bard, grandson of the last human king near the Mountain, leads the townspeople and finally kills Smaug. Armies of men and Elves then arrive and are about to battle the dwarves for the treasure, when suddenly Elves, dwarves, and men must join to fight the common menace of goblins and wolves. The goblins are defeated, and Bilbo returns home, rich, happy, and freed from his former complacency.

889a   *The Lord of the Rings.* Published in three volumes: *The Fellowship of the Ring* (1954); *The Two Towers* (1955); *The Return of the King* (1956). Boston, Houghton Mifflin.

889b   *The Lord of the Rings.* 2nd rev. ed. Published in three volumes: *The Fellowship of the Ring; The Two Towers; The Return of the King.* New York, Ballantine, 1965.

889c   *The Lord of the Rings.* Collector's edition. Boston, Houghton Mifflin, 1974. 423, 352, 440 p.

These three editions of Tolkien's great work are not substantially different from one another; the second edition corrected a few minor errors and added an index; the Collector's edition was issued in one volume, with a slipcase, beautifully bound in red with the design of a magical tree stamped on it, to commemorate Tolkien's invented "source" for the history of the War of the Ring, the Red Book of Westmarch.

The story centers around the ring that Bilbo found in the caves of the goblins and took from Gollum, its former possessor. This ring turns out to be the One Ring of the Dark Lord, Sauron of Mordor, who had poured a great part of his evil power into it when he made it, millenia before, and now wants it back. With it, he will be invulnerable and able to conquer the world. Bilbo's nephew Frodo, aided by Elves, dwarves, men, and his hobbit friends, takes the dreadful responsibility and risk of bearing the Ring to Mordor itself, so that it can not be merely kept from Sauron, but altogether destroyed. While Frodo and his faithful gardener, Sam, quietly penetrate into the heart of Mordor, the forces of the Free West, led by the wizard Gandalf and the future King, Aragorn, engage Sauron's attention in battle. When Frodo achieves his quest, Sauron is defeated, but the West's victory is not unmixed with sorrow, for the Ring-bearer and the Elves must leave Middle-Earth for the Elves' divine homeland, the Undying Lands of the Uttermost West.

890　*Tree and Leaf.* Boston, Houghton Mifflin, 1964. viii, 112 p.

Contains the essay "On Fairy-Stories" (1938), discussed in the Introduction above, and the allegorical short story "Leaf by Niggle."

891　*Farmer Giles of Ham.* Embellished by Pauline Diana Baynes. Boston, Houghton Mifflin, 1949. 79 p.

How Farmer Giles, a citizen of the ancient British Little Kingdom, defeated the dragon Chrysophylax, kicked out the lazy and greedy King Augustus, and set himself up in the world. A tongue-in-cheek story with many jokes on scholarly matters, and graceful medieval-style illustrations.

892　*The Adventures of Tom Bombadil, and other verses from the Red Book.* Illus. by Pauline Baynes. Boston, Houghton Mifflin, 1962. 64 p.

Sixteen poems, some of them in *Lord of the Rings*, purportedly written or "translated" by the hobbits. Most are light comic verse, but No. 15, "The Sea-Bell," is the closest thing to a serious poem Tolkien ever wrote.

893　*Smith of Wootton Major.* Illus. by Pauline Baynes. Boston, Houghton Mifflin, 1967. 62 p.

A quiet fairy tale about a cook from Fairyland and a boy who wore a Faerie star on his brow. A meditation on the meaning of enchantment.

894　*The Road Goes Ever On, a song cycle.* Music by Donald Swann. With decorations by J. R. R. Tolkien and Samuel Hanks Bryant. Boston, Houghton Mifflin, 1967. 68 p.

Musical settings of several of Tolkien's verses from *Lord of the Rings*, followed by translations and explanations of two of Tolkien's poems in Elvish. The music, unfortunately, is rather banal.

895　*The Tolkien Reader.* New York, Ballantine, 1966. xvi, 281 p.

Contents: "Tolkien's Magic Ring," by Peter S. Beagle; "The Homecoming of Beorhtnoth Beorhthelm's Son," a verse play on the aftermath of the Battle of Maldon; *Tree and Leaf; Farmer Giles of Ham;* and *The Adventures of Tom Bombadil.*

896   *Smith of Wootton Major and Farmer Giles of Ham.* Illus. by Pauline Diana Baynes. New York, Ballantine, 1969. 156 p.

897   Lobdell, Jared, ed. *A Tolkien Compass, including J. R. R. Tolkien's "Guide to the Names in* The Lord of the Rings." La Salle, Ill., Open Court Publishing, 1975. 201 p.

Eleven essays by amateur writers on Tolkien, none of which are of any value, and the priceless Guide, which is a series of notes made by Tolkien for the benefit of translators and is fascinating both linguistically and psychologically.

898   Beard, Henry N. and Kenney, Douglas C. of the *Harvard Lampoon. Bored of the Rings, a parody.* New York, Signet/NAL, 1969.

A classic parody distinguished by a collegiate preoccupation with *double-entendres* and by its names: Arrowroot for Aragorn, Dildo and Frito for Bilbo and Frodo, Twodor and Fordor for Gondor, and so on.

899   Foster, Robert. *A Guide to Middle-Earth.* Baltimore, Mirage, 1971.

An annotated directory which explains every proper name in Tolkien's work.

900   Carter, Lin. *Tolkien: A Look Behind* The Lord of the Rings. New York, Ballantine, 1969. vii, 212 p.

The historical background of Tolkien's work, including a history of fantasy from ancient times, which confuses epic literature with modern fantasy; a chapter on Tolkien's names; biographical information on Tolkien; and a summary of each book of *The Hobbit* and *The Lord of the Rings.* Some of Carter's observations are interesting, but he is too often inaccurate.

901   Ellwood, Gracia Fay. *Good News From Tolkien's Middle-Earth.* Grand Rapids, Mich., Eerdmans, 1970. 160 p.

902   Evans, Robley. *J. R. R. Tolkien.* New York, Warner Paperback Library, 1972. (Writers for the Seventies Series). 206 p.

An unimaginative gloss on Tolkien's ideas.

903   Helms, Randel. *Tolkien's World.* Boston, Houghton Mifflin, 1974. 167 p.

An excellent structural analysis of Tolkien's novels is followed by an equally excellent Freudian analysis. Helms asserts that Tolkien's mythology is as useful as Blake's.

904   Isaacs, Neil D. and Zimbardo, Rose A. *Tolkien and the Critics.* South Bend, Ind., University of Notre Dame Press, 1968. 296 p.

A compilation of scholarly essays.

905   Kocher, Paul H. *Master of Middle-Earth: the Fiction of J. R. R.*

Tolkien. Boston, Houghton Mifflin, 1972. 247 p.

An inconclusive, but highly suggestive and useful group of essays, reasonable and scholarly in tone—that is, neither silly and adulatory nor overcritical.

906   Miller, Stephen O. *Middle-Earth: a World in Conflict.* Illus. by James Shull. Baltimore, T-K Graphics, 1975.

A synopsis of *Lord of the Rings,* with a commentary on every turn of plot which is notable mainly for its obviousness.

907   Ready, William Bernard. *The Tolkien Relation, a Personal Inquiry.* Chicago, Regnery, 1968. 184 p. (Also published in paperback under the title *Understanding Tolkien and The Lord of the Rings*).

A masterpiece of confusion, irrelevance, and jargon.

908   Ryan, J. S. *Tolkien: Cult or Culture?* Armidale, N.S.W., Australia, University of New England, 1969. xv, 253 p.

A heavily annotated doctoral dissertation covering Tolkien's life, friends, work, and success.

909   Sale, Roger. *Modern Heroism: Essays on D. H. Lawrence, William Empson, and J. R. R. Tolkien.* Berkeley, University of California Press, 1973. xi, 261 p.

Argues that Tolkien, in spite of his adoration of the past and dislike of the present, is a typically modern author concerned with the dissolution of the old tradition of heroism.

910   Stimpson, Catherine R. *J. R. R. Tolkien.* New York, Columbia University Press, 1969. 48 p. (Columbia Essays on Modern Writers No. 41).

A critical essay with some good insights but with a polemic anti-Tolkien attitude. Still, her essay is a good corrective for the more common unthinking adulation.

911   Urang, Gunnar. *Shadows of Heaven.* Philadelphia, Pilgrim Press, 1971. xvi, 186 p.

912   West, Richard C. *Tolkien Criticism: an annotated checklist.* Kent, Ohio, Kent State University Press, 1970. xv, 73 p.

Lists all of Tolkien's published work, including scholarly articles, as well as briefly annotating many critical works.

913   Glover, Willis B. "The Christian Character of Tolkien's Invented World." *Criticism,* Vol. 13, No. 1 (Winter 1971), pp. 39–54.

Discusses the religious implications of Tolkien's work as well as the invented religion of his Middle-Earth.

914   Kirk, Elizabeth. " 'I Would Rather Have Written in Elvish:' Language, Fiction, and *The Lord of the Rings.*" *Novel,* Vol. 5, No. 1 (Fall 1971), pp. 5–18.

Discusses Tolkien as a writer whose art functions to unify experience, rather than define a new consciousness.

915   Monsman, Gerald. "The Imaginative World of J. R. R. Tolkien." *South Atlantic Quarterly*, Vol. 69, No. 2 (Spring 1970), pp. 264–278.

Compares Tolkien's linguistic achievement with *Finnegans Wake*. See also Nos. 260, 599, 600, 601.1, 602–604 above.

TRAVERS, PAMELA L., 1906– .

916   *Mary Poppins*. Illus. by Mary Shepard. London, G. Howe, 1934. xii, 206 p.

917   *Mary Poppins Comes Back*. Illus. by Mary Shepard. New York, Reynal and Hitchcock, 1935. xi, 268 p.

918   *Mary Poppins Opens the Door*. Illus. by Mary Shepard and Agnes Sims. New York, Reynal and Hitchcock, 1943. xi, 239 p.

Three identically structured books dealing with the entrance of Mary Poppins into the bosom of the Banks family, and with her departure each time she has things running smoothly. Mary is sharp, impertinent, no-nonsense, vain, and infinitely superior, as well as being the honored friend of magical beings everywhere. Like all good nannies, Mary Poppins smells of toast and apron starch and takes the children for walks in the Park; unlike any other, she will be found dancing in the Zodiac or receiving honors from the Greek gods. An unforgettable fantasy. Followed by

919   *Mary Poppins in the Park*. Illus. by Mary Shepard. New York, Harcourt, 1952. 235 p.

A group of stories, rather than a novel.

TREVINO, ELIZABETH BORTON DE, 1904– .

920   *Beyond the Gates of Hercules, a Tale of the Lost Atlantis*. New York, Farrar, 1971. viii, 247 p.

Aurora and her twin Atlanta, a Sea Priestess, are unwilling witnesses to their brother Baka's evil dedication to science, which eventually causes the destruction of the continent of Atlantis. The story is incredibly pretentious, the characters are all good, wise, noble, pure, trusty, and reverent, except the sadistic Baka, and the conclusion of the plot has nothing to do with the technology Baka has developed.

TURKLE, BRINTON, 1915– .

921   *Mooncoin Castle, or Skulduggery Rewarded.* New York, Viking, 1970. 141 p.

The ghost of a cowardly Irish peer, a talking raven, and a witch join forces in order to prevent the ancient Mooncoin Castle from being demolished and made into a shopping center. The subtitle of this very funny tale is a pun that reveals how they do it. Charming and clever.

TURNBULL, ANN.

922   *The Frightened Forest.* Drawings by Gillian Gaze. New York, Seabury/Clarion, 1975. 125 p.

Paul, Stephanie, and Gillian realize that Gillian's expedition under the Devil's Table—a small local hill—through the old railway tunnel has let the power of a witch loose on the countryside. They try to defeat her by believing in the tramp Davy Sylvester, whom the country people call the Lord of the Wood, and who manages to reimprison her after a final confrontation. The characters are credible but sketchily developed, and the two magical beings are never shown in their magical guises.

TURTON, GODFREY, 1901– .

923   *The Festival of Flora.* Garden City, N.Y., Doubleday, 1972. 360 p.

A Roman mosaic on his property is the gateway to the past for a young Englishman, who enters Roman Britain and becomes involved with a girl, Flora. Although Flora is a Roman and is engaged in fighting off the unwelcome attentions of the visiting Emperor, she spends most of her time gaily dancing on the green with her British friends. Sentimental and anachronistic.

TWAIN, MARK, pseudonym of Samuel L. Clemens, 1835–1910.

924   *A Connecticut Yankee in King Arthur's Court.* Afterword by Edmund Reiss. New York, Signet/NAL, 1963 (1889). 334 p.

A modern American is transported back to the time of King Arthur, where his outspoken ways get him in deep trouble at first, until he convinces the superstitious natives that he is not a demon. For a while everything goes well: he runs the country, accepted as The Boss, marries the pretty Alisande, and introduces all sorts of modern conveniences. But he has aroused the enmity of the great lords, the priests, and Merlin, who combine against him and cause his defeat, thus returning the country to the Dark Ages. In spite of the many opportunities for humor of which Twain took advantage, the overall tone of the book is dark, sardonic, and bitter. One of Twain's fiercest denunciations of human nature.

925   *The Mysterious Stranger and other stories.* With a foreword by Edmund Reiss. New York, Signet/NAL, 1962 (1916). xv, 253 p.

Another embittered, sardonic piece. An angel—named Satan—comes to a small sixteenth-century German town and proceeds to upset the equilibrium of the boys who know who he is by pointing out the obvious contradictions in their beliefs.

UTTLEY, ALISON, 1884– .

926   *A Traveller in Time.* Illus. by Christine Price. New York, Viking, 1939. 287 p.

Penelope, a little girl staying in a country farmhouse, finds herself stepping into its past as a great manor owned by Sir Anthony Babington, who headed a plot to free Mary Queen of Scots, but was caught and executed. Penelope is not involved with the Babington Plot, nor does she see its horrifying end; she is concerned, rather, with the vanished life of the past, which she finds infinitely preferable to her own. At last she returns permanently to the present, forever changed by her wondrous, mystical experience. A beautiful nostalgic fantasy with a memorable heroine and an air of quiet melancholy.

927   *Magic in My Pocket, a Selection of Tales.* With decorations by Judith Brook. London, Faber and Faber in association with Penguin Books, 1957. 239 p.

Short stories about little red hens who do housework, silly rabbits, and runaway carousel horses, all in a rural English setting. Taken from seventeen of Alison Uttley's books for small children, including *John Barleycorn, Cuckoo Cherry-Tree, Sam Pig and Sally,* and *The Country Hoard.*

VAN LEEUWEN, JEAN, 1937– .

928   *The Great Cheese Conspiracy.* Illus. by Imero Gobbato. New York, Random, 1969. 87 p.
Three mice who live in a movie theatre, after seeing too many old Bogart movies, decide to form a gang to knock over a cheese store. After various misadventures, the kindly old owner and his extremely lazy cat decide to adopt the gang.

WALLOP, D.

929   *The Year the Yankees Lost the Pennant.* New York, Norton, 1954. 250 p.
The book that became *Damn Yankees*—how middle-aged Joe Boyd signed a pact with Mr. Applegate (the Devil) and became the baseball star Joe Hardy, savior of the blundering Washington Senators. Although Applegate changes Joe back at the most crucial moment possible, the Senators win the pennant, and the World Series, anyway, and Joe goes home to his wife.

WALTON, EVANGELINE.

930   *The Island of the Mighty: the Fourth Branch of the Mabinogion.* Formerly titled *The Virgin and the Swine.* Introduction by Lin Carter. New York, Ballantine, 1970 (1936). xvi, 368 p.
A retelling of the Fourth Branch of the Welsh epic, from a modern, psychological perspective. The wizard Gwydion tricks his sister Arianrhod into bearing a son, brings the boy up, and tricks his mother into naming him Llew Llaw Gyffes and giving him armor. When Arianrhod curses the boy, saying that he shall never marry any woman, Gwydion makes a wife for him out of flowers, Blodeuwedd. Blodeuwedd and her lover Gronwy plot to kill Llew, but Gwydion magicks him back to life; Llew kills his rival in the same way he was killed, and Blodeuwedd becomes an owl. This strange, distorted story is all that remains of an ancient Celtic myth of the Triple Goddess; Walton has turned it into a modern novel with shrewd psychological observation.

931 *The Children of Llyr.* Introduction by Lin Carter. New York, Ballantine, 1971. xiii, 221 p.

Another retelling, this time from the Second Branch. Branwen, sister of Bran, king of Britain, marries the king of Ireland, but soon her husband begins to treat her badly, and finally he forces her to become a servant in her own household. When Bran finds out about this, he takes a great army to Ireland; but horror follows horror until all the Irish, all but seven of the British, and Branwen herself are dead. Where *Island of the Mighty* was an essentially optimistic character study, this book is a grim, barbaric epic of jealousy, hatred and revenge, written with strength and energy.

932 *The Song of Rhiannon, the Third Branch of the Mabinogion.* Introduction by Lin Carter. New York, Ballantine, 1972. xiv, 208 p.

An accurate, but much less involving, retelling of the most episodic and queer of the strange Welsh stories, in which the survivors of the Irish war return to Britain with the head of Bran, which can still talk although separated from his body. The story of the birth of another survivor, Pryderi, is also told here so as to introduce his mother, Rhiannon, who later marries Bran's brother Manawyddan. After seven years, the wanderings of the survivors end, and they go to their own homes. Both the original story and this retelling are confusing; Walton's ability to clarify the original and flesh it out seems to have gotten lost.

933 *Prince of Annwn, the First Branch of the Mabinogion.* New York, Ballantine, 1974. 178 p.

How Pwyll, the father of Pryderi, changed bodies with Arawn, Lord of the Underworld, and, though sorely tempted, did not use his appearance to dishonor Arawn's wife; how Arawn helped him fight against the demonic Havgan; and how his victory aided him in winning Rhiannon of the Birds for his wife. In this Walton combines the ancient Welsh mythology of the Great Mother with the Babylonian myth of Nergal the Destroyer, by pitting them against each other in the struggle of Pwyll and Havgan. But the book as a whole lacks the internal logic and the unity of her narration of the Second and Fourth Branches.

WARBURG, SANDOL STODDARD, 1927– .

934 *On the Way Home.* Illus. by Dan Stolpe. Boston, Houghton Mifflin, 1973. 137 p.

Not a fantasy, but a confused, incoherent, and pretentious allegory about Alexi, a boy who wakes to life in the frozen waste, the Bear who comforts him, the identical twin who takes him to the palace of the evil Monkey King, and the humble fisherfolk who listen to his tale. Warburg is not content to let his story tell itself, but keeps adding signposts pointing to his moral intentions.

WATSON, SALLY, 1924– .

935   *Magic at Wychwood.* Illus. by Frank Bozzo. New York, Knopf, 1970. 128 p.

A fairy tale about a princess who refuses to stay home knitting and a prince who hates going on quests, and how each managed to give the other what he or she wanted. Frivolous and funny, with a remarkably practical and caustic-tongued heroine.

WERSBA, BARBARA, 1932– .

936   *A Song for Clowns.* Drawings by Mario Rivoli. New York, Atheneum, 1965. 101 p.

Humphrey Tapwell's minstrelsy attracts no customers in the oppressed kingdom. When he begins to sing songs about oppression, the King has him arrested, but he escapes, makes the King reform, and finally discovers who he really is. Well-written, but the plot is disorganized and the characters wholly undistinguished.

WHEELER, THOMAS GERALD.

937   *Lost Threshold, a Novel.* New York, S. G. Phillips, 1968. 189 p.

James MacGregor falls from his own cellar into a new world and cannot get home again without the greatest difficulty, since the only entrance he knows is above a perpendicular cliff. He decides to stay, and with the aid of the homely people of the River, the wise Brothers, and the magnificent, albatross-like Pilot Birds, he defeats the evil Graen, who have been taking tribute by force. The premise of the story is original, but it is awkwardly developed.

938   *Loose Chippings.* New York, S. G. Phillips, 1969. 190 p.

An American professor on a visit to England loses his way and stumbles into the friendly village of Loose Chippings, or Chipping Loo, as the inhabitants call it. There he is welcomed as a friend and introduced to the village's many surprising secrets. But when he leaves to return his rented car, he can't get in again, and no one believes any of his story—because "loose chippings" means "soft shoulder" in British usage. This well-planned story with its surprising twist is light-hearted, pleasant, and readable.

WHITE, ELWYN BROOKS, 1899– .

939   *Stuart Little.* Illus. by Garth Williams. New York, Harper, 1945. 131 p.

After several appropriate adventures for a person of his size—sailing in the Central Park pond, falling down a drain, and the like—Stuart, the mouse son of Mr. and Mrs. Little, goes to New England in his little car, looking for a friend, the bird Margalo. Stuart had once saved her life by shooting a cat in the ear with a tiny arrow. He doesn't locate her, but at the end he is cheerfully driving on, sure that he is doing the right thing for himself. This light little story is notable for Stuart, who is strong, clever, friendly, and resourceful.

940   *Charlotte's Web.* Pictures by Garth Williams. New York, Harper, 1952. 184 p.

When Wilbur the pig finds out that he is going to be killed and eaten, he is terrified, but his friend Charlotte, a spider, saves the day by weaving the words "Some pig" into her web above the pigpen. Thanks to Charlotte, Wilbur wins the prize at the State Fair and is allowed to live in piggish comfort for the rest of his natural life. A loving story of real problems overcome by friendship, written in White's dryest, most tongue-in-cheek New England style.

941   *The Trumpet of the Swan.* Pictures by Edward Frascino. New York, Harper, 1970. 210 p.

How Louis the trumpeter swan, who played the trumpet like Louis Armstrong, got his trumpet in the first place, and how it and he got into the zoo to live. White's style is as good as ever, but his characters and their situation are contrived.

WHITE, TERENCE HANBURY, 1906–1964.

942   *The Sword in the Stone.* With decorations by the author and end papers by Robert Lawson. New York, Putnam, 1939. 312 p.

The boyhood of Wart, who grew into King Arthur. Wart's tutor, Merlyn the magician, "eddicates" him by turning him into various animals and taking him to see various interesting people: he becomes a fish in the moat and has to escape from a monstrous pike; he witnesses a joust between the nearsighted King Pellinore and the old tilting blue, Sir Grummore; he becomes a falcon, a snake, and a badger; he and Kay go with Robin Hood, or Wood, to rescue Friar Tuck and the Dog-boy, and Kay kills a griffin. Grown up, and with all his friends cheering him on, he draws the Sword from the Stone and becomes the King. The miraculously right anachronisms and the sly, imitation-pompous tone give the story its distinctive atmosphere. Great literature and great fantasy.

943   *The Once and Future King.* New York, Putnam, 1958. 677 p.

A rewritten, much weaker version of *The Sword in the Stone* is the first part of this tetralogy. *The Queen of Air and Darkness* describes how Arthur's sister Morgause, mother of Gawaine, Gaheris, Agravaine, and Gareth, seduced her brother and conceived Mordred. *The Ill-Made Knight* tells how the ugly boy, Lancelot, tried to become the best knight in the world; became Arthur's friend; fell in love with Guenever; was seduced by Elaine; and led the other knights on the Grail quest, which, however, he was not allowed to complete. *The Candle in the Wind* concludes the Arthurian story, telling how Mordred caused the dissolution of the Round Table and of Arthur's dream of Might serving Right. This magnificent work is the best version of the Matter of Britain, and one of the best fantasies, ever written. Scenes of Jovian humor and scenes of passionate intensity balance, even blend with one another into a work whose emotional impact is incalculably great.

944   *Mistress Masham's Repose.* Illus. by Fritz Eichenberg. New York, Putnam, 1946. 255 p.

Orphaned, ten-year-old Maria, living in the gigantic but rundown ducal palace of her ancestors, is afflicted by a hypocritical guardian and a cruel governess, Mr. Hater and Miss Brown; but she finds happiness with a colony of Lilliputians living in secret on the estate. But Mr. Hater and Miss Brown want to show the People in a circus, and imprison Maria in the ducal dungeon. How her friend the Professor (a self-portrait of White) and the People rescue her and expose the scheming pair, and, incidentally, restore all of Maria's lost fortune, concludes this outstandingly witty, satisfying fantasy.

945   *The Elephant and the Kangaroo.* New York, Putnam, 1947. 254 p.

The Archangel Michael comes down the chimney and tells Mr. White and his landlords, the feckless Mikey and Mrs. O'Callaghan, to build an ark. After countless difficulties, they get it afloat, but have to be rescued by the daily boat from Liverpool. That is the plot, such as it is, but the real interest of the book lies in White's sadistic, unkind, raucously funny, pathetic characterizations of the O'Callaghans (based on real people), and his fascinating discussion of just how one builds an ark in the modern world.

946   Garnett, David, ed. *The White-Garnett Letters.* New York, Viking, 1968. 318 p.

Record of a long correspondence between these close friends.

947   Warner, Sylvia Townsend. *T. H. White.* New York, Viking, 1967. 352 p.

A moving portrait of White's unhappy life and his joyful work.

948   *America at Last: the American Journal of T. H. White.* Introduction by David Garnett. New York, Putnam, 1965. 250 p.

White's diary of his triumphant lecture tour of the United States.

949   Lott, Herschel W. "Social and Political Ideas in the Major Writings of T. H. White." *Dissertation Abstracts Index,* Vol. 31 No. 8, pp. 4126A–4127A.

WIBBERLEY, LEONARD, 1915– .

950   *Mrs. Searwood's Secret Weapon.* Illus. by Warren Chappell. Boston, Little, Brown, 1954. 294 p.

Mrs. Searwood's secret weapon is the ghost of an American Indian, who always warns her in advance when the Germans are going to bomb the neighborhood. To defend herself against being thought a spy, she and the Indian steal a fighter plane and take photographs of the Nazis' French V-2 base, which she presents to the (unnamed) Prime Minister. Silly and contrived.

951   *The Mouse That Roared.* Boston, Little, Brown, 1955. 279 p.

The Duchy of Grand Fenwick badly needs money, so it declares war on the United States in order to get reparations after it loses. Duchess Gloriana's boyfriend, Tully Bascomb, leads an invasion force of crossbowmen to New York, where the population is undergoing an atomic air-raid drill. When Tully captures both the eccentric Professor Kokintz and his ultimate weapon, the Q-bomb, Grand Fenwick is horrified to realize that it has won the war. A pleasant, gentle little satire on the fantastic nature of modern war and diplomacy. Followed by

952   *Beware of the Mouse.* Illus. by Ronald Wing. New York, Putnam, 1958. 189 p.

How a cowardly Irish knight helped the fifteenth-century Duke of Grand Fenwick defeat the entire army of France and married the

Duke's lovely daughter. Average, but enjoyable. Followed by

953   *The Mouse on the Moon.* New York, Morrow, 1962. 191 p.

954   *The Mouse on Wall Street.* New York, Morrow, 1969. 159 p.

Two further modern stories about Grand Fenwick, which is growing a little thin as a premise. In the first, Grand Fenwick beats all the other countries to the Moon in a rocket ship fueled by its famous wine, Pinot Grand Fenwick; in the second, Duchess Gloriana's desire for a fur coat nearly destroys the economy of the Free World.

955   *McGillicuddy McGotham.* New York, Morrow, 1956. 111 p.

A leprechaun is appointed as ambassador from the Little People to the U.S. in order to protest against an airport being built over their pots of gold. Blarney and luck overcome the same old narrow-minded bureaucrats and get McGillicuddy into the Oval Office.

956   *The Quest of Excalibur.* New York, Putnam, 1959. 190 p.

King Arthur's return, as a ghost, is complicated by Cibber Brown's arrest for using a government spade to poach rabbits, Princess Pam's running away from her boring royal duties, and Chuck Manners's disbelief in ghosts. *Another* set of stuffy bureaucrats has to be defeated before things are righted in England and Arthur can go back to wherever he came from.

WILDE, OSCAR, 1854–1900.

957   *The Happy Prince and other stories.* Illus. by Lars Bo. Introduction by Micheál Mac Liammóir. Baltimore, Penguin, 1962 (1888). 186 p.

Wilde's strange, melancholy, overemotional, sometimes bitter fairy tales with their queer mixture of glamour and religiosity. The glowing, optimistic "The Selfish Giant" and the cruel, heartwrenching "The Birthday of the Infanta" are among the best of modern fairy tales; "The Remarkable Rocket" is a prescient, witty story that strongly echoes Wilde's own remarkable career.

958   *The Picture of Dorian Gray.* With an introduction and bibliography by Jerry Allen. New York, Harper Perennial Classics, 1965 (1890). xviii, 206 p.

A beautiful young man whose portrait is being painted wishes that it could age while he remains forever young. His wish is granted, and he embarks on a life of degeneracy, corruption, and crime. Finally, in an access of sudden rage, he tries to destroy the portrait which hides his secret; he falls dead, a shrunken, hideous figure of evil, while the portrait hanging above him reverts to its original beauty. A fascinating, macabre, melodramatic Faustian story of pride and its punishment.

959   Pearson, Hesketh. *Oscar Wilde, His Life and Wit*. New York, Harper, 1946. 345 p.

WILKINS, VAUGHAN, 1890–1959.

960   *The City of Frozen Fire*. New York, Macmillan, 1951. 250 p.

A stranger—badly wounded and carrying a ruby crown—who can speak nothing but Latin and Medieval Welsh appears in early-nineteenth-century Wales and casts himself on the mercy of the Standish family. When the crown is stolen, the Standishes and their friends set out in a brand-new experimental steamship to recover it and to aid the inhabitants of hidden Cibola, who are descendants of the twelfth-century expedition of the Welsh Prince Madoc. A first-class pirate adventure yarn with glorious villains in the evil Captain Darkness and the vacillating Mr. Yemm, the story is disfigured by some peripheral racism. Removal of the racist comments would not alter the plot and would greatly enhance the book's already great readability.

WILLARD, NANCY.

961   *Sailing to Cythera*. Illus. by David McPhail. New York, Harcourt, 1974. 72 p.

Three stories of the magic adventures of a little boy, Anatole. In "Gospel Train" Anatole and his cat go to Aunt Pittypat's ninth-life christening party; in "The Wise Soldier of Sellebeek" Anatole helps the soldier return to his home, then persuades the Sun to restore the soldier's memory; in the title story Anatole enters his grandmother's wallpaper, with its pattern based on the famous painting, and returns with the friendly monster Blimlin. Beautifully written, but precious and insubstantial.

WILLIAMS, ANNE SINCLAIR.

962   *Secret of the Round Tower*. Drawings by J. C. Kocsis. New York, Random, 1968. 87 p.

Melisande's colt Champion looks just like any other horse, but she is convinced that he is a unicorn in spite of his lack of a horn. When Elvine the witch gives him unicornity tests, he does prove to be a unicorn, which causes all sorts of trouble until Melisande realizes that she must set him free. Better than average in spite of over-formal dialogue.

WILLIAMS, CHARLES WALTER STANSBY, 1888–1945.

963   *War in Heaven.* Grand Rapids, Mich., Eerdmans, 1972 (1930).

The discovery of a murder victim's body in a publishing office sets off a chain of events involving an evil publisher's occult studies, Prester John, and the Holy Grail. A young couple and their toddler son, a poetry-writing Catholic Duke, a publisher's reader, and a country clergyman are the collective heroes whose lives are irrevocably changed by the appearance of, and struggle over, the Grail. One of Williams' most optimistic and joyful novels.

964   *Many Dimensions.* Grand Rapids, Mich., Eerdmans, 1974 (1931).

An unscrupulous scientist bribes the Persian keeper of the Stone of Solomon, which he wants for its immense powers: the holder can travel through space and time, heal illness, and read minds. But it is a sacred object, not to be used in the service of greed or pride. The Lord Chief Justice, who knows the scientist, and his secretary, Chloe, try and fail repeatedly to keep the Stone from being used or stolen. Finally Chloe gives herself willingly to the power of the Stone through love, destroying it, and herself dying in the process, thus achieving Heaven. The story is essentially a "thriller," a mystery with a surprising resolution, showing the dangers of unlimited power.

965   *The Place of the Lion.* London, Faber and Faber, 1965 (1931). 206 p.

The escape of a lioness from a circus coincides with a holy man's trance to provide an entrance into the world for the angels of the elemental virtues, who take the form of huge animals—a lion, a butterfly, a snake, and so on. The lives of all the local people are permanently changed by this: the heroine, Damaris, a scholar whose main motivation is vanity, is almost destroyed by a pterodactyl. Her lover Anthony is the only person who can cope with the crisis, which he does by assuming the burden of Adam, naming and taking dominion over the beasts. A complicated, confusing, not quite coherent plot is enlivened by several scenes of terror, and Damaris's struggle to understand herself is well-drawn.

966   *Shadows of Ecstasy.* New York, Pelligrini and Cudahy, 1950 (1933). 260 p.

A sinister man, Nigel Considine, comes from Africa with his followers and announces that he has the secret of eternal life, and that
he intends to cause the overthrow of the Western governments who
rule Africa. A period of terror follows as Considine's black followers
attack whites, riot in the streets, and make London unsafe, but a vicar
and his mixed bag of faithful friends defeat him. The story is really
about the fascination of evil, but the theme is swallowed up by the
racist framework in which blacks and African religion are equated with
evil.

967   *The Greater Trumps.* Preface by William Lindsay Gresham.
New York, Avon, 1969 (1934?). 221 p.

A girl and her family are swept into a misguided struggle for
power through her fiancé, a gypsy, whose uncle guards a set of strange,
golden figures endowed with mysterious life. When a supernatural
storm arises from the fiancé's abuse of the Tarot cards which control
the figures, only the girl's saintly aunt can still it. Sanctimoniously
written, with an unconvincing ending, and a fair amount of unpleasant
glee at the sufferings of the girl's stupid father.

968   *Descent into Hell.* New York, Pellegrini and Cudahy, 1949
(1936?). 248 p.

The most difficult of William's novels. The powerful story compares the spiritual development of two neighbors, a young woman,
Pauline, and a middle-aged historian, Wentworth. Pauline rids herself
of a frightening *Doppelgänger* by assuming the burden of a martyred
ancestor's pain; Wentworth's selfishness entraps him in a destructive
relationship with a succubus. A cerebral, abstruse, philosophical book,
more a character study than a story.

969   *All Hallows' Eve.* Introduction by T. S. Eliot. New York,
Avon, 1969 (1948). 239 p.

The ghost of Lester, a young married woman, becomes the means
of salvation for another girl, Betty, who is under the control of a
wicked magician. Lester's repentance for her past lack of concern for
Betty, her love for her husband, and Betty's forgiveness combine to
destroy the magus's hold over Betty's mind and the minds of his
duped disciples. This is the best of Williams's novels, coherent, well-
plotted, with excellent studies of interpersonal relationships, and full
of striking, memorable scenes.

970   Hadfield, Alice M. *An Introduction to Charles Williams.* London, Hale, 1959. 221 p.

971   Heath-Stubbs, John F. A. *Charles Williams.* London, Long-
mans, 1955. 44 p.

972   Shideler, Mary McD. *The Theology of Romantic Love: a*

Study in the Writings of Charles Williams. New York, Harper, 1962.
248 p.

973   Bolling, D. T. "Three Romances by Charles Williams." *Dissertation Abstracts Index,* Vol. 31 No. 9, p. 4755A.

See also Nos. 260, 599–604, 649, and 911 above.

WILLIAMS, JAY, 1914– .

974   *The Hero from Otherwhere.* New York, Walck, 1972. 175 p.

Two junior-high-school boys are enemies until they are magically summoned into another world, where together they must defeat the wolf Fenris. Derivative and dull.

WILLIAMS, MARGERY.

975   *The Velveteen Rabbit.* Illus. by William Nicholson. Garden City, N.Y., Doubleday, 1922. 44 p.

The Boy loves the Rabbit so much that he thinks the toy is Real. After the Boy has scarlet fever, he gets another Rabbit, and the old Rabbit is set out to be burned; but the Nursery Magic Fairy comes and makes him Real. A simple, touching fairy tale deservedly beloved by generations of children.

WILLIAMS, URSULA MORAY, 1911– .

976   *The Moonball.* Illus. by Jane Paton. New York, Meredith, 1965 (1958). 138 p.

A group of children playing one summer evening find the Moonball, which proves to be a tiny spaceship inhabited by mysterious but kindly beings. Their efforts to keep this news a secret leads them into some troublesome situations.

977   *The Three Toymakers.* Illus. by Shirley Hughes. New York, Nelson, 1970. 156 p.

When the King announces a great toy competition, old Peter the Toymaker and his adopted son, Rudi, both enter, but so does the wicked Malkin in the next village. Malkin makes a talking doll, Marta, who looks sweet and lovely, but is really rude and mischievous. When Marta, who has won the prize, insults the King and runs away, Malkin is disgraced and Peter and Rudi win the prize.

978   *Malkin's Mountain.* Illus. by Shirley Hughes. New York, Nelson, 1970. 159 p.

Malkin has fled to the next kingdom and is now magically moving the mountain from which the good toymakers get their wood. Rudi tries to save the village, but is captured and imprisoned. Rudi's twin children and his brother find a way to reach him; they smuggle gold in to him, with which he makes the key that controls the mountain's heart, and stops Malkin's evil plan. The plot is full of false climaxes and *deus-ex-machina* contrivances.

979   *Castle Merlin.* Nashville, Thomas Nelson, 1971. 142 p.

Susie, visiting Castle Merlin on a holiday with many other children, befriends the lonely, introverted, unpredictable Bryan. Exploring the castle, the two enter a dungeon which contains a chained prisoner, whom they do not realize is a ghost. Trying to help him only gets both of them in trouble; Bryan steals a famous book on merlins (falcons) for him to read, and then disappears, while Susie has to cope with the results of his action. An intricate, well-plotted story.

WILLIAMSON, JOHN STEWART (JACK), 1908– .

980   *The Reign of Wizardry.* New York, Lancer, 1964 (1940). 142 p.

The story of Theseus, here known as "Captain Firebrand," who defeats Minos of Crete, master of black magic. The plot is exciting, but the writing is abysmally bad.

WILSON, GAHAN.

981   *Harry, the Fat Bear Spy.* Illus. by the author. New York, Scribner, 1973. 120 p.

Harry and his friend Fred, spies employed by the government of Upper Bearmania, must find out why all the macaroons at the National Macaroon Factory are green. An absurdly funny lampoon of adult spy stories, with gloriously nonsensical illustrations.

WINTERFELD, HENRY, 1901– .

982   *Castaways in Lilliput.* Illus. by William M. Hutchinson. Translated by Kyrill Schabert. New York, Harcourt, 1960 (1958). 188 p.

Three Australian children drift away from their seaside home on a rubber raft and land in Lilliput, which has become modern and up-to-date, with helicopters, hot running water, telephones, police, and (presumably) ulcers, inflation, and urban sprawl. A gimmicky story.

WOOLF, VIRGINIA, 1882–1941.

983   *Orlando, a Biography.* Afterword by Elizabeth Bowen. New York, Signet/NAL, 1960 (1928). 224 p.

An Elizabethan boy grows up, falls in love with a Russian princess who leaves him, becomes a scholar and a diplomat, is sent to Constantinople by Queen Anne, where he turns into a woman, returns to England, falls in love again with an explorer, and finally is seen as a middle-aged lady in the 1920s. The book is an affectionate tribute to Virginia Woolf's friend, the poet V. Sackville-West. A witty, clever, dreamy, intricate, and memorable fantasy. The complex character analysis for which Woolf is renowned is clearer and more accessible than in any other of her books.

WRIGHT, AUSTIN TAPPAN, 1883–1931.

984   *Islandia.* New York, Holt, 1942. 1,018 p.

A young American, John Lang, goes to Islandia as consul, thanks to his friendship with Dorn, the son of a great Islandian noble. Lang soon grows to love Islandia and to contrast its quiet, pastoral, stable, and liberated way of life with that of his greedy, hustling countrymen. When he helps prevent an invasion by the savage Bants to the north, the Islandians reward him by allowing him to stay and presenting him with Islandian citizenship and a farm of his own. Islandia is like Tolkien's Middle-Earth in one respect: the country itself came before the story. The book as published, in spite of its great length, is only one-third of its original size; most of the cut material dealt with Islandia's customs, history, language, and geography. Wright's great achievement is Islandia's society, with its complex systems of interdependence and customary behavior, its simple, logical morality, its orientation to the land and the family group, and its "three loves": *alia*, love of family and home; *ania*, love of husband and wife; and *apia*, sexual love with its creativity and destructiveness. *Islandia* is a utopian fantasy—not a utopia, a model for our own society, but a living picture of a lost and better past.

985   Saxton, Mark. *The Islar, a Narrative of Lang III*. Map by Samuel Hanks Bryant. Boston, Houghton Mifflin, 1969. ix, 308 p.

A sequel to *Islandia*, written by Wright's original editor, this story narrates John Lang's grandson's adventures in an Islandian civil war. King Tor, the son of John Lang's first love Dorna, is murdered by his own son, who invites an army from an enemy country into Islandia. Lang III and his friends prevent the invasion, but recognize that Islandia must change in order to be safe from the rest of the modern world. This is a good tale whose reverence for the original neither obtrudes into the story nor disappears at the crisis, and is a tribute to the genuineness of Wright's original vision.

WRIGHTSON, PATRICIA, 1921–   .

986   *Down to Earth*. Illus. by Margaret Horder. New York, Harcourt, 1965. 222 p.

A boy from a distant planet, visiting the Earth, is befriended by a group of Australian children, who find themselves in difficulties when a well-meaning truant officer tries to put him into an orphanage. The story is almost science fiction, but for a rather silly and distracting fantasy element.

987   *An Older Kind of Magic*. Illus. by Noela Young. New York, Harcourt, 1972. 186 p.

Some children living in Sydney meet friendly beings out of Australian aboriginal folklore—playful water, tree, and earth spirits. The plot is tenuous, but the Australian faerie beings are original and fascinating.

988   *The Nargun and the Stars*. Map by Noela Young. New York, Atheneum, 1974. 184 p.

Orphaned, city-bred Simon goes unwillingly to live with his middle-aged cousins on a station in the outback, but finds friends in the Pot-koorok, a tricksy little water-sprite, the Turongs, who swing and twitter in the trees, and the Nyols, tiny earth-spirits. As Simon, his cousins, and the friendly sprites work together to save the station from the elemental, savage earth-creature, the vicious Nargun, Simon gradually becomes reconciled to his new life. A tight, suspenseful plot and excellent characters—especially the practical-joking Pot-koorok and conscientious, shy Edie—adorn this imaginative, innovative fantasy.

WYLIE, ELINOR HOYT, 1885–1928.

989   *The Venetian Glass Nephew.* New York, George H. Doran, 1925. 182 p.

An innocent, elderly cardinal in eighteenth-century Italy asks a villainous glassblower, who has the secret of making glass figures come to life, to make him a nephew. The nephew falls in love with the beautiful Rosalba, who, in a horrific reversal, is made into a china figurine. If a book can be horrifying, dainty, and precious at the same time, this is it.

YOLEN, JANE, 1939– .

990   *The Girl Who Cried Flowers and Other Tales.* Illus. by David Palladini. New York, Crowell, 1973. 55 p.

Five beautifully written fairy tales in a serious, calm, melancholy, stately style.

991   *The Magic Three of Solatia.* Illus. by Julia Noonan. New York, Crowell, 1974. unp.

Four related and continuous short tales: how Sianna got the three magic buttons from the sea witch, Dread Mary; how she had to use them to protect herself from the evil King Blaggard; how her son Lann first saved her father from death, then his own true love from enchantment. The same beautiful style found in the previous book cannot, however, save this pretentious, didactic fantasy, although the story of Dread Mary is worthwhile.

YOUNG, ELLA, 1867–1956.

992   *The Unicorn With Silver Shoes.* Illus. by Robert Lawson. New York, McKay, 1957 (1932). xiii, 215 p.

Ballor's Son, prince of the Fomor, goes to the land of the Ever-Young, where he meets the laughing god Angus, the boy Flame of Joy, and the mischievous Pooka. When the Djinn, Eblis, falls into the Civilized World one day—that is, into early-twentieth-century Ireland —the friends set out to rescue him, with shape-changing, storytelling, and encounters with quaint peasants. The lyrical writing makes Ireland sound like Paradise, and the fantasy makes imaginative, solid use of Irish folklore.

ZELAZNY, ROGER, 1937– .

993   *Nine Princes in Amber*. Garden City, N.Y., Doubleday, 1970. 188 p.

The first book of a projected series of five novels about the adventures of Corwin, Prince of Amber, which is the only real world; all others, including our own, are Shadows. The nine princes are in conflict, and Corwin is bent on revenge for his wrongs. This novel, and the two following to date, all possess the same characteristics: great amounts of violence; Byzantine intrigues and treacheries; episodic, attenuated action; cliff-hanging climaxes; postponed resolutions; total lack of humor; and pseudo-picaresque *machismo*. Followed by

994   *The Guns of Avalon*. Garden City, N.Y., Doubleday, 1972. 180 p.

995   *Sign of the Unicorn*. Garden City, N.Y., Doubleday, 1975.

Neither of these books is at all comprehensible without its predecessor.

996   *Jack of Shadows*. New York, Walker, 1971. 207 p.

Jack is a thief from Darkside, the half of Earth that never sees the sun; it is ruled by magic, while Dayside is ruled by science. To win the lovely Evene, Jack tries to steal a famous jewel for her, but is betrayed, and his revenge eventually causes him to destroy the mechanism that holds the world still, thus introducing the alternation of day and night. The book is written with considerable vigor, and the contrast between the wily, vengeful Jack and the stiff, compulsive, machine-like Daysiders is good.

INDEX OF NAMES AND TERMS

(Index of Titles follows)

References to the three-digit item numbers of the Bibliographic Guide are printed in **boldface**. All other references are to page numbers and are printed in regular type.

AUTHORS, EDITORS, TRANSLATORS, ETC.

ILLUSTRATORS

TERMS

INDEX OF TITLES